Reader responses

I really liked what I read. It was God-centered and Spirit-led. The concepts were simple and real. The questions were powerful. If you are motivated and serious about determining the right direction and strategy for your life, this book is a must-read.

—Steve Douglass,
President, Cru
Author of numerous books

An abundance of original thought and challenging insights; incredible! From the first chapter I could sense my interest growing as I am drawn to processes that have clear objectives and evidence critical thinking. The writing is clear and concise, complimented with visual examples. This is a unique book filling a much-needed void with something not available to us previously.

—Terry Smith,
Founder QoreAnalytics

I've lost count of how many times I have been asked to address an audience of Christian executives and engineers in Silicon Valley on the subject of integrating their work, life and family. *Truventure* answers this question. I believe there is a real market among Christians who can't seem to integrate family, work and Biblical principle into life.

This is a guide for executives and engineers. The material contained in the Appendix alone is worth the price. The Truth and Lies chapter is powerful and key. The Quiet Time Diagrams and the Master Question lists are brilliant.

—Walt Wilson,
Founder Global Media Outreach

Truventure is unique in content, delivery, and calling for a very personal response by the reader. That moves it from being a good read to a challenge to rethink how we personally relate to our world; our careers, and our God.

—*Eric Hartlen,*
Business executive and Pastor

This book is substantial and needed in the marketplace. No one has integrated biblical faith and business strategy this well. Outstanding, powerful and God centered. Authentic personal stories turn content into living truth. It is practical, easy to follow and implement. Your tools here are extremely helpful, original, unique and instructive. I believe this work is worth a great deal and of extreme eternal implications. God is up to something important here.

Passionate—your commitment and zeal for the content which led you to turn great theories into living truth are obvious and your sense of urgency behind this is amazing. Personal—transparent and authentic personal stories and examples of how you have fleshed out the *Truventure* over your adult lifetime are very helpful and potent.

—*Dr. Ron Jenson,*
Founder & Chairman,
High Ground
Author of 24 books

The criterion for a good vision is golden.

—*Tom Waller,*
Founder Mentors Forum,
CEO Summit Tea

Making godly decisions/choices long before being tested, *Truventure* forces us to make these decisions based on a deeper relationship with our Lord and a deeper understanding of His direction for our lives. *Truventure* forces us to define our value system, which will determine who and what we aspire to be today and to become tomorrow.

—*Terry Smith,*
Founder, QoreAnalytics

I am in awe of the fingerprints of God all over this. This book is amazing, what I've been longing for in my life. It is really helping me connect the dots in a lot of areas past and present.

—Shannon Meadows Allison,
Supply Chain Executive

"A healthy intolerance for actions that did not match what I believed"— powerful and heart stopping!

—GeGe Showalter,
Founder Giddy Up Gals

Truventure works! As a 5 year practitioner of the content, I can confidently say *Truventure* contains practical tools for knowing and staying on point with what matters most, walking in agreement with God in every area of life. Managing my life and business from a 1-page strategy has truly been transformational!

—Tim MacDonald,
Co-founder Chrysalis

This is not a Christian book, and it's not supposed to be. It's an apostolic voice to the marketplace community to come to Jesus, a perfect tailoring of the gospel to an unbeliever in the marketplace.

—Thomas Hale,
Academic Dean,
Embassy School of Leadership

The issues identified are clear, well thought through, and personal enough to attract a personal response. I was delightfully stunned by the meticulous manner in which you use your personal experiences; this moves the concepts from objective truth to personalized truth.

—Eric Hartlen,
Business executive and Pastor

You managed to write an eminently practical book with ample flexibility, avoiding rigidity, in personal application. Your book provides immeasurably greater stimulation to my spirit than the most potent espresso, to my brain. It came as a personal guidebook for my future. I want to extract every ounce of treasure this book holds for me in shaping my own *Truventure*!

—*Kathy Ross,*
Co-founder, Reasons to Believe

I believe your book will bring vision to many people who know there is something tugging at their heart that they are not yet able to articulate. They just know the irritation from the way they are living now and believe there is a better way, but not sure what that is or how to "get on the track" so to speak to search it out. For others, who are already on their journey, it will provide the tools and teachings on how to even better pursue what they are already doing. Your tools are very practical and easy to understand.

—*Chris Gross,*
Founder, Gross Profit

Hearts for the Lord shine through in the pages. It is obvious you wish for readers to fall more deeply into an integrated love relationship with our Lord. That is always a great strategy.

—*Gene Wood,*
Founder, Word4Asia
Author of several books

Truventure

Strategy for Wildly Successful Living

Mark Modjeska
Angela Owen

Truventure is dedicated to the One and the one.

⌐

Each chapter points preeminently to the One
and is written for the one who pursues their
true adventure with Truth Himself.

Contents

Appendices

Acknowledgments

I would like to acknowledge those whose fingerprints are on *Truventure*: the late authors Watchman Nee and Jerry Bridges, the late Dr. and Mrs. Bright who modeled their personal contract with God, Dave Hannah who caste visions of eternal significance, and Phil Davis who created the term *Truventure*.

I would like to acknowledge the long list of men who left an indelible mark on me for good. The list begins with Enoch, who walked with God, and more recently Tom Waller, John Hemken, Tim MacDonald and Chris Kraiss, who relentlessly walk out their pursuit of God.

Truventure would not exist without three indispensible women. It would not be remotely readable without Kristan MacDonald, a phenomenally gifted editor who applied expertise with enduring excellence. It would not be worth reading without Angela Owen, whose interpersonal IQ, personal professionalism, and spiritual depth make her co-author extraordinaire and invaluable member of any team. My *Truventure* would have come to naught without Janet, wife of my youth, love of my life, and huckleberry. I credit Janet for the seed that would eventually become my *Truventure*, a healthy intolerance for actions that did not match what I believed.

Reserved for prominence: I would like to acknowledge the influence of my late father who modeled remarkable integrity, my mother who models what it looks like to fully give one's life to Christ and their marriage in which they only had eyes for each other.

—Mark Modjeska

Acknowledgments

I extend heartfelt gratitude to Mark Modjeska, strategist extraordinaire who supported me in my own *Truventure* journey and then invited me to sojourn side by side in writing this book. I thank John Hemken for believing in me and helping me find my wings as an entrepreneur. I thank Gordon Murray and Phil Davis for daring to dream alongside me.

For their patience, encouragement, and deep words of wisdom, I thank my husband, Todd, high school sweetheart and the love of my life; our beautiful children, Lexy and Tyler, who daily bring light to my world; my gorgeous mother, Bernice Powell, who models a life of integrity and compassion; and four extraordinary friends who faithfully remind me who I am and Whose I am—Mary Carter, Kathleen Hemken, Jeanette Kraiss, and Danette Brinkley.

I thank my late father, Jerry Powell, for his unfathomable love, his passion for life, his compassion for people, and his belief in me. I am honored to forever be "Daddy's Little Girl."

And finally, but most importantly, I thank my God and Savior, Jesus Christ, the King of Glory.

—Angela Owen

Introduction

What is Truventure and Is it for Me?

I worked diligently for years applying strategy in the marketplace,
why wouldn't I apply it to what I care about most?

Strategy determines the preferred path to a desired destination. *Truventure* determines the desired destination by asking God to reveal the true you wildly successful per His grand plan. He knows what the true you wildly successful looks like. *Do you?*

Truventure captures what worked when I applied strategy to life, business and ministry. During the past decade, the content proved effective for a wide spectrum of people. *Could a God-centered, personalized, simple approach work for you?*

Truventure—short for true adventure—is a truth-based adventure of eternal significance. *Who wouldn't want that?* It is a lifelong pursuit of one's True Quest, co-venturing with Him, His way. Ask and He will answer; trust the Trustworthy to discover the true you wildly successful. Becoming who you were designed to be *guarantees eternal significance*.

Each of us has the opportunity to thrive when we make truth tractive, unconstrained. *Are you thriving?* For traction, I use *Prerequisite Principles* as lens to adjust my perspective to God's, vehicles of *Strategic Intentionality* to close gaps between truth and behavior, and my *Strategic Pyramid* to land my Creator's vision of me being wildly successful per His grand plan.

True adventure awaits those who want (or at least want to want) closer intimacy and deepening alignment with God authentic. *Truventure* was written for you because *you* were created for eternal significance. This is for those who want a straightforward way to apply strategy to what they care about most, their life and life's work. It's your life. *Isn't it worth being strategic and intentional about?*

Embark on your true adventure and *see what God will do!*

Prologue

Wilderness to Eternal Significance

The Norwegian Wilderness

A remote cabin in Norway was the trailhead of my *Truventure*. The Norwegian wilderness afforded solitude with God to discuss questions like, *How do I make my life count?* With only the wilderness to distract me, I indulged extravagant time to ask, *What are my priorities?* Delving into such questions, candid conversations with God, and living out the answers became my true adventure. The more we candidly talked the more I wanted to view everything from His perspective. This revealed uncomfortable, fiord-sized gaps between my lifestyle and what I believed. I exchanged nominal efforts—what felt like quasi intentionality—with undeterred efforts to maximize this life for eternity.

My Daunting Question

I returned from the Norwegian wilderness to corporate life with a healthy distaste for going through the motions. I exchanged meandering through mind-numbing corporate requirements with strategic intentionality by creating strategy on one page in the form of a *Strategic Pyramid* for my division. The effectiveness of the *Strategic Pyramid* quickly moved me up the corporate ladder, but success in the marketplace created a personal crisis. A daunting question plagued me: *If the marketplace is worthy of strategic effort, isn't my life?* The arduous efforts required to land a vision and strategy only amplified the question, *Why would I work that hard at developing and implementing strategy in the marketplace—and not in my own life?*

As in the Norwegian wilderness, I spent time asking God His perspective. This time the question was, *What is the picture of me being wildly successful?* The question intimidated me but as soon as I took the question to the One Who Knows, His response alleviated what had felt so daunting. Asking God for straightforward answers to strategic questions became the modus operandi of my *Truventure*.

We determined the vision for my life, strategies to land the vision, and target metrics. I placed these in my personal Strategic Pyramid. The process of jointly developing strategic specifics with God centered me and my Strategic Pyramid became a useful grid to examine to the extent I was aligning my life with His plan for me.

A Key Question

One of the most frequently asked questions I hear is, *How do I live out my principles in the market place?* The problem is internal, not the marketplace, just ask those working in ministry. Furthermore, none of us are immune to the difficulty of living out authentic Christianity in our home. The question soon becomes, *How do I authentically live out my Christianity in every aspect of life?*

Christ paid for us to authentically live our Christianity in every aspect of life. He waits for us to yield to Him living His life in and through us to accomplish this very thing. So how does this cooperating with Christ work in daily life? Trained as a research scientist, I documented my findings; trained as an engineer, I refined what worked. Some elements of applied strategy are original; others are picked up from the corporate heap of "we did that last year." I simply implemented the tractive ones for the rest of my life.

Consequently, *Truventure* is my handbook of strategic intentionality in my quest to see things from the Creator's perspective, to cooperate with the Holy Spirit, to align with Truth Personified, to eliminate the gaps between my lifestyle and His Truth, to maximize this life for eternity. My purpose is not to instruct others to copy my journey, but rather invite them into their own journey with the Lover of their soul. I am not prescribing steps; I am describing a lifestyle that flows from a personalized, Spirit led quest to find one's own path with Truth Himself.

The Value of *Truventure*

Another frequently asked question is asked several ways, but at the heart of each way the person is seeking to understand value. The most general way is when one asks, *What is different before and after one embarks on their Truventure?*

- Living truth versus merely knowing truth.
- Ruthlessly living out truth in every aspect of life versus selective application.
- Intentionally bringing Christ into every circumstance rather than occasionally.
- Having a divinely designed vision that resonates with how one was personally designed rather than a vague sense of what success looks like.
- Having a clear plan with simple strategies, target metrics, and measured progress versus hoping for the best.

The differences before and after one embarks on their *Truventure* have significant, remarkable, and eternal impact.

The marketplace tends to be more direct, *What is the value (proposition)? Truventure* delivers target clarity and tractive execution unto eternal significance. Delivery is truth-based, Spirit-led, and simple. The most difficult thing in this strategy handbook is asking God and yielding to what He says. Others also find it easy; a group of artists declared, *I can do this!*

Some of us live by the motto, "In God we trust all others must bring data." We want measured value rather than words. For measured progress in landing my vision I use a composite metric. Before I developed my Strategic Pyramid, I could not articulate the vision of me being wildly successful per God's grand plan. Within one year of implementing my Strategic Pyramid, my composite metric increased from zero to 63%, then to 80% the second, and 95% the third. But wait, it gets better! What God is doing behind the numbers is more meaningful today than yesterday.

A Subterranean Memoir

Truventure is written in the first person so another frequently asked question concerns co-authorship. At a subterranean level, *Truventure* is a memoir. The main thing is what worked for me (Mark) when I applied strategy to life; my story is simply an imbedded stream that runs beneath it. Almost a decade ago, Angela Owen stepped up her Spirit-led quest using the content of *Truventure*. For six years we discussed a pertinent aspect on a weekly basis. This process distilled the essence of similar yet highly personalized *Truventure*s. Angela does what I hope readers will do: explore the essence of what worked and implement it in a way that works best for them. Angela, the consummate coach to high performance teams, wrote the Traction Sections and the Epilogue.

A Spirit-Led Quest

For me to adequately address the question, *How do I make my life count?* I had to embrace rather than suppress a healthy intolerance for actions that did not match truths I believed. I had to see God uncensored and embrace that He cannot lie and live accordingly—engaging Truth Himself in every aspect of life. With Him, anything is worth doing poorly on the way to doing it well. As I accelerate to the finish line, I embrace the truth that life is a vapor and need act accordingly. What began with a question from a remote cabin in Norway has become a Spirit-led quest for eternal significance—a true adventure, co-investing my short life for all eternity.

How satisfied are you with the one life you have to invest for all eternity?

PART ONE

Prerequisite Principles

Physical chemistry was my most difficult undergraduate course, but I made it nearly impossible by skipping one of the prerequisite courses, third-year calculus. As a result, the meaning of *prerequisite* left an indelible impression on me. *Prerequisite Principles* are the lens we need to accurately understand and apply *Truventure*— to accurately understand how to think about each topic and how to tractively apply each lifestyle. I ask the Holy Spirit to use the content within each *Prerequisite Principle* to adjust my paradigm as I pursue a strategically aligned life with my Creator, and I endeavor to yield to Him as He embeds the content of each into the fabric of my being.

Chapter 1

Grace
Resting as a Lifestyle

Everything in *Truventure* must be understood and applied through the grid of grace. In my pursuit of a strategically aligned life with my Creator, I cannot afford any variation of earning God's favor. My pursuit is highly intentional, but my intentionality must be grace-based in order to accurately align with God. My intentionality must ride entirely on what He has done, and on what He will continue to accomplish. I enter into resting as a lifestyle when I move from summoning *my* wisdom and power, to allowing *Jesus's* wisdom and power to live through me. *Truventure* leaves behind what I produce in my strength to discover what the Gardener wants to produce through me. I intentionally yield as He prunes self-reliant effort.[1] *Truventure* applies grace-based, strategic intentionality to life with a pact—everything by grace alone, through faith alone, in Christ alone, resting in Jesus living His life in and through me.

The Gist of Grace

The gist of grace is that I can do nothing to earn God's favor. His favor and my worth are based exclusively on His nature and work—not at all on my nature or work. Every good thing about me and every good I do is 100% reliant on Christ's merit. Christ's currency pays for everything. Human effort to earn God's favor is the mortal enemy of grace. Trying to earn God's favor by being good or doing good is directly opposed to the Gospel.[2] It is not God's truth but the enemy's lies that I believe when

I allow myself to remain in a vague sense of God's disapproval. God is never vague. My job is to simply yield to Him, so He can live His life in and through me.[3] Grace-based intentionality yields and rests in what Jesus accomplishes, not in what I accomplish apart from the Vine. My intentionality is in response to God's complete provision in Christ. All my intentionality is via Christ living His life in and through me.

Identifying Less Than Full Grace

If your parents demonstrated unconditional love and mentored you in genuine grace, I identify with you. Yet even under such pristine conditions, innate desires to earn God's favor became latent seeds of destruction. I was appalled at myself when I read Jerry Bridges's book, *Transforming Grace*. Intellectually I knew all the right answers, but my gut response to some statements proved I did not viscerally know grace. My theology was sound, but an honest look at my actions disclosed patterns that were inconsistent with grace. For example, sometimes I was reluctant to approach God after failing Him, even after repenting. At other times I had a vague fear that I would not receive God's favor if I did not have devotions that day.

Even one inconsistency in my thinking means my lifestyle is not fully resting in the merit of Jesus. Ninety-nine percent is not equal to one hundred percent. Jesus fully accomplished the work, and He is faithful to continue His work in me: "For by that one offering he made forever perfect in the sight of God all those whom he is making holy."[4] I was living by grace to some degree, but not nearly as much as Christ's death had purchased. The longer I allowed any distortion of full and genuine grace, the longer I allowed the enemy to dim the light of truth.

Truth Himself wanted to take the truths of grace deeper in me. He used the writings of the late Jerry Bridges to plumb the depths of genuine grace in my life. True grace liberates, so I make it a habit to frequently ask the God of all grace to help me candidly answer Jerry-esque questions, such as:

- *Am I hesitant to ask God for something after I have failed Him?*
- *Are there any ways I am still trying to earn God's favor and acceptance?*

• *Do I worry that if I do not have my devotions God will not accept me as much as if I did?*[5]

If you sense the God of all grace wanting to take the truths of grace deeper in you, then before continuing *Truventure* draw near to Him, ask Him to generously give you His insight. Consider reading *Transforming Grace* and *The Cure*.[6] Only after receiving a divine breakthrough in grace, continue *Truventure*—where everything is by grace alone, through faith alone, in Christ alone. He is our Singular True Quest: He is our Only Way.[7]

Doing While Resting

I am a servant of God, the Generous Landowner; He calls me to work in His fields, to do things that please Him. He is pleased with me when, by His wisdom and power, I yield to Jesus doing them through me. I can receive and feel His pleasure through what Christ accomplishes in and through me. I have no ability to earn His pleasure; I simply reciprocate His love, which pleases Him. I intentionally reciprocate God's love as my antidote for striving to earn anything from Him. His pleasure and favor are completely satisfied with the overflowing cup of Christ. Nothing I add can make the totally full cup fuller—it is already super-abundantly, continually overflowing with the merit of Christ alone. My job is to carry the overflowing cup of Christ wherever I go.

Enter His Rest

The legacy of believers through the ages is entering into God's rest—resting exclusively on His protection, provision and presence in all things, all the time. *Truventure* journeys into the heart cry of the Father in the Old Testament and the heart cry of the Son in the New Testament: "Enter my rest!"[8,9] With grace-based intentionality, we enlist the Holy Spirit to discard any attempts to earn His favor. This means that applying any strategic concepts or vehicles in *Truventure* in order to earn God's favor is anathema.[10] We challenge ourselves and each other to rightly align with the Father and the Son in the context of our pact—everything by grace alone, through faith alone, in Christ alone, resting in Jesus living His life in and through us.

Introduction to Traction

It is my (Angela's) privilege to guide you in the Traction Sections where you will encounter challenges to:

1. Hear God's voice as you talk to Him

2. Trust God to help you be strategic as you understand the chapter content

3. Go higher in your own *Truventure* journey as you apply the chapter content

To get the most out of *Truventure*, take time to thoughtfully process the Traction Sections. Each section represents a milestone on the journey that is uniquely yours. The significance of each milestone will be directly proportional to the time you invest and will ultimately determine how far you are able to go.

"Journey into the Wildness of God" dons the upper right corner of each Traction section's opening page. Perhaps you are wondering what this phrase means. Maybe you are even struggling to reconcile the idea of God's "wildness" with docile Sunday school pictures of Jesus. Let me tell you why this phrase is so meaningful for me.

You see, for much of my life, I had an incorrect view about myself that ultimately limited my perspective of God's plans for me. *I'm not good enough, not strong enough, not smart enough...*You get the picture. Shame and low self-image shackled me to a deceitful post of doubt and discouragement. But God in His mercy would not leave me in chains. He used a particular scripture to arrest me into truth and ultimately set me free.

> *We all, with unveiled faces, are looking as in a mirror at the glory of the Lord and are being transformed into the same image from glory to glory.*
> *—2 Corinthians 3:18*

In my state of bondage, I had been looking into the wrong mirror. Instead of looking into the mirror at all of my shortcomings, I needed to fix my eyes first on Jesus, and trust Him to transform me into His image. This truth rocked me to my core, and I began a fervent search of the scriptures to find out more about *who* He is. I was hungry to see Him clearly and to understand His ways. In my quest to better know and understand Jesus, I discovered

that placid images found in most renderings fell far short of capturing His wonder and majesty. After all, the One who died as the sacrificial Lamb also conquered as the reigning Lion of Judah!

To see yourself clearly and to understand God's plans for you, you must first see God more fully. Allow the Traction tagline, *Journey into the Wildness of God*, to help you anticipate a *fresh* perspective on God. Avoid putting God in a box. Set aside anything that confines the life that He designed for you. You will find adventure with Him is a close as your next breath.

You don't have to be on exotic location to experience adventure with God, but you will need some gear for the trek ahead. In addition to this book, gather a journal, and a pen. You will also need a mirror—but not just any mirror—you need a mirror that reflects the truth of His glory. I must warn you that mirrors of this kind tend to highlight blemishes in the most obvious ways, but rest asserted that it is always for the purpose of refining and making us more like Him so that ultimately He is reflected in and through us.

You have an opportunity to be wildly successful for eternal impact. *Shall we begin?*

Grace: *Resting as a Lifestyle*

Everything in Truventure *must be understood and applied through the grid of grace.*

True grace liberates...

I intentionally reciprocate God's love as my antidote for striving to earn anything from Him.

Jesus is your Quest...and you are His. Soak in this idea for a moment. Write a prayer expressing what it means to be pursued by the King of Glory.

Ask & Listen—Talk it over with God

One can know and even believe what God says about grace yet live trying to earn God's acceptance. Quiet your heart before God and ask Him to show you an example of a time you attempted to earn His favor in place of simply receiving His love in grace. Describe below a time when your actions belied the truth that you do not need to earn God's acceptance or favor. (For example, *After I failed God, I didn't ask Him for anything for a while.*)

Who won when you allowed yourself to react in a way inconsistent with grace?

___ God?

___ You?

___ The enemy?

Ask God to reveal anything causing you to take your gaze away from Him. Did He reveal anything that might be hindering you feeling totally accepted by Him and His love? If so, what did He reveal? On a scrap piece of paper, list anything God revealed that is hindering you feeling totally accepted by Him.

Traction

Now take this list of hindrances and symbolically place them on the altar before God. Tear the list into small pieces and toss them into a trashcan. Ask God to help you fully release these hindrances to Him and to be quick to remind you to return to grace should they raise their ugly heads again.

Ask Him now to show you an example when you have done something because you are fully accepted by God because of His Son. Write a sentence describing a time when you have done something while resting in the fact that you never need to earn God's acceptance.

What are two ways that you can bring this testimony of grace-walking to remembrance when tempted to earn God's favor? Record them below.

    1.

    2.

Essence

Resting as a lifestyle is how we *truventure*. Grace makes possible every step of the journey ahead. Talk with God about resting in the fullness of His love as you *truventure* with Him. Take the crucial step of summarizing what you've learned.

Everything by grace alone, through faith alone, in Christ alone, resting in Jesus living His life in and through us.

Chapter 2

Lordship

A Lifestyle Yielded to My True Owner

I n my pursuit of a strategically aligned life with my Creator, I want to see lordship[1] as *He* sees it before I spend any time on strategy. I want to be crystal clear on my position relative to God, because that affects everything I strategize and how it is implemented. As a strategist, I find one jugular point about lordship particularly helpful to adjust my paradigm to God's perspective: *this is not my life.* He is the Potter; I am the clay.[2] This is the life He allows me to experience and co-invest with Him for eternity, and while I am privileged to co-strategize with Jesus, in the final analysis whatever He says goes. *Truventure* is my strategic pursuit of a lifestyle that shows it.

Intellectual Honesty

Aligning with my Creator requires intellectual honesty to align with everything He says, rather than focusing only on certain passages I favor. Much of God's Word is written in Semitic, wisdom literature, and often uses hyperbole to emphasize a truth. As a result, I may encounter seemingly contradictory statements in His Word, but God expects me to seek Him for understanding. The classic example is side-by-side verses, such as Proverbs 26:4-5, "Don't answer a fool according to his foolishness or you'll be like him yourself. Answer a fool according to his foolishness or he'll become wise in his own eyes." *So am I to answer a fool or not?* I must search the entire Word of God to understand. Often such seemingly contradictory statements are not found side by side, which requires me to be more astute. I do not want to be like Thomas Jefferson, who cut out portions of Scripture which did not fit his worldview.[3] At least he was honest about it, but that does not demonstrate the intellectual honesty I seek. I prefer to seek God Himself and His Word when I encounter truths that I need to hold in tension rather than ignore.

Truths in Tension

Many of God's realities are in tension with each other, yet are simultaneously true. On the topic of lordship, one of those truths in tension is: I am both Jesus's friend and His slave. Jesus Himself highlights our profound identity as His friends when He says, "I do not call you slaves anymore, because a slave doesn't know what his master is doing. I have called you friends, because I have made known to you everything I have heard from My Father."[4] And that is just the beginning—we are also God's children, heirs of God and coheirs with Christ.[5,6] And yet the Bible also calls us His slaves.[7,8,9] Paul,[10] James,[11] Peter,[12] and John[13] described themselves as slaves of Christ, and the first sentence of the book of Revelation declares, "The revelation of Jesus Christ that God gave Him to show His slaves what must quickly take place. He sent it and signified it through His angel to His slave John[.]"[14] I would rather be a slave who is truly free[15] than a freeman who is truly enslaved,[16] and I cannot afford to overemphasize being a friend of Christ and underemphasize being a slave of Christ, any more than I can afford to do the reverse.

Another truth in tension when it comes to lordship is that while God is my True Owner, He grants me a partnership.[17] God's unrivaled position grants Him decision-making authority in my life. And yet, He grants me the role as steward of the life he gave me. By His own nature, by the very definition of God, the irrevocable truth is that He alone is the decision maker.[18] And yet, my Benevolent Boss makes some decisions, others He delegates to me, and on others we collaborate. Effective strategy development and implementation require crystal-clear decision making, so I need to know who rightly makes what decisions in my life, and how are they made. My *Truventure* is a journey in partnership with my True Owner. I have freedom in Him to make choices as He allows, and at the same time I remain ready to obey Him no matter what He says. As steward of my life, I have a fiduciary responsibility to always only consider, and always only execute, *His* best interests in every aspect of this life.[19]

I want the fullness of a lifestyle embracing all His truths—even those that seem to be in tension. I take indescribable comfort in knowing the One who owns everything[20] also owns me.[21] He owns all my problems too, and that is a relief. Whereas I used to cringe at Exodus 21:5-6,[22] now I get it—now I want to declare, *I love my Master.* God is good, and He always treats us with the dignity of one created in His own image.[23] His benevolence makes me want to respond in reciprocal love and submission. Once I get over myself, I embrace that He is the decision maker because I know He is always right and always has my best interest in mind. For me to focus on any aspect of biblical truth at the minimization of another yields a lifestyle of partial truth. Aligning with all of God's truth, aligning with the Truth Himself as Lord, is fundamentally how I *truventure.* The more I *truventure* with Him, the more I relish His truths in tension.

Crisis and Capitulation

Gaps between my theology and my lifestyle are most often revealed in crises. He takes me to my limit to reveal the gaps between all He means by lordship and my current reality. I actually make this easy for Him, since most of my crises are largely self-induced. Here is one example of how God taught me to submit to His agenda in all circumstances.

After repatriating to the United States from an assignment in China, I ran a global business for several years, and was genuinely content. But then I was promoted to oversee a large portfolio of businesses and manufacturing sites. Overnight I was catapulted higher in the corporation than I ever expected; however, I failed God's success test by allowing a prestigious promotion to incite selfish ambition. Selfish ambition became my crack cocaine, and prestige became the high of my addiction. I took being a workaholic to an art form. It was not long before God leveled off my career and began removing trappings of prestige.

The chasm between my heartfelt belief—that this is not my life—and a life consumed with selfish ambition became so corrosive to my spirit and caustic to my soul that I couldn't take it any more. One day I was walking from my car to the office, when I finally conceded the battle raging within me—the battle between obsession with prestige and contentment in God, the battle between my agenda and His agenda, the battle between *my* life and *His* ownership of me. I could not wait to get to my office and write out what I called my "Great Exchange." I chose to never become a corporate VP, or VIP, in exchange for contentment in God alone.[24]

Even after my Great Exchange, circumstances continued to degrade; I experienced sequentially lower lows, which tested and retested the authenticity of my capitulation. Surrendering my agenda to His is a reoccurring theme in my life-long journey to viscerally align my lifestyle with my theology. Eventually, I had peace in place of internal striving. Eventually, I desired humility rather than projecting myself in a superior light. Six years later, I was open to what God wanted to do with the rest of "my" life. Twelve years later, I realized there is four times the risk to prestige than the upside I had arduously pursued. I still regularly pray through my Great Exchange document because I want submission to His agenda imbedded into the fabric of my being. The lessons keep coming as I pray through my Great Exchange.

The bottom line is, I cannot afford longings for things that are not His plan for me. I must consciously abandon my preconceived notions of what "my" life should be, so that I can become receptive to, submit to, and embrace His providence—however He chooses to unfold it. I am jealous for a lifestyle where God is truly my Singular Possession. I prayerfully choose—in advance of a crisis—to be totally content in my Singular Possession and progressively listen to what He means by His lordship and to align with that truth.

Scaling the Right Wall[25]

A lifestyle yielding to my True Owner is essential to *Truventure* and is presupposed in everything that follows. *Truventure* seeks to align my lifestyle with Truth and apply strategy to my life. Therefore, I want to be wary of when my lifestyle usurps Christ's rank[26] and when my strategizing usurps His ownership of me. Lordship is a *Prerequisite Principle* because spending time on strategy while holding—even subconsciously—to lies that my life, ministry, or business belongs to me is scaling the wrong wall. Anything deviating from the jugular truth that this life is not my own furthers a false narrative; God categorically refuses to lead false narratives. Unless I am yielding to my True Owner, I am going down the wrong road, proceeding without Him. I find His way much better; I prefer to scale the right wall with Him.

Lordship: *A Lifestyle Yielded to My True Owner*

This is the life He allows me to experience and co-invest with Him for eternity, and while I am privileged to co-strategize with Jesus, in the final analysis whatever He says goes.

I have freedom in Him to make choices as He allows, and at the same time I remain ready to obey Him no matter what He says.

Gaps between my theology and my lifestyle are most often revealed in crisis.

Ask & Listen–Talk it over with the Lord

Jesus is Lord...and He also calls you "friend" (John 15:15). Keep His deep love for you in mind as you adventure further into the land of Lordship. Take a few minutes to quiet your mind and heart. *Turn your eyes upon Jesus. Look full in His wonderful face, and the things of earth will grow strangely dim in the light of His glory and grace.*[*] Write a prayer asking Him to lead you as you journey toward deeper realization of the interplay between His love and lordship.

Step 1: Identify the Gaps

Ask God to reveal any areas of your life where the truth of His Lordship is stifled in any way. List any gaps between the truth of Lordship and your lifestyle that Jesus reveals. *(In the left hand column of the table)*

Gaps	Actions to Take

---

[*] Helen H. Lemmel. "Turn Your Eyes Upon Jesus." 1922.

Figure 2.1 Truth of His Lordship Gaps

Ask yourself, *If I'm not submitted to Jesus, then to whom am I ultimately obeying and submitting?* Put a percentage on each choice below.

Who	Percentage
Jesus	
Self	
The enemy	
Boss	
Parent	
Boyfriend/girlfriend	
Children	
Friend	
Other_____	

What does this say about your level of complete submission?

> *Therefore there is now no condemnation for those who are in Christ Jesus.*
> Romans 8:1 (NASB)

Remember our pact? That everything *Truventure* is based on grace and grace alone? Revelation of any gaps between your lifestyle and God's truth serves to *call you up* to who you are as a new creation in Christ. Confess any feelings of guilt or condemnation and return to the resting place of grace. Record any insights you receive from God during your time of confession.

Step 2: Close the Gaps

Choosing to reject condemnation and guilt, ask Jesus to show you how to address each gap between your lifestyle and the truth of His Lordship. Record the insights He shares with you for each gap in the column on the right beside each respective gap in Figure 2.1.

Consider what it means to truly live out what it really means for Him to be Lord. What does daily life with Jesus as Lord really look like? List three examples in the space below.

1.

2.

3.

Essence

Living a lifestyle yielded to the True Owner is how we *truventure*. Talk with God about what it means to joyfully yield to His Lordship as you journey with Him each day. Take another decisive step and summarize what you've learned.

⇁

I want to be wary of when my lifestyle usurps Christ's rank
and when my strategizing usurps His ownership of me.
Lordship is a Prerequisite Principle because spending time
on strategy while holding—even subconsciously—
to lies that my life, ministry, or business belongs
to me is scaling the wrong wall.

Chapter 3

Truth and Lies

A Lifestyle Clearing the Decks

As we pursue a strategically aligned life with our Creator, we embrace His grace and submit to His lordship; nevertheless, we get tripped up because we live in a war zone. Our lives are the prized battleground between epic combatants—God, the Author of Truth, and Satan, the father of lies. Consequently, our ability to discern both truth and lies is an essential *Prerequisite Principle* of our *Truventure*.

Most of us readily assert that God tells the truth, but it's not as easy to maintain in real life. As we press into God, our Logos, He points to attitudes and actions that reveal we do not take Him at His word. Although He is the One Who Cannot Lie,[1] few of us align every aspect of our lives to every truth He proclaims. I desperately want to be such a man, but I often walk out lies with a head full of doctrinal truth. I behave as if hurts, fears, and feelings trump God's clear and well-supported declarations. I get sucked into living by sight rather than by faith.[2] I must intentionally choose to believe the Author of Truth; otherwise I default into believing the father of lies, to my peril. *Peril* is a strong word, but appropriate because the root of each lie maligns and challenges the pristine nature of God.[3] So it is essential that I follow Jesus in a lifestyle that clears the decks of lies in order to align with Truth.

Clearing the Decks

Throughout the ages seamen bellowed, "Clear the decks!" to prepare their vessel for unhindered action, primarily battle. Likewise, I must clear the decks of my primary battleground, my mind, to stand free alongside my Commander. This is vital to my war strategy; I must enlist Him to vigilantly, ruthlessly address lies that contradict truths I claim to believe. Otherwise I am complicit with the enemy, intentionally or by default. Unless I want to be ambushed trying to do this alone, I must enlist the only One who can win. Recall our grace pact—everything by Christ living His life in and through me.

It is easier to leave the decks of a ship sloppy than to clear the decks. It is easier to believe lies than to walk out truth, but ease is not the priority. My Commander determinedly sacrificed everything for me,[4] and keeps fighting for His design of my life in its purest form. How invaluable: I want to wholeheartedly cooperate! He wants to give me a quintessential life in return for cooperating with Him in a lifestyle of clearing the decks. No more settling for something less, no more under-targeting, no more shortchanging myself from all He designed. Clear of contradictions and lies, I can be me, unconstrained.

The Truth About Truth and Untruth

Considering how my Commander fights for me and the quintessential life He designed for me, I recommit myself to a lifestyle of clearing the decks in order to align with Him. To this end, I enter the war college eager to learn the strategic concepts of knowing truth and discerning lies.

Truth is pure. Adding the slightest impurity yields untruth. Our adversary uses this against us. He adds smidgeons of untruth to the truth we know. He adroitly nudges our perspective until we no longer focus clearly, and then we no longer center ourselves exclusively on Truth. Additionally, the laws of logic assert that something cannot be simultaneously true and untrue. Our adversary also uses this against us, inciting even the slightest inconsistency between what we believe and our behavior, knowing inconsistencies germinate. As I engage my Creator, He uses His consistent, true nature to expose and eradicate untruths in me.

Untruth follows the law of entropy, tendency toward disorder. Untruths progressively degrade perspective. I see things less accurately when I accept untruth. Consequently my decisions increasingly diverge from truth. I feel fuzzy, messy, and uncentered. This never reaches equilibrium. Like dark energy, untruth pulls me farther away from my True Center.

According to the law of entropy, energy must be put into the system to reduce disorder. Untruth is no exception. Truth Himself must expose and dispel untruth. I must receive His light and allow it to expose lies. It also requires me to expend the energy of repentance, to yield to Truth living His life in and through me. This is how I prove in my lifestyle, not merely in my theology, that I believe the One Who Cannot Lie.

God illuminates vital truths,[5] and He intensely wants to be believed. Satan also wants to be believed, and he floats fatal lies.[6] Truth points to the Truth; lies point away from it. In fact, lies don't care where they point; anywhere is fine as long as it is not the truth. But God cares intensely! God abhors our adversary's subtle lies that distort our perspective, blur our vision, muddle our mind, and hamstring our walk. Satan abhors our Savior's truths that straighten, illuminate, order, and unleash every aspect of us to follow God. Therefore, I never quit applying "The Truth about Truth and Untruth" because I want to be a skilled warrior, adept at listening to my Commander, discerning truth, and clearing the decks as I follow Him in this battle we call life.

Two Kinds of Wedges

Our war college manual illustrates how our ambidextrous adversary wields violence and subtlety with equal expertise. He clobbers with violent attacks and seduces with covert operations. Merciless attacks on Job exemplify Satan's ruthless desire to incite us to question God's character.[7] Our adversary used subtle lies against Samson to hamstring the strongest man on earth, a judge and defender of Israel. Samson swallowed the succulent lie that his strong muscles and undefeated victories were about *him* and the power *he* possessed, rather than about God and God's power for Israel's deliverance. The unchecked lie, though covert, was sharp enough to gouge out his eyes—a scary warning.[8] Each of us can relate to feeling knocked down by Satan's attacks.[9] Likewise, each of us can relate to being seduced by his lies. More like Samson than I care to admit, my pride gets pricked, indicating I swallowed the lie that it is all about me. But I have the opportunity to turn the eyes of my heart to my centering truth, "I have been crucified with Christ and I no longer live, but Christ lives in me."[10]

We are in the battle zone for life, and the battle is for our integrity. Our relentless adversary, despising Truth, wields violent attacks and covert operations to drive wedges between us and Truth Himself. We are called to be alert and sober minded because our enemy prowls around like a roaring lion looking for someone to devour.[11] Since "someone" means you and me, and since everything out of his hellish mouth is a lie, let's explore a lifestyle clearing the decks of lies.

Our Commander Clearing the Decks

Christ, my Commander, brilliantly demonstrated how to clear the decks of lies when admonished to forgo the cross: "Get behind Me, Satan! You are an offense to Me because you're not thinking about God's concerns, but man's."[12] Jesus quickly rejected the lie subverting His call. He decisively dealt with the lie denying His need to die. He vehemently nailed the jugular issue by asserting He could not fulfill God's plan man's way. Jesus emphatically doubled down on obedience, recommitted submission to His Authority Figure, and embraced crucifixion rather than let Satan's lie take root.

Jesus's response stands in stark contrast to mine. Jesus set His face like flint to the cross, but I squirm to avoid daily taking up my cross.[13] Our Commander, ever vigilant, never had to deal with a lie He swallowed, but I do. His example compels me to more diligently reject lies that come crawling across my deck, long before they take root.

An Epic Life Well-lived

Covert lies trip up even long-time stalwarts of the faith, but their stories can show us how to perceive lies and stand on truth. This is the story of John, my friend and hero. John had enlisted for life with his Commander decades before this story begins. Together they dared and accomplished great things. This story begins with violent attacks *and* covert subterfuge. Outwardly, John faced cascading financial loss. Inwardly, he swallowed incognito lies. Eventually, our hero lost hope. The story reveals the Commander rescuing John, and five critical steps John took to walk victoriously in hope.

Act 1: An Incognito Lie

Fortified with a midwestern work ethic, it only takes a modicum of hope for John to bulldoze through obstacles. After a great career in corporate

America, an enviable executive pastor role, and entrepreneurial success, he found himself strapped for cash. Equally comfortable in the church and marketplace, this minister of God knew all the right answers, but an incipient lie came crawling onto his deck: *he needed to settle.* The lie was so innocuous that even today it is hard for him to definitively articulate what *settling* meant. It left a vague impression that God had passed him by. Perhaps he could help others dare great things for God, but the lie convinced John it was too late to dare great things for his own life.

The incognito lie—*you need to settle*—insinuated that financial constraints, especially this late in life, nullified God's big dream for him. The root lie was a double whammy: *circumstances are bigger than God, therefore God can't be trusted.* The father of lies rarely floats the root lie, but persistently passes off less objectionable versions tethered to the root. None of the versions announce themselves or overtly overthrow truth. Our enemy sows seeds of falsehood and doubt, then watches them grow alongside truth.

Act 2: An Avalanche

John wasn't merely strapped for cash—he experienced an avalanche of financial disasters, followed by prolonged fiscal struggles. Being financially constrained is an amoral condition;[14] allowing oneself to continue feeling that way is a slippery slope. The father of lies, ever ready to exploit slippery slopes, tossed John a subtle lie supported with indisputable data: vanishing income, growing expenses, unabated debt, and past the prime of life.[15] The accuser embellishes lies with accusations, and for John they sounded something like this: "You've messed up too much. You have too much debt. God has passed you by."

The accuser was slick enough to not overtly blame God, but pressed John's history of mistakes. Of course this courageous man of God had made mistakes. He had dared great things with God, and whether we like it or not mistakes are a part of life. God uses our mistakes to teach; our enemy wields them as banderillas, sharp barbed sticks thrust in the flesh to weaken and distract. Likewise, our enemy did not overtly depict God as smaller than circumstances; he harped on John's lack of finances. John allowed thoughts of financial constraint to fill up his bandwidth.

Even as I watched my friend diligently cooperate with God in every aspect of life, we both missed his unwitting reception of the incognito lie that he had to settle for something less—a lie that implied financial constraints at his age trumped God's plans, and the double-edged lie that neither John nor God could be trusted. Our enemy didn't care what version of the lie was chosen, and he was equally happy to see John ping-pong between them.

This stalwart of the faith regarded circumstantial evidence and its inferences as factual. Bank balances and age are facts; God fears no facts. When we listen to lying inferences conflated with facts, we have a problem. An avalanche of financial constraints does not mean God is smaller, nor do prolonged financial struggles mean our Redeemer has passed us by, but the accuser insinuated these to squelch John's freedom to dream.

Intellectually, our hero knew God's plans for him were based on God, for whom nothing is impossible, not John's bank balance or age. Any of us could answer that quiz correctly. John truly believed in God *Almighty,* and yet he lost hope. His lifestyle contradicted the truth he believed. It began innocuously when an incognito lie—*he needed to settle*—veiling a fundamental lie—*circumstances are bigger than God*—cloaking a secondary lie—*you can't be trusted and neither can God*—wrapped in an accusation—*you've made too many mistakes*—came crawling across his deck. John did not recognize the Trojan horse, so Satan's lies buried themselves deep in his psyche.

Act 3: A Penetrating Light

I cringe when I remember John sitting in his sunroom one afternoon saying, "I lost hope." Crushed for him I exclaimed, "Why didn't you tell me!" His response illustrates the impact of our enemy's violent-covert combo strategy: "I didn't realize the depths I had gone until I was coming out of it." While avalanching finances distracted him, slithering lies stole John's hope before he realized it was gone.

Satan relished driving our great hero to his knees, but then our Commander, Brilliance Himself, exposed the ungodly darkness of lost hope. Our Commander drew John's attention to Himself, revealing that He, the God for whom nothing is impossible, had not passed John by. He revealed that John need not settle, and that He wanted John to dare great things again, despite his bank balance and age.

The vital turning point came when our hero intentionally acknowledged that God never dilutes truth to equilibrate circumstances.[16] The tractive turning point came when our hero agreed with the One Who Cannot Lie, and subscribed to what God says about Himself, what He says about John, and what daring plans He had for John. Our hero *insisted* on these, enlisting the Spirit of Truth to eradicate lies and dispel untruth. In this way John aligned with truth, cleared his mind of lies and stood tall alongside his Commander.

Act 4: Five Steps

When John overcame, he employed five critical steps to cooperate with God to vigilantly, ruthlessly stand firm against lies intended to pull the rug out from under him.

Critical step #1: Soak in the truth. Our enemy favors the religiosity of reading God's Word as a task. It is essential to read God's Word *with God*, inviting Him to reveal truth and expose discrepancies between what we intellectually believe and what is evidenced by our attitudes and actions. It is essential to escape the clamor against our souls, diligently escaping external distractions and internal disquiet. John found it essential to simply ask God what *He* meant by each truth, and to listen as God revealed His answers.

Critical step #2: Become self-aware. I cannot clear the deck of lies I do not perceive. Sometimes I blissfully gloss over inconsistencies that contradict truths I believe. But ignorance is no excuse. I am called to be alert and self-aware.[17] In John's case, being alert and self-aware meant watching his hope meter to see when hope *begins* to deflate, long before it goes to zero. Becoming more self-aware includes a) learning what kind of meter we need (e.g. hope, fear, joy, and pride), and b) upgrading the meter's sensitivity so awareness kicks in sooner. This is an example of engaging our mind with the mind of Christ and our spirit with His Spirit to intelligently obey His commands to be alert and self-aware.

Critical step #3: Identify triggers that make us susceptible to believing lies. John had two triggers, financial constraints and the feeling of failure. Now aware of these triggers, John quickly gets off these slippery slopes and leaps onto the Rock. John takes feelings of financial constraints and failure to his Promised Sufficiency, Full Provision, and Complete

Protection. We are in a battle zone. It is essential we proactively prepare for battle by knowing our personal triggers.

Critical step #4: Vehemently reject the lies. We are in the fog of war, where faulty inferences and false accusations cloud the issue, and it is hard to see clearly. Therefore we must have the mind of Christ to unambiguously reject enemy diversions and attacks—like Jesus,[18] and like Shadrach, Meshach, and Abednego[19]—all of whom implacably refused to bow down to a lie. John now decisively turns away from subtle hints that he should settle, and actively turns toward daring exploits with God.

Critical step #5: Double down on truth. Jesus quickly rejected lies, emphatically doubled down on obedience, resubmitted Himself 100% to the Father, and embraced His own crucifixion. It is best to double down on truth by using the truth countervailing the root lie. In John's story, the root lie was that circumstances trump God, rendering both John and God untrustworthy. The countervailing truth is that God Almighty easily trumps circumstances; therefore we can trust God no matter what. John doubled down on truth by soaking in it, rejecting the accuser's lies, and resubmitting himself to the Father's daring plan for him.

Act 5: Heroic Hope

Our tried and true hero walked with God through three careers. Although he knew the truth, the time had come to viscerally learn truths at a deeper level. John learned the following verse deeper than ever: "'For I know the plans I have for you, *John*'—this is the LORD's declaration—'plans for your welfare, not for disaster, to give you, *John*, a future and a hope.'"[20] Our hero once swallowed lies unknowingly, but now he sees them come crawling onto his deck. He upgraded his hope meter to be sensitive to micro deflations. He also upgraded his hope meter to have a higher upper range because now he advances with joy, confident in his Hope, *daring with God to change the world.*

John recently spent his 58th birthday strategizing with his Creator to understand the pure, highly concentrated essence of John being wildly successful, unconstrained. He would not let me close his epic tale without encouraging you to get alone with God and ask Him three vital questions: *What lies have I accepted? What truth am I to replace for each lie? What gift does God want to give me in return?* I can see John's children and grandchildren gathered around as John says, "Let me tell you a story. It is the parable of our Gracious Father, His lavish response, and His desire to give us truth and gifts when we come home to Him."[21]

Determining the Pace

Differentiating between truth and lies determines the pace of our *Truventure*; it gives us warrior cleats in our pursuit of a strategically aligned life with our Creator. Some Christ followers relentlessly wrestle *every* fact and feeling into congruity with God's Word, and others—well, not so much. Some apply tenacious faith to see God All-wise untangle the complexities of life, and others—well, not so much. The former intentionally engage the One Who Cannot Lie to align their lifestyle with what they believe; the latter become comfortable with a lifestyle that contradicts truths they claim to believe.

We all experience avalanches, receive covert attacks, encounter complex problems, and find ourselves on slippery slopes. We all get tripped up; we live in a war zone where our integrity is the prized battleground between epic combatants—God, the Author of Truth, and Satan, the father of lies. *Truventure* is for those compelled to tractively align their life with Truth. The pace-determining step[22] is clearing the decks to enter into truth. Only then do we find traction to *truventure* with Him in the battle.

Truth and Lies: *A Lifestyle Clearing the Decks*

Although He is the One Who Cannot Lie,[1] few of us align every aspect of our lives to every truth He proclaims. I desperately want to be such a man, but I often walk out lies with a head full of doctrinal truth. I behave as if hurts, fears, and feelings trump God's clear and well-supported declarations.

I must clear the decks of my primary battleground, my mind, to stand free alongside my Commander.

Differentiating between truth and lies...gives us warrior cleats in our pursuit of a strategically aligned life with our Creator.

Ask & Listen–Talk it over with the One Who Cannot Lie

Jesus answered, "...for this reason I was born, for this I came into the world, to testify to the truth." John 18:37 (NIV) Read the word *with* God. Ask Him what He wants you to know today as you read this verse together. Record below the revelations that God unveils.

Invite Him to help you identify any areas where lies have crept in and made their way on the deck of your life. Make note of any lies exposed.

List 3 ways these lies are showing up in your attitudes or actions.

1.

2.

3.

Traction

Ask God to help you identify any triggers making you vulnerable to these lies. List them below. (For example, *financial hardship*)

Refuse to receive any whispers of condemnation that may be slithering nearby. Ask God to reveal the truth that annihilates each lie and record below what you hear Him say. (For example, *God promised to supply all my needs.*)*

Vehemently reject the lies and double down on truth. Declare the truth over yourself and your situation. Record your declaration in the space below.

Essence

Living the lifestyle clearing the decks is how we *truventure*. Picture God smiling in pride for your willingness to expose and clear the deck of lies! Ask Him to heighten your self-awareness and be quickly alerted to any lie that would threaten in the future. Talk with Him about a plan of action to expose and reject lies swiftly, decisively and vehemently. Summarize what you've learned in this chapter and imagine yourself and God trekking up the mountain of truth with warrior cleats, rejecting every lie

**The pace-determining step [of *Truventure*]
is clearing the decks to enter into truth.**

---

* Philippians 4:19

Chapter 4

Mind and Spirit

A Lifestyle of a Branch in the Vine

When I fully rest in Christ's provision, fully surrender to His ownership, and fully commit to differentiating between truth and lies, I am positioning myself for intimacy with the Lover of my soul. This most intimate of relationships works as long as I am candid with the One who knows everything anyway. By His very nature, God is personal and He communicates personally. "Mind and Spirit" explores how to engage in two-way communication with Him. For me, the pursuit of a strategically aligned life with my Creator is accomplished by intentionally addressing every aspect of life in the context of asking the One Who Knows, discussing it with Him, and following His lead.[1] Consequently, another *Prerequisite Principle* of *Truventure* is a lifestyle of engaging my mind with the mind of Christ and my spirit with the Holy Spirit.

First Principles First

How well we *truventure* is dependent on our ability to listen to and follow our True Quest. Hearing God's voice is not difficult if we are willing to shut out distracting noise inside and outside our heads. A lifestyle clearing the decks certainly helps too. It also requires contrite, humble, submissive dependence on Him as Lord, believing that He exists and that He rewards those who diligently seek Him.[2] He commits Himself with promises like, "Draw near to God, and He will draw near to you,"[3] and "Call to Me and I will answer you and tell you great and incomprehensible things you do not know."[4] God's Message to mankind is replete with admonitions to, and examples of, hearing His voice and walking with Him. Numerous Christian classics unpack these truths.[5]

Concerns with Spirit-led Strategy

Truventure, my pursuit of a strategically aligned life with my Creator, is my handbook for applying strategy to life. An astute question I often receive is, "How do you strategize and be led by the Holy Spirit?" As straightforward as this question appears, there are disparate presuppositions behind it.

Waste of Time or Diminished Dependence

When some people ask, "How do you strategize and be led by the Holy Spirit?" it is a way of articulating their view that strategy is a waste of time. They think that if one is led by the Spirit, then strategy is unnecessary. However, they might not apply the same "spiritual" strictness when they do not know how to drive to a desired destination.[6] And of course that is what strategy is—determining how to get from where you are to where you want to be. If we check a map or GPS to route our journey, we should also be comfortable with intentionally asking God questions about His direction for our lives.

Others fear strategizing will diminish dependence on the Holy Spirit, or that people will become more committed to their strategy than to obeying the Holy Spirit. These are legitimate fears. Man has an innate bias to not align with the Spirit, and a species-proven tendency to become more infatuated with what we think than what the Spirit of God says. I wholeheartedly agree with the paramount value placed on being led by the Spirit, and am against the application of strategy that is anything less than desperately dependent upon, and entirely subject to, the Holy Spirit.

My approach is Spirit-led strategy and ongoing submission to the Sovereign as He progressively reveals it. My approach is co-strategizing and co-executing strategy in the context of hearing God lead, and continually checking with Him and submitting to Him moment by moment, willing to change anything at any time. With this approach, strategy is not a waste of time, but rather it is essential to making the most of the time God gives me. This approach does not diminish dependence on the Holy Spirit, but *requires* it.

Oil and Water

Others ask, "How do you strategize and be led by the Holy Spirit?" because they consider strategy and being led by the Spirit as two completely different aspects of their lives. They do not see a connection between the two, nor do they see the need for them to be in the same sentence. They have never considered being strategic and simultaneously being led by the Spirit. Theirs is an oil and water perspective.

This perspective presupposes that one strategizes by engaging the brain, while being quasi-unengaged with the spirit. The presupposition that either our spirit or our brain be shifted toward neutral for the other to function at peak performance is a subtle lie that I reject. Similarly, I reject the notion that we ought to attain a balance of functioning with some level of strategy and some level of being Spirit-led. That is antithetical to my view. In my view, it is fully "both and," not "either or."[7] In other words, I see it as full-bore, Spirit-led co-strategizing, engaging my mind with the mind of Christ and my spirit with the Holy Spirit—not half-and-half.

God gave man both a mind and a spirit. Throughout His entire Message God calls man to question, analyze, test, and cognitively discover if He is true or not. He also calls us to discern with our spirit. As I submissively engage my mind with the mind of Christ and simultaneously engage my spirit with the Holy Spirit, I come to understand His view on strategic life issues and how I fit in His grand plan. Rather than oil and water, mine is a flourishing branch and vine perspective, where the branch can neither survive, nor produce, if not attached to the Vine. For me, my co-strategizing with Jesus is no less "in Him" than any other action I take.

Essentials for Spirit-led Strategy Development

There are three things I keep in mind as I practice a lifestyle of a branch in the Vine, as I co-strategize with Jesus, as I *truventure* with my True Quest.

1. Remain in dependent, humble submission to His agenda—no matter what.
2. Seek to understand His perspective—everything from His perspective.

3. God is interested in relational, progressive revelation of truths originating from His nature—not merely handing over requisite information.

This branch in the Vine lifestyle is not merely thinking and then taking the ideas to Him. Rather it is thinking and doing everything in the context of simultaneously asking Him, *What do You think about this?* Everything means every thing because "In Him we live and move and exist."[8] This is not a platitude; rather it is how we are to live every aspect of life. It is where the rubber meets the road. *Truventure* happens in the context of continually asking my Master Instructor, *Is this right?*

A Personal Example

For me all of this is lived out by simply "hanging out with Jesus,"[9] and discussing whatever is currently relevant to Him or me. I respond to whatever is on His mind and ask His opinion regarding what is on my mind. This is how I engage in two-way communication with God; this is my lifestyle of being the branch in the Vine.

Jesus is my Confidant. The more I interact with Him as my true Confidant, the easier it is to engage my mind with the mind of Christ while simultaneously engaging my spirit with His Spirit. It flows naturally. I start by writing out my questions, followed by His impressions. Then I pray through these, allowing the Editor to edit and re-edit until I have peace that I see the critical aspects from His perspective. It can be about anything, but the key point is that I simply process it with Jesus so I am following His lead. I process everything—every aspect of life, every issue, at any time—with Jesus. Sometimes my mind will ask, *Am I praying?* To which I reply, *Who cares; I am hanging out with Jesus, discussing important issues. Let me get back to that.*

Historical Examples

I see God strategizing and giving strategies throughout history. God gave Abram a personally specific strategy, *go west*,[10] which resulted in becoming the father of many nations. God gave the Israelites the strategy of isolation for national formation and spiritual purity.[11] God gave Gideon the strategy to defeat an innumerable army: dwindle his troops to 300.[12]

God gave Nehemiah a strategy for rebuilding the wall, with a sword in one hand and a trowel in the other.[13] And God gave Paul a tent-making strategy to undercut adversaries, exemplify the Christian work ethic, and demonstrate the proper motivation for work.[14] In these examples, God dealt with each man intellectually and spiritually. In fact, each story feels like a simultaneous intellectual and spiritual dialogue between God and man.

The Perfect Example

Jesus modeled the *Prerequisite Principle* of hearing God's voice by simultaneously engaging mind and spirit—intentionally addressing every aspect of life in the context of asking the One Who Knows. No matter what Jesus was doing, even though He is the Vine and we the branch, the Vine Himself modeled the lifestyle of the branch in the Vine for us by remaining in the Father. Our Perfect Example restricted Himself to one-ship with the Father, to will only what the Father wills, to judge only as the Father judges, to say only what the Father says, to do only what the Father does. Wow! That's what I want, too! I want to yield to my True Quest living His life in and through me. I want to engage in two-way communication with God about everything. As I become increasingly candid with the One who knows everything anyway, I come to realize how personal God is, and how He genuinely wants to communicate and journey through life with me. I want to intentionally, tractively follow Him in my pursuit of a strategically aligned life with my Creator.

Mind and Spirit: *A Lifestyle of a Branch in the Vine*

How well we truventure is dependent on our ability to listen to and follow our True Quest.

God gave man both a mind and a spirit.

The more I interact with Him [Jesus] as my true Confidant, the easier it is to engage my mind with the mind of Christ while simultaneously engaging my spirit with His Spirit—it flows naturally.

Ask & Listen–Talk it over with the Vine

"Trust in the Lord with all your heart and lean not on your own understanding" (Proverbs 3:5 NIV). Ponder this scripture and underline any key words that stand out to you. Invite Jesus to give you insight into what it means to fully engage your mind while being led by His Spirit. Listen for His wisdom to speak to your heart. Record below what you hear Him say.

Think about decisions that you've made recently...places you've gone... things that you've said and done. Ask Him to show you where your self-dependence superseded total dependence upon Him and write below what He brings to mind.

How might the things you identified via the preceding question have been different had you asked God, *"Is this right? What do you think about this?"*

Picture something that you do every day...something quite ordinary like simply driving to the office, getting the kids ready for school, or studying for a test. What might it look like to fully practice a lifestyle of a branch in the Vine in these very ordinary things?

Now, picture something more complex...maybe a major life decision that you must make, a significant task to complete at work, a difficult teenager to lead and guide. What might it look like to fully engage your mind and spirit in life's challenging decisions?

Mark talks about hanging out with Jesus, taking everything to Him. How would you describe the kind of relationship you desire with Him? Trust Him to lead you and make note of key ideas He brings to mind.

Essence

Living the lifestyle of a branch in the Vine is how we *truventure*. Imagine engaging your mind and spirit with God's, which is how He wants to journey with us. For me, this feels like coming into a pristine space. How about you? Summarize what you've learned from engaging your mind and spirit with His.

**He [God] genuinely wants to communicate
and journey with me through life.**

Chapter 5

The True You

A Lifestyle Embracing the Truth about You

C onsider the path we have taken as we near the end of part 1. We explored how to use the *Prerequisite Principles* of grace and lordship to accurately align with our Singular Provision and True Owner. We rejected lies that contradict truths we claim to believe, and we engaged our mind with the mind of Christ and our spirit with His Spirit. Now, in the "The True You," we invite our Designer to reveal His special design of each of us, and adjust our paradigm so we accurately see and wholeheartedly embrace His design of the unique you and the unique me.

My pursuit of a strategically aligned life with my Creator starts with seeing everything from God's perspective—including myself. It is vital to my lifelong strategy that I see how He sees me, accept the full truth of what He says about me, and honor my Creator by embracing the unique design package that is *me*. Seeing my True Quest as He describes Himself, and seeing me as He describes me, are essential to tractively advancing in my *Truventure*.

Divine Intentionality

God created each of us as a unique person. This means more than having a unique set of fingerprints. He created each of us with a complex synthesis of interests, expertise, personalities, talents, gifts, values, callings, relationships, passions, and priorities. He did this with divine intentionality. He did this for the fulfillment of His perfect grand plan, not by mere happenstance or rolling genetic dice. Our Creator is heavily invested in

His plan for each of us, and He does not leave us alone to figure it out. He yearns that we discover what wildly successful looks like so we fit in His grand plan—an incredible mosaic of unique designs.

Paragon Parent

Growing up, I wanted to be Roy Rogers, "King of the Cowboys." With his movie-star looks, fast draw, and fast horse, Roy was always on the right side of the law. Roy always won. I wore my cowboy hat and six-shooter with pride. The sawhorse my grandfather made me was painted palomino gold just like Roy's horse, Trigger. Yet clearly, I fell short. Set aside the Hollywood aspects, who other than Roy Rogers can be Roy Rogers? Now I realize that God specifically designed me to uniquely fit in His grand plan. Not even Roy Rogers could perform as God's purposed design, fit, and function of Mark Modjeska.

Even now, I sometimes find myself wanting to be someone I'm not. For example, I would like to be the most well-read man on earth. I feel guilty for not reading more, and what I do read is not what I aspire to read. I aspire to read the classics and biographies of great people. But I tend to read books on physics, the stock market, international intrigue, and a few classics. The classics that I read, I tend to re-read over and over again. But that is a hint about the true me. The true me is drawn to gain traction on existential truths. I am not saying which is better, but I am pointing out that understanding and embracing the truth about me—whatever that truth is—is key to the Great Artist's masterpiece rendering of the true me being wildly successful.[1]

Like the Paragon Parent that He is, God stands able and ready to help us unwrap the truth about you and me. This is staggering and breathtaking, with mind-boggling implications. It is liberty. Liberty is what I feel as I abandon my own identity agenda for the identity He constructed for me. Good can be the enemy of the best. What I want to identify with may be good (be the most well-read man in the world), but if it does not align with my Paragon Parent's design for me (be wildly successful at gaining traction on existential truths), then my good becomes the enemy of His best.

When I apply the *Prerequisite Principle* of engaging my mind and spirit with His, I am able to hear His voice teaching me the difference between my good and His best. Because I subscribe to the *Prerequisite*

Principle of lordship, I am able to relinquish my desired design of me and embrace His purpose for me. When I employ the *Prerequisite Principle* of rejecting lies and embracing the truth, I live out who I am, unconstrained. Because of the *Prerequisite Principle* of grace, I know none of this happens because of my own effort, and I have peace with no striving. As a result, I am thrust into God's perfect mold for me. I am truly me, and I bring joy to my Paragon Parent.

Identity: Universal and Unique

The existential question, *Who am I?* has universal and unique components. We were designed to discover both the common identity we have in Christ, and the individual person He specifically designed each of us to be.

As Christians, we share a common faith and truth, a common command and commission, a common purpose and goal, a common identity and victory. We share a common enemy and common weapons for standing in the victory Jesus won on our behalf. We share similar struggles and battles. And we often share the same lies that come crawling across our decks. God's Word emphatically and exhaustively emphasizes our common identity in Christ and the transformative, triumphant truths we share as believers. One can never go deep enough into all God conveys about being *in Christ*.[2]

The Great Artist creatively converges common and unique as He draws from the common identity components we have in Christ and the diverse set of traits He designed into each of us. He helps each of us become like Christ in similar and distinctive ways. The variety within the body of Christ exemplifies this, but it does not stop there. We see it through the ages.

The Bible is a kaleidoscope of people discovering and embracing how they were designed. Esther was designed to use her beauty in God's plan for His people's deliverance; while John the Baptist made a reverse fashion statement, wearing camel hair and preparing the way for the Messiah. David, the poet warrior king, was drawn to poetry and music, providing timeless inspiration in between countless battles; his son, Solomon, was drawn to knowledge and wisdom literature during a lifetime of peace. Daniel was designed to stand down hungry lions and corrupt administrations;

Hosea to withstand the heartache of betrayal to demonstrate the passionate pursuit God Himself feels for us. These illustrate great diversity of unique designs, which God sketches across the millennia.

These illustrative examples grab me by the lapels, shake me and demand to know: *What is the truth about God's design of me?* I am one of the characters He designed with divine intentionality to fit in His grand plan. I must align with the truth about me—the truth about me from His perspective.

What About You?

What makes you tick? Like Copernicus, Blaise Pascal, Robert Boyle, and Hugh Ross, some of us are drawn to science to leverage innate scientific curiosity for the glory of God. Some of us are compelled to connect with people, some with nature. Some are drawn to apologetics, some to politics, and others to athletics. In the movie *Chariots of Fire*, Olympic runner Eric Liddell says, "I believe God made me for a purpose, but He also made me fast. And when I run, I feel His pleasure."[3] We have the privilege to explore the question, "When I (fill in the blank), I feel His pleasure."

The picture of you or me being wildly successful comes into view if and only if we accurately perceive the distinctive ways we were each uniquely painted. The Master Artist paints one-of-a-kind portraits of us, each with a distinctive character all its own. He creatively expresses His image in us, each with our own special design to reflect His image with the specific passion He has for our unique life. He reveals His heart, the heart of the Great Artist, in each of us. As a result, we are a thing of beauty—individually and collectively. DC Talk says it this way:

> *A piece of canvas is only the beginning for*
> *It takes on character with every loving stroke*
> *This thing of beauty is the passion of an Artist's heart*
> *By God's design, we are a [...] kaleidoscope.*[4]

The Creative Artist blends in each of us the common identity we have in Christ and the unique identity components that He purposefully imbued in each individual. We do not all get Roy Rogers's good looks.

After all, God's own Son was considered unimpressive, was unrecognized by many, and was decorated with a crown of thorns.[5,6,7] And yet all these attract us even more. As we embrace how He paints us, we become even more attracted to Him than when we insist on being painted our way. The things we have in common in Christ flourish as we align with the specific person He designed each of us to be. In this way, we cooperate with the Master Artist's hand-painted panorama across the ages, purposed to fit in His grand plan.

Sub-optimized on Several Levels

The quest for a meaningfully significant life is sub-optimized when we don't see and align with God's design of us. What a tragedy it would be to miss out on the unique person God created us to be. The ripple effects of a disconnect regarding who we truly are and why God made us touch our spouses, our friends, our descendants—even reaching across generations. In addition to the personal impact, there is a societal impact. The Christian community bemoans the control of hyper-ungodly influences in the media, arts, science, entertainment, education, government, judiciary, and business. Many Christians find themselves yelling at their television as daily news stories betray abject foolishness of man's blatant rejection of a biblical worldview.

However, we have this culpability: for generations we patted ourselves on the back for pushing full-time Christian ministry at the exclusion of intentionally investigating what God created each of us to be and do. The unspoken can be powerful; as a result, many have felt guilty for aspiring to vocations other than the mission field. I grew up under sound Christian teaching but do not recall any teacher asking if I sensed a call to the mission field of the media, arts, science, entertainment, education, government, judiciary, or business. If we had done the latter, I believe there would be more Christians of godly influence in those fields today, and still have just as many who should rightly be in full-time Christian work. Did God need us to oversell full-time Christian work? I believe we could have better taught believers how to become all God created them to be, to mature in Christ and influence their world—whether it be an unreached people group, or their sphere of influence in society. Knowing the true you is that important.

It's Not About Me

I am not advocating personal, humanistic introspection. Instead, I advocate listening attentively to the Designer Himself. This investigation of the unique, true me is not for me—it is for Him. I simply want to see things—even myself—from His perspective, congruent with His truth, so I can tractively align with Him.

I had to learn and relearn that God is not committed to my design of me. My design included professional ascension; surely God would be glorified the higher I rose, right? But my desire to rise was based on a fallacy; it was based on my design of me, tweaked by personal ambition, and whitewashed with "spiritual" rationalization. It took successive demotions to make it clear that God was committed to His design for me, and not at all committed to my design of me. For years after my design did not work out, I struggled against the feeling that God had put me on the shelf. Unabashedly, He revealed that He intentionally put the trappings of my personal ambition on the shelf—not me. He revealed that I had so identified with a coveted title, executive office, large organization, and my own design for me that I felt put on the shelf along with them.

In 1997, God took great efforts to teach me to live the life Christ wants me to live; not the one I desire. Throughout the following years and decades, God took great pains to teach me many similar lessons even deeper. All these can be summarized under an umbrella lesson: God is committed to His design of me, and not at all committed to my design of me. After successive humiliations and demotions, I capitulated at successively deeper levels. I learned in deeper ways that it is all about Him and what He wants to accomplish in His design of me. *It is never about me.*[8]

Divine, Personal Revelation Brings Freedom

Our *Truventure* thrives on divine, personal revelation[9]—those times when God seems to download His truth into our mind and spirit. Divine, personal revelation is the sustenance of my true adventure.[10] By it He causes His truths to resonate within, and by it He exposes the lies that keep me from being all He created me to be.

When my thoughts about myself do not align with God's thoughts about me, His divine, personal revelation is the truth that exposes the untruth. Once the untruth is exposed, I need to choose the truth. If I harbor pride (thinking more highly of myself than I should), false humility (putting myself down when it is appropriate to admit my strengths), insecurities (not trusting God and His design of me), and pining comparisons (wishing I were like someone else), I yield to the enemy's distraction rather than submitting to God.

If I harbor any of these while maintaining that God designed me with agape love, unlimited power and complete wisdom, I am being intellectually dishonest. It is blatantly dishonest for me to mention how much He loves me or quote that His ways are higher than my ways, [11] and remain mentally disgruntled with how I am designed. I'm not saying we are not dealt tragedies that break our hearts, but I am saying that choosing to align with the Sovereign Lover of our soul takes spiritual and intellectual honesty. And for this we need divine, personal revelation in ever-deeper ways from the One who is Truth.

One such time for me was when He downloaded the obvious fact that *God does not do mediocre.* At first I thought, *Of course.* But think about it—that includes you and me. The fact that God does not do mediocre has staggering implications and unleashes all sorts of possibilities when I pursue a strategically aligned life with my Creator's plan. Even now, God reminds me that He will accomplish His design for this book. In so doing, He counters my insecurity that writing this book is way above my pay grade. Of course it is! "It is not that we are competent in ourselves to consider anything as coming from ourselves, but our competence is from God." [12] This is a great relief as I co-write with the One who does not do mediocre.

As He and I co-write, I embrace the truth about Him and the truth about me. It is freeing to embrace the things I both like and dislike in His creation of me. It is freeing to wean myself from the subtle, sometimes unconscious, longings to be something or someone else. It is freeing to clear the decks of subtle lies that defy the truth about my Creator and His creation, the true me. [13] This is part of letting Jesus, the untamed Lion of Judah, be Lord and Liberator.

Walking in the Light

As I *truventure* I am irresistibly drawn to the Light. In His light, I see things—including myself—from my Creator's perspective for a lifestyle that embraces the truth about me. As I tractively journey with God, I become more like Him.[14] Interestingly, my uniqueness flourishes rather than diminishes. His grand plan draws me into Himself to explore what wildly successful looks like for the life He intended. As I release the baggage of what I am not, I cry "Freeeeedom!"[15, 16]

Take the journey. Pursue a strategically aligned life with your Creator. Discover the unique person He designed you to become, the one-of-a-kind who fits exquisitely in the Creative Artist's awe-inspiring panoramic masterpiece. Only you can discover the true you.

Figure 5.1. She appears skeptical but I was one tough cowboy, really.

The True You: *A Lifestyle Embracing the Truth about You*

We invite our Designer to reveal His special design of each of us.

God stands able and ready to help us unwrap the truth about you and me.

God does not do mediocre—that includes you and me.

Ask & Listen—Talk it over with the Creator

"For we are His creation, created in Christ Jesus for good works, which God prepared ahead of time so that we should walk in them" (Ephesians 2:10 NASB). Imagine Jesus, the Master Designer, gazing upon you, His master creation. What is the truth about God's design of you? Ask Him what He sees when He looks upon you, His masterpiece. Record below what you hear Him say.

Review the following list of untruths and check any that you have allowed to influence your view of yourself:

☐ Pride (thinking more highly of self than you should)

☐ False humility (putting yourself down when it is appropriate to admit your strengths)

☐ Insecurities (not trusting God and His design of you)

☐ Pining comparisons (wishing you were someone else)

☐ Other _____

Write a statement renouncing each of the untruths that you checked above. My example is that *I renounce the insecurity and doubt that I feel when speaking in front of others and replace it with the trust that God will give me the words to share and the courage to speak in public with confidence.*

Mark emphasized the opportunity for Christians to serve in mission fields such as media, arts, and business. Similarly, Bill Bright, founder of Campus Crusade, and Loren Cunningham, founder of Youth With a Mission, taught of the importance of building influence in the seven mountains of society. On a scale of 1-5 with 5 being the highest, how strongly do you feel called to each of the seven mountains as listed below?

Media	1 2 3 4 5
Arts & Entertainment	1 2 3 4 5
Family	1 2 3 4 5
Business	1 2 3 4 5
Education	1 2 3 4 5
Judiciary/Government	1 2 3 4 5
Religion	1 2 3 4 5

God's divine fingerprints are evident in your unique creation. Describe yourself beside each category in the table below:

Passions & Interests	
Skills & Expertise	

Personality	
Values	

Mark writes that *God does not do mediocre —and that includes you and me.* Ask God what personal implications this statement has for your life. Write down what you hear Him say.

Essence

Living a lifestyle embracing the truth about you is how we *truventure.* Fix your eyes upon Jesus. Take the next bold step, and fully embrace the true you God revealed to you as you walked together through this chapter. Describe your favorite part of the true you below.

∽

Only you can discover the true you.

Prerequisite Principles

5. The True You:
A Lifestyle Embracing
the Truth about You

4. Mind & Spirit:
A Lifestyle of a
Branch in the Vine

3. Truth & Lies:
A Lifestyle Clearing
the Decks

2. Lordship:
A Lifestyle Yielded to
My True Owner

1. Grace :
Resting as a
Lifestyle

Personalized Truth Markers

For each chapter, write a *personal application* of the recorded truth:

◖▶ *1.* **Grace**—*Resting as a Lifestyle*

I enter into resting as a lifestyle when I move from summoning *my* wisdom and power, to allowing *Jesus's* wisdom and power to live through me.

For me, it means _____

_____

_____

_____

_____

◖▶ *2.* **Lordship**—*A Lifestyle Yielded to My True Owner*

I want to be wary of when my lifestyle usurps Christ's rank and when my strategizing usurps His ownership of me

For me, it means _____

_____

_____

_____

_____

◖▶ *3.* **Truth & Lies**—*A Lifestyle Clearing the Decks*

Differentiating between truth and lies determines the pace of our *Truventure*; it gives us warrior cleats in our pursuit of a strategically aligned life with our Creator.

For me, it means _____

_____

_____

_____

_____

❥ 4. **Mind & Spirit**—*A Lifestyle of a Branch in the Vine*

The more I interact with Him (Jesus) as my true Confidant, the easier it is to engage my mind with the mind of Christ while simultaneously engaging with His Spirit—it flows naturally.

For me, it means_____

_____

_____

_____

_____

❥ 5. **The True You**—*A Lifestyle Embracing the Truth about You*

It is vital to my lifelong strategy that I see how He sees me, accept the full truth of what He says about me, and honor my Creator by embracing the unique design package that is me.

For me, it means _____

_____

_____

_____

_____

PART TWO
Strategic Intentionality

My undergraduate courses taught me the importance of prerequisites, competitive swimming taught me the benefit of being intentional, and the marketplace taught me the value of thinking strategically. Consistent intentionality in daily swim practice makes the difference between clocking a personal best time or not in the championships. Thinking strategically often makes the difference between growing a business or bankrupting it. In the same way, *Strategic Intentionality* makes the difference for me between meandering through life and purposefully aiming at being wildly successful in God's plan for me. While *Prerequisite Principles* provide a lens to correct my paradigm, *Strategic Intentionality* provides tractive vehicles for me to strategically align with my True Quest. He uses the vehicles in *Strategic Intentionality* to reveal where I gloss over inconsistencies between my lifestyle and His truth—gaps He wants to close. I use each vehicle to practice hearing His voice and actively yield to His lead. As I followed His lead, He forbade me to think of these vehicles as "tools" to be a better Christian. He impressed upon me that His higher priority for me was intentionally, wholeheartedly journeying with Him to maximize this life for eternity. God invites us to explore vehicles of *Strategic Intentionality* to maximize our alignment with Him and our role in His grand plan.

I use the term *Connected Integrity* to emphasize to myself that I want every aspect of me to accurately align with Truth Himself. This is God's highest good for me—zero gaps between His character and mine. But here's the problem—my highly developed ability to rationalize glosses over inconsistencies between my lifestyle and His character. I also use the term *Connected Integrity* to contemplate God's nature: the Venn diagram of His character, words, and actions overlay perfectly. If the Venn circles of my character, words, and actions overlay perfectly with God's, then I have *Connected Integrity* with Him. When they do not, I am entertaining selective obedience. How do I escape the oxymoron of selective obedience, despite my uncanny ability to rationalize? I yield to the Lover of my soul, who uses vehicles in part 2 with super abounding grace to deliver me from selective obedience and gain traction for a lifestyle of *Connected Integrity* with Him.

Chapter 6

Personal Covenant with God

A Lifestyle of Deepening Surrender

The deepest surrender possible was demonstrated by my Savior, who surrendered His life for me. I want to reciprocate in full, releasing every aspect of my life to Him. For this I use my personal covenant with God—where I relinquish all of me in a succinct document. We focus entirely on how *He* defines lordship and what that looks like in my life. In it we go for the jugular; we make it my most singularly focused, concerted attempt to submit, align, and cooperate with Him as my Lord. In my pursuit to align with Jesus, I tried different things, and though my first covenant was drafted in desperation, it has become an incredibly tractive vehicle of strategic intentionality. I use it to actively align and intentionally hold myself accountable to make Jesus Lord with specificity.

A Stake in the Ground

I was at the end of my rope when I drafted my first covenant with God. I had been at the end of my rope many times before, but this time felt worse. I felt I had more to lose than ever. I had a death grip on the rope of career advancement, while watching it unravel. Then, from the end of my unraveling rope, I remembered something. At a conference years ago, I heard Bill Bright[1] share that he wrote a contract turning everything over to God. Clutching to the end of my rope, I asked, *Why wouldn't I do that?* It was not the first time I surrendered all—more like the millionth. But my first draft brought traction to my quest for deepening surrender. This is typical of *Truventure*: I did not need more head knowledge on lordship; I needed the truths I already "knew" imbedded into the fabric of my being.

In my covenant, I transferred every aspect of "my" life to God. I turned over 100% ownership and complete management to Him. That is why you see quotes around *my* modifying *life*. It is not mine.[2] In the million times I had surrendered to Jesus before, I had meaningfully relinquished all to Him. Even if I eventually took some bits back and had to surrender them again, there was nothing inherently wrong with those surrenders, but to gain traction I needed more. The *more* I needed was proactive, tractive, ever-deepening surrender. I needed to proactively learn from God what genuine surrender looks like to Him; I needed to discuss with Him every implication of His 100% ownership of me, and I needed to learn what Jesus's complete management of me looks like.

My first draft was a remedial step but essential for sustained advancement. I simply tried to delineate His lordship in simple, concrete words. The original three paragraphs, signature and inventory are captured in Figure 6.1.

Covenant

This validates my total surrender, full submission, and irrevocable release of all aspects of this life to the lordship of Jesus Christ.

This life is best described as the life God allows me to live. It is not my life! It belongs to God alone. He is Owner. I forfeit it to become His lifetime slave. I own nothing and have no rights.

With everlasting gratitude, I choose to humbly lack what You withhold, relinquish what You take, suffer what You allow, receive what You give, to be what You require.[3]

Mark Modjeska
Date: 17 October 2003

Inventory:

Mind, Heart, Eyes, Tongue, Hands, Feet

Authority, Rights, Will, Decisions

Beliefs, Convictions, Attitudes, Thoughts

Ambitions, Hopes, Dreams, Desires

How I spend my time, What I watch, listen to, and read

Health, Security, Family, Friends, Ministry

Wealth, Finances, Social Security, Insurance, Retirement

House, Furnishings, Electronics, Cars

Swimming, Skiing, Vacation, Eating

Figure 6.1. Mark's Original Covenant

That succinct document was my stake in the ground. It was like writing on my mirror, "God alone is Owner!" My context of *ownership* came from high-level contract negotiations where we delineated who owns what, who is responsible for what, and who gets what in the exchange. In my experience every contract was enthusiastically negotiated by both parties, every transfer of ownership gladly embraced. Writing my covenant with God with the gravitas of a contract felt good. It felt good to declare I would no longer abide self-in-control, because I never wanted self to usurp God's ownership of me. It felt good to declare I would no longer abide the incongruity of claiming His lordship yet managing my life. It felt good to seal the deal in a way that was meaningful to both parties, explicitly embracing creed-like terms in black and white. He wanted to write it in stone, but we settled on an electronic version.

The most proficient Manager I could ever find graciously accepted to make management decisions in my life: some of which He would make, some of which He would delegate to me, and others He would collaborate on with me. There is a wonderful soft side of sovereignty that I see when the Father asks, "What would you like the decision to be?" But no matter what the decision, no matter which decision-making process my Manager employs, surrender is not fractional—it is a whole number. The only acceptable terms of surrender to God are 100%.

An amazing thing happened as I prayed through my covenant. It became a living document, a vehicle my Lord could use to further unwrap what lordship and surrender mean to Him. I invited Him to use this document to dig deep in me, to unearth and address fractional surrender in me. Therefore, my covenant is a progressive vehicle exploring deepening surrender. Exploring lordship on His terms, with concrete specifics, started with the first draft: innumerable drafts thereafter are successive stakes in the ground marking the continued expedition. Like compounding dividends, each step of deepening surrender makes the next step more valuable.

It's Not What You Call It That Matters

I called my covenant a contract because that's what the late Bill Bright, a man I respect for his integrity, called his. Like Bill, I love the gravitas of a good contract, clearly defining roles and responsibilities, benefits and obligations. Personally, I need a strong name to send a binding message to myself, and I savor the intense clarity of well-written contracts. While Bill, others, and I value our experience with contracts, others cringe at the word. It can connote fine print, legalese,[4] and confusion—clearly the opposite of the intended purpose. Please call it whatever appeals to you. *Covenant* is rich in relational connotations; alternate terms include *agreement,* or *vow.* It makes no difference what you call it. It makes all the difference how you mean it, what you include, Who you allow to edit it, and how you progressively use it. Your covenant should be succinct, honest, tractive, and uniquely yours.

Plumb the Depths

I need to proactively plumb the depths with God if I am to have *Connected Integrity* with Him. To do this, I get alone with God to discuss my covenant with Him one phrase at a time. As we examine each creed-like statement—what it means to Him and how it relates to my life—He unpacks fundamental truths, explains how each is to play out in my life, and points out gaps between His truths and my reality. I respond with ironclad language in my covenant as I attempt to more deeply surrender to what He wants of me.

I am not in a hurry to get through the document. Often I do not. My goal is to camp out on whatever phrase the Holy Spirit chooses to impress upon me in the moment. This is the fertile ground of *Truventure.* I must be in the moment, actively listening. I ask the Holy Spirit to make the words He lifts off the page truer of me in deeper ways. My overriding objective is to be as honest with Him as possible. I share where and how I am struggling. I consciously push the bounds of candor, and consciously reject my highly developed ability to rationalize, so I can be genuine and real with my Confidant.

When we spend time together, Jesus highlights areas in me that are not surrendered to Him. I hate their existence, so I love that He pinpoints each one. As a result, my current version includes clauses like these:

- I have no latitude to yield to any temptation.
- I have no latitude to harbor any longings contrary to Christ.
- I have no latitude to squander time.

I ask Jesus to bring His magnifying glass to our times together. I need Him to look at each aspect of me in detail, to assess my lifestyle vis-à-vis His, with granularity. Granularity is the level of detail in the data. He looks at the data and reveals the gaps between my lifestyle and His. He reveals His solution as well. He always brings the solution: He Himself is the Solution. Together we plumb lordship on His terms, with increasing granularity. One expression of such granularity is my inventory of what I have surrendered to the Owner. It intensifies my surrender by adding specificity. When I review my inventory with Him, I ask after each item, *What else?* I am actively listening for Him to respond; He inevitably does. My inventory invites God, the Counter Party of my covenant, into every specific aspect of me with increasing granularity for renewed, ironclad, and ever-deeper surrender. I find it essential and in my best interest to assess with the Owner whether I have taken anything back. He responds with pertinent specificity.

He plumbs the depth of a phrase one day, plumbs it deeper another day, and deeper still on another. He addresses a breadth of issues: one day He deals with who He is, another with my identity, another with what it means to believe Him. One day He deals with my thought life, another with my speech, another with my time management, and another with my eternal significance; the list goes on. One day He dropped in my lap a five-point plan for how He wants me to trust Him as Lord. I transcribed each point into my covenant. He continued to refine each point as I actively listened with *Strategic Intentionality.* Another day I explained that my love for Him was not motivating me as powerfully as I wanted. He responded with focused, far-reaching insights in four succinct paragraphs, which I titled "A Lifestyle of Reciprocal Love." He never overwhelms me with too much to address; He always overwhelms me with His sufficiency.

As He reveals His insights and revelations to me, I find myself *co-editing with God.* No edit is too small; every edit is made in hope of even more clarity and a lifestyle of even deeper surrender to my Liege Lord. Every phrase is continually distilled to be more precise per His insights. This is not fully accomplished this side of eternity, so my latest draft is never treated as final. I reject every inclination to think of my covenant as a finished product. Rather, it is a document depicting the current step in my *Truventure* with Him. A decade-plus of co-editing my covenant with the Lover of my soul is found in appendix A, along with Angela's. Even though we have been discussing it for years, He continually reveals something new. He always has more to reveal, more to unpack concerning what His 100% ownership and complete management of me looks like. And it is pure pleasure for me to pray into the joy of a lifestyle of deepening surrender.

My objective in praying through my covenant is to proactively journey with Him, to follow His lead in my pursuit of *Connected Integrity* with Him. I am interested in the distance traveled within me, not the distance I travel through the document. As I pray through what integrity looks like, we plumb the depths as the Holy Spirit points out unaligned aspects of my lifestyle. I want the gaps between us exposed so I can yield to a lifestyle of *Connected Integrity* with Jesus, where every thought, belief, word, and action align with Truth Himself.

Deepening Grace

Praying through my covenant is never a task. It is a meaningful, productive adventure each day with the Lover of my soul. I want to do it daily but never legalistically. I endeavor to pray through at least a portion of my covenant *on a routine basis* that more nearly approximates *daily* than *weekly*. Recall our grace pact: I disavow *daily* in a legalistic way, and I ask that grace-pact-keeping readers do the same.

Per our pact, everything in our journey is through grace alone, by faith alone, in Christ alone. Christ alone can accomplish a lifestyle of deepening surrender. He works in us to will and do His good pleasure.[5] Each of us is held accountable to say yes to Him, but even our yes is by His grace. There is no striving to construct, no endeavoring to earn. In *Truventure* we strive and endeavor, but *how* we do it is jugular—by simply yielding to Him, doing what He wants by His mighty power and grace, for His eternal glory.[6] *He* does the deepening in us; we simply cooperate, yielding to His control, letting go of ours. Like everything in *Truventure,* it is not about the covenant itself. It's about getting alone with Jesus to understand His perspective, to align with the Lover of my soul.

Ironclad Rails to Freedom

As I surrender, He steels ironclad rails destined for *Connected Integrity* with Him. In order to accurately target a lifestyle of deepening surrender,

I invite my Counter Party to assess whether I am living up to my side of our covenant. Fortunately, the Counter Party is also my Advocate, who works in me to fulfill my covenant with Him. And my Counselor, the Holy Spirit, points out how we are going to cooperate to close the gaps between my theology and my reality. This is *Truventure*, the ultimate transformational, tractive, and intentional journey of strategically aligning with my Creator in every aspect of life. The ironclad language of my living covenant becomes ironclad rails for my path to freedom, the freedom of fully yielding control to my Liege Lord.

Personal Covenant with God:
A Lifestyle of Deepening Surrender

I did not need more head knowledge on lordship; I needed the truth I already "knew" imbedded into the fabric of my being.

I ask Jesus to bring His magnifying glass to our times together.

I want the gaps between us exposed so I can yield to a lifestyle of Connected Integrity with Jesus, where every thought, belief, word, and action align with Truth Himself.

Ask & Listen—Talk it over with God

Discuss with God what you will call your living document. Select from the list below or fill in the blank with your own key word.

- ☐ Covenant
- ☐ Contract
- ☐ Agreement
- ☐ Vow
- ☐ _____

Rather than trying to figure it out on your own, ask God what key elements He wants you to include in your personal covenant. List them here.

Release all self-induced pressure of getting this right and just imagine talking to God as you write your living document. What matters is candidly asking God what it means for Him to be Lord or your life. The specifics He brings to mind are important. Jot them down as a draft covenant on one of the blank pages at the back of the book.

Traction

Select one phrase from your first draft. Ask God if there is anything else He wants you to know about this. Discuss it with the Lord, asking Him to give you a picture of deepening surrender. Describe below the picture He unveils.

Essence

Living a lifestyle of deepening surrender is how we *truventure*. You've taken the tractive step of surrender in composing your covenant with God. Closing any gaps between your theology and your reality is worth engaging your mind and spirit with His in your covenant. Describe how praying through your covenant with God will help you gain traction for a lifestyle of deepening surrender.

As I surrender, He steels ironclad rails destined
for Connected Integrity with Him.

Chapter 7

Strategic Intent

A Lifestyle Doing the Next Right Thing

was clueless about a lot of things early in life. Some eight-year-olds know what they want to be when they grow up. At age eighteen, I had not given it much thought. After college, graduate school, and a decade in the marketplace, I felt called to continue in business, as a leader doing what Christ would do if He were in my shoes. He was happy to show me how to do the next right thing, as long as I yielded my mind to the mind of Christ and my spirit to His Spirit. Doing the next right thing requires making choices. Strategy is about making intelligent, tractive choices. Strategic intent[1] is a business concept I picked up during the Advanced Management Program at INSEAD,[2] a concept that yields sustained traction in business. Strategic intent guides each employee, empowers all divisions, and focuses every company within a conglomerate toward a shared stretch objective.

The undeniable effectiveness of strategic intent in the workplace brought me to a question. As you will see in subsequent chapters, it became a perennial question: *If it works that well in business, why wouldn't I use it for what concerns me most—my own life?* With trepidation I asked, *What is the strategic intent of my life?* The question resonated with my desire to pursue a strategically aligned life with my Creator and to have a focused, over-arching, life-long objective that would tractively harness my options and intelligently guide my decisions.

Examples, Classic and Personal

Readers of *Harvard Business Review* will recognize Komatsu as the classic business example of a company using strategic intent to harness visionary aspirations. For most of the 20th century, Caterpillar was the leader in heavy earth-moving equipment in nearly every country, with a massive product portfolio and global infrastructure supporting over 400 products. Komatsu was one-third the size, had essentially one product line, and was predominantly a one-country company. But Komatsu leveraged its strategic intent—*Encircle Caterpillar*—to focus its employees' energies with this long-term, stretch objective. In doing so, Komatsu became a formidable competitor.[3]

My own strategic intent—*Wholeheartedly devoted to God*—filters my options and examines my decisions. My strategic intent simply and effectively focuses me on what and how Christ would lead in the marketplace if He were in my place. It gives me a filter to reject man's way of doing things, so He can live His life in and through me in my world. *Wholeheartedly devoted to God.* I like that it is theocentric. I like that it is a heartfelt call to action. I like that as it becomes increasingly true, everything comes under submission to Christ. I like that it would take a lifetime to plumb the depth and breadth of its full meaning, and yet every second of my life I can know if it is currently true. In a simple way, it infuses my life with Strategic Intentionality. OK, I like it more than you do. But that is my point; God makes it resonate within *me*, to fulfill His call on me.

A friend whom I deeply respect has a great strategic intent. I have never heard him use the term, but clearly his strategic intent is, *Just say yes to Jesus.* It is Nike's slogan, *Just do it*, inescapably applied to lordship. It presupposes God's authority and demands unequivocal obedience no matter the circumstance. It refocuses the mind on the jugular point—it is always Jesus's decision, not mine. It reliably tests life's complexities and options. It is decisive. It invokes the right answer, even if leaning away from it. It is simple, succinct, divinely revealed, and incredibly useful to motivate, guide, and curb wayward tendencies. It is brilliant! Even better than brilliant, he owns it.

Daniel's Strategic Intent

Daniel, the Jew exiled to Babylon in 605 BC, is an epic example of living out a personal strategic intent. Daniel's lifestyle was in stark contrast with the Babylonian culture. Despite power politics and a godless culture, Daniel faithfully chose to align with God's commands. This is *Connected Integrity*, and Daniel's was impeccable.

As he begins to tell his own story, Daniel reveals his strategic intent—*I am determined not to defile myself.*[4] Throughout the entire plot, those seven words guide Daniel's choices. He remains true to his strategic intent, even when doing so threatens his advancement and his survival. Instead of caving to the prevailing immoral culture, which pulls at every natural desire, Daniel successfully determines not to defile himself. It starts with food and drink, but as Daniel chronicles his life, we witness a man living out his strategic intent in a variety of situations.

In the famous lions' den episode, we see Daniel determine not to defile himself. Despite an irrevocable edict forbidding all citizens to pray to anyone other than the king, Daniel visibly prays to his God, knowing he is signing his death warrant. He is cast into a den of hungry lions for disobeying the king's edict and miraculously survives, unscathed. Daniel would tell us the choice, not the outcome, matters. Even so, let the record show the lions do not harm Daniel, yet immediately devour his rivals.

As Daniel's story unfolds, subtler and more eternally dangerous challenges emerge. Temptations of pride, glory, and corrupt gain lurk. Successive successes make the temptations even greater. Daniel is mightily used by God. He is clearly the smartest man in the room. He is promoted to the top echelons of power in the most powerful kingdom on earth. Yet he determines not to defile himself with pride.[5] Daniel gains the reputation of having God's spirit. He receives angelic visions. Nonetheless, Daniel determines not to defile himself by usurping one iota of God's glory.[6] Daniel is surrounded by prosperity, self-gratification, and self-serving corruption. Nonetheless, he determines not to defile himself with self-indulgence and selfish gain. Success often exposes cracks in one's integrity; successive successes almost ensure it. But *Connected Integrity*, though exceptionally rare, is possible—and God proves it in the life of Daniel.

Daniel's life-long faithfulness to core beliefs and values reveal what a lifestyle of *Connected Integrity* looks like, even under the most adversarial circumstances to one's soul, career and life. Daniel turned the initial decision not to defile himself into a lifelong lifestyle. He embraced his strategic intent and applied it to every aspect of life. Daniel's strategic intent presupposed God's preeminence and centered him on God's call to do the next right thing. Daniel never deviated from his strategic intent. Daniel finished well—undefiled, his integrity connected to his preeminent God.

Cacophony of Oughts and Options

The story of Daniel's strategic intent is one of *preemptive* integrity despite prevailing culture, danger, and temptation. But strategic intent is also essential in the face of good. Following one's strategic intent is essential for doing the next right thing in the midst of life's cacophony of oughts and options, even when they're all good.

I ought to be this; I ought to be that. I ought to do this; I ought to do that. I ought to be more this; I ought to be less that. I ought, I ought, I *ought*. While the oughts may be good, the barrage is debilitating, not empowering. Oughts would not tug at us if they did not have an element of good, but when given too much clout they compete with what is best. It is unacceptable for me to do loads of good things, only to miss His best plan for me.

Strategic intent helps me make intelligent choices and quiet the cacophony of oughts. A God-given, personalized strategic intent can push the proliferation of oughts to the outskirts of consciousness. The oughts become irrelevant because there is something far more valuable to pursue: one's over-arching, life-long objective.

Optionality is a good thing; as a strategist I love optionality. But the proliferation of options can numb our assessment of what is important. If we want to be strategic, we cannot afford to be overwhelmed by the number of options, oblivious to the most important possibilities. Strategic intent intelligently focuses one's time, energy, and resources to harness life's proliferation of options so our decisions align with God's call. The result is strategic, laser-like focus towards a lifestyle of *Strategic Intentionality* for the fulfillment of His grand plan.

Discovering One's Strategic Intent

Cooperating with Jesus for the fulfillment of His grand plan requires a faithful response to His call. Therefore, it is essential to investigate the overarching objective He wants exemplified in me, a.k.a. my strategic intent. So I simply ask Him the question, *What do You want to characterize me more than anything else?* His answer is priceless. Getting alone with God is priceless. Our journey and where He leads is priceless.

If priceless, why don't I see everyone going after it? It is easier to do a lot of good than hold yourself accountable for what is best. To co-decide one's own strategic intent requires courage. It takes courage to receive God's trust. He trusts us to be wise and strategic with His call. It takes courage to be visionary with the life entrusted to us. Visionaries have the courage to embrace a higher calling. They focus on that higher calling at the expense of everything the rest can't leave behind. Choose to be visionary in this way: embrace the overarching, lifelong objective He designed to resonate within you. His strategic intent for you delivers clear direction in every circumstance. It can prioritize the proliferation of oughts and options, so you can do the next right thing.

I encourage you to get alone with the One who designed you. Get a cup of coffee or tea, get comfortable, and get quiet for uninterrupted strategizing with Jesus. Yield your mind to the mind of Christ and your spirit to His Spirit. Identify together His strategic intent for you to align with His call. Embrace His answer. By His grace, He will respond to these questions asked in contrite humility:

- When sorting through challenges, questions, confusion, and difficulties, is there a go-to phrase or concept that always seems to help me do the next right thing?
- What concept or phrase does God bring to mind when I face the proliferation of oughts and options?
- Is there a guiding-light concept, phrase, or call that describes my life?
- If I could be one thing, what would that be? What do both He and I want to characterize me, more than anything else?
- What does God continually impress upon me that harmonizes what He wants of me overall?

- In summary, what simple statement succinctly articulates the key points my Designer said as I asked these questions?

A great strategic intent is simple, straightforward, and personally compelling—a clarion call that inspires you to do the next right thing. It links your personal daily life to a timeless, higher call in a way that resonates with you. Great examples include *Just say yes to Jesus,* and *I am determined not to defile myself.* In each example, the respective man of God leveraged the simplicity of his strategic intent for sustained traction for a lifestyle of *Connected Integrity.*

Maximized Significance

In the millennia of history there are few Daniels. God yearns for more. He yearns for wise, intentionally strategic responses to His highest call on each of us. He yearns for us to experience a lifestyle of *Connected Integrity* with Himself. But just as for Daniel, it does not happen without extreme intentionality to intelligently focus on Him, decisively cut through distractions, diligently harness options, and faithfully align every decision with His call. I may have started out clueless in life, but I have no intention to stay that way. Join me; venture with Jesus to seize the day with your strategic intent. Experience Daniel's undeterred lifestyle of *doing the next right thing* as you *truventure* with your True Quest.

Strategic Intent: *A Lifestyle Doing the Next Right Thing*

The proliferation of options can numb our assessment of what is important.

My own strategic intent filters my options and examines my decisions.

Strategic intent helps me make intelligent choices and quiet the cacophony of oughts.

Ask & Listen–Talk it over with God

Your Designer anxiously awaits the joy of conversation with you. Pen a prayer asking Him to help you quiet your heart and hear His voice.

When sorting through challenges, questions, confusion, and difficulties, is there a go-to phrase or concept that always seems to help you do the next right thing?

What concept or phrase does God bring to mind when you face the proliferation of oughts and options?

If you could be one thing, what would that be? What do both He and you want to characterize you, more than anything else?

What does God continually impress upon you that harmonizes what He wants of you overall?

Circle key phrases in the answers you captured above and write a simple statement succinctly summarizing them into your strategic intent.

Strategic Intent

Essence

Living a lifestyle of laser-like focus is how we *truventure*. The laser-like focus of your strategic intent will help you filter options and examine decisions as you move forward. Describe how your life's journey will be different after you apply your strategic intent to the cacophony of oughts and important decisions.

⌒

**Venture with Jesus to seize the day
with your strategic intent.**

Chapter 8

Core Principles

A Centered Lifestyle

H*e lost his way.* We know it when we see it: principles abandoned, integrity lost, character entropied. Personally, this scares me—greater men than I have lost their way. So I ask the One who designed me: *What truths, values, and principles do You want to rule my choices, transform my character, and be imbedded in the fabric of my being?* The answers, which resonate so profoundly in me that I want them to rule how I respond to every situation, are my core principles.

It takes energy to reverse entropy, but this is not a problem. God created energy, and His strategic intent for mankind is *Christ-like sons and daughters.*[1] The Ultimate Force Himself powerfully infuses core principles into His *Truventurers* to regain abandoned principles, reverse the trajectory of integrity lost, and realign a disordered life. He uses core principles for a lifestyle centered on Him so we can *find* our way, not *lose* it.

Developing Core Principles

To identify my core principles, I get alone with the One who designed me and ask Him what they should be. He identifies, clarifies, refines, and intensifies the core principles He selects for me. He connects my core principles to current situations. He repeats this process in a variety of contexts. In each context He highlights the value of the core principle, emphasizes its connection to Himself, and helps me visualize what a lifestyle centered in Him looks like. Personally, I find this process tractively intensifies my love and commitment to Him.

I keep my core principles document in my quiet time folder so I can pray through them on a daily basis. When I do, Jesus connects His teachings and my life situations, making my core principles more alive and relevant. The Editor edits as we discuss them. Over time, He deepens my core principles within me—cognitively, viscerally, and practically, until my lifestyle demonstrates His character. As I relinquish instant self-gratification in favor of lifelong integrity, He sinks my core principles deeper into my consciousness, heart, will, and lifestyle into the fabric of my being. This is how He centers me in Him for a lifestyle centered on Him.

Thirty years ago, as a young engineer in the Norwegian wilderness, I asked God to help me identify my core principles. Originally we came up with nine. Recently I added three. I finally identified them as core principles when I realized I had been asking God to imbed them in the fabric of my being for years. This is key to identifying core principles—if you get alone with God and listen, He will bring to mind, unwrap, and refine the core principles you continually *yearn* for. The subject matter of my core principles changes little over time, but they are not "once and done." God continues to deliver deeper insights into what each core principle means to Him, and how to better cooperate with Him so that each is increasingly evidenced in my life.

He reveals more of Himself in each of my core principles, thereby creating in me an ever-intensifying desire for a life centered in Him. They become less about stand-alone principles, and they become increasingly about Him being reflected in me more and more. Various organizations use team-building exercises. Jesus takes this to the stratosphere using core principles to intensify the quality of my relationship with Him.

I share my approach to core principles, but your approach and core principles should uniquely reflect your own *Truventure*. The process is simple, but needs to be intentional and diligently relational—getting alone with Jesus to discuss the principles, values, and truths most important to you both. Consider how He has impressed you in the past. Listen to how He impresses you now. Make a list, prioritize it, and together pick the top choices. Allow the Editor to edit as you pray through your core principles daily.

Rewired Circuits

High frequency traders shorten the physical distance between their servers and the stock exchange to make their high-speed connections even faster. I look at my core principles this way; God "rewires my circuits" to shorten the connection between principle and action, to close the gaps between my lifestyle and His character. As I cooperate with my Circuit Master we become closer, more connected, and more centered in Him. He uses core principles to accelerate this impact on me.

Jesus's personalized core principles for me include: 1) Believe God and all that entails, 2) *Connected Integrity*, and 3) Everything from God's Perspective. They are more vibrant and vital to me now than when He first gave them to me over three decades ago. Let me illustrate with my number one core principle, *Believe God and all that entails*. These six words pack a lifelong, accelerating punch for me.

Believe God means I innately trust His nature. To innately trust God, I must reckon myself crucified in Christ to truly reckon myself resurrected in Christ. The ego-centered nature can never fully trust God, but the new creation in Christ can. *Believing God* is more than implicit trust; it is implicit trust lived out explicitly by *acting* accordingly to His truth in all things, all the time. *All that entails* means I embrace His zero-gap policy when it comes to believing Him and acting like it. Zero gaps are impossible for me to attain; I enlist Jesus to close every gap between His Word and my lifestyle.

Believe God and all that entails requires infinitely more than cognitive accuracy and pristine theology—it requires that I align with Him moment by moment, in every aspect of life, by His grace. Imagine believing everything in God's Word—no filters, incorrect presuppositions, or personal bias. Imagine disavowing every lie, no matter how subtle. *Believing God and all that entails* shortens the distance between principles and action.

In Advance

In advance are two words that preempt defeat with victory. Soldiers do not wait for the day of battle to train, athletes do not wait for the race to get into shape, and students do not wait for the exam to learn. I need to cooperate with Jesus *now* to imbed core principles into the fabric of my being *in advance* of upcoming tests.

Praying through my core principles, I seek to understand the essence of each and pour out my desire to live them out. This is how I cooperate with Jesus to pre-surrender to Him, living His life in and through me *in advance* of inevitable testing. The trained athlete has hope for finishing strong. I want to spend plenty of time with my Hope, cooperating with Him, so my core principles are fully imbedded into the fabric of my being that I might be faithful, accelerating God's way to the finish line. The more I pray through my core principles and yield to Christ living His life in and through me, the more He shifts the odds *in advance,* so that when tempted and tested, I increasingly choose to remain where God placed me—in Christ, authentically living out His purpose and design of the true me.

I want pre-decided to become pre-settled, pre-settled to become pre-grounded, pre-grounded to become pre-imbedded, so that Christ is actually living His life in and through me in advance of any challenge. This is my attempt at being pre-centered in Christ for a lifestyle that is centered in Him.

From Me-centric To God-centric

God uses my core principles in the lifelong arc from *me-centric* to *God-centric*. As a results-oriented follower of Christ, I know results come from God and I fervently pray for results. But if I focus on how they reflect on *me*, I bastardize the virtue of being results-oriented. In my own life, when I reflect on the long arc from me-centric to God-centric, I see—countless prayers along the way that are emblematic of *disconnected* integrity. I desperately wanted God's will, while not fully dying to me-centric desires. God's approach to this was to answer many of my prayers with what I considered disaster. His strategy was to root out self-centric elements in me. I had to realize that God does not support the self-centric. Praying through my core principles during those times—when God's answer was no, when I was demoted rather than promoted, when external accomplishments escaped my grasp—helped me cooperate with God to root out self-centricity in me.

By "praying through" my core principles, I mean I pondered them; I explored what they mean to Jesus, and tried to understand them from His perspective. Those times with Him became an eye in the storm as

He unpacked each core principle, linking each one with verses from His Word, and connecting them to real-life situations. And then, the most amazing thing happened. I found myself wanting to apply my core principles infinitely more than I wanted to achieve results. I wanted a centered lifestyle based on core principles much more than I wanted outward success. Workplace pressures did not lessen, organizational conflicts did not subside, and stakes did not diminish. Yet I was transformed into caring more about reflecting God through my core principles than about polishing my image. I still pray for results, but I endeavor to align with God's priority, which is rooting out self-centric elements in me. I have come to appreciate His no answers to my requests more than coveted yes answers. Temporal outcomes are secondary when core principles take effect. My priority becomes living them out to reflect Jesus in every situation.

Identity

Traversing the arc from me-centric to God-centric boils down to a lesson in identity. Everyone knows our true identity is not about external accomplishments, but it is easy to identify with them. Objective observation reveals that I can easily slip into subconsciously identifying with "my" accomplishments, and whether or not God answers my prayer requests the way I want. Understanding the priceless value of when God says no was key for me to correct that false identity. I had to experience the deep, meaningful satisfaction of living out my core principles—viscerally, not merely intellectually. I had to identify more with the core principles He was ingraining in me than with external appearances.

There is a common identity we all share in Christ, vital to God's strategic intent of *Christ-like sons and daughters.* Layered onto that, each of us receives a personalized set of Designer-selected core principles that He causes to resonate within us. God engages each of us to become like Christ, *and* He personalizes each of our identities with core principles that are uniquely ours. So my identity has two components, both centered in Jesus. The first is getting closer to the common identity I share with all Christ followers. The second is embracing the unique identity He creates in me to fit in His grand plan, which includes the core principles He causes to resonate within me. When these dual components of my identity are increasingly aligned with my True Quest, my *Truventure* leads me to a centered lifestyle.

An Even Keel

I love the picture of a ship sailing straight through a tropical storm with sixty-mile-per-hour winds, thirty-foot waves, and torrential cross currents. I want to be that ship! I want to sail straight with an even keel, despite tumultuous circumstances. Core principles are the vehicle God uses to give me an even keel. Through them, my character is honed so I better reflect Him, and I experience His peace in turmoil. It is not a matter of simply receiving personalized core principles from my Designer. We also investigate what each core principle means in detail, what each means to Him, what each means in the turbulence of life. Together we walk them out during calm seas, and we walk them out through gale-force winds.[2] And a surprising, yet biblical thing happens: we cut through the storm, centered on Him. When I am focused on Him living His life in and through me in discernable ways, tumultuous circumstances remain but are no longer my focus. I have a higher focus—to be so centered in the truths of my core principles that I can sail straight with the One who is my Even Keel, irrespective of circumstances. What a life!

What's Important and What's Not

It is not important to worry about what is a principle, versus a truth, versus a value, versus a character trait. Core principles are a mixture of all these. Truventure is not an academic or semantic exercise. Its focus is accurate, strategic alignment with our Creator. Furthermore, if "core principles" is not the right title for you, then change it. I called mine "priority principles," but readers may more intuitively understand *core*. I also like "centering principles." What we call them does not matter, but where we find them does—in the One who designed them to resonate deep within us. Everything in *Truventure* is about journeying with Jesus. Core principles are a way to spend exceptionally strategic, tractive, and meaningful time with God.

Reverse the Trajectory

I do not want to be that man who lost his way—principles abandoned, integrity lost, character entropied. Nor do I want to meander through life simply *hoping* to be principled. Trying to live a principled life does not cut it, and it's not God's solution. God's solution is His Singular Solution, His Son living His life in and through me. To rewire my circuits for a closer connection to God, to prepare in advance for life's challenges, to traverse the arc from me-centric to God-centric with an identity established in Him, to become the storm-tossed ship sailing with an even keel, to become a man of integrity centered in Christ, I find the only way is the Way Himself and in Him I *find* my way instead of *losing* it.

Core Principles: *A Centered Lifestyle*

He sinks my core principles deeper into my consciousness, heart, will, and lifestyle into the fabric of my being.

I need to cooperate with Jesus now to imbed core principles into the fabric of my being in advance of upcoming tests.

God uses my core principles in the lifelong arc from me-centric to God-centric.

Ask & Listen: Talk it over with the Father

Who doesn't feel the need to be more centered? God wants to help you get centered. Write a prayer asking Him to guide you in discovering your core principles.

What principles have you found resonate with you in times past? List these principles here.

Now step into the present and ask Him what principles He would like to impress upon you now. List these impressions here.

Look through the two lists you've identified thus far. Ask God to help you collectively prioritize the lists and number each item in order of priority (with 1 being the highest priority). Identify your top three to five and place them below.

1.

2.

3.

4.

5.

Review the prioritized list, and ask God to help you select a core principle to help guide your choices. Write it in the space below.

Core Principles

Is there another core principle that He would like you to add to the list? ☐ Yes ☐ No

If yes, add it now. (Repeat this cycle of asking if there is another to add until you feel confident that your list is complete.)

Do the core principles you selected center you? ☐ Yes ☐ No

If no, keep talking with God and refining your list until you can answer with a resounding "yes!"

Essence

A centered lifestyle is how we *truventure*. Unexpected twists and hidden dangers often mark the trails of life. Applying core principles to every situation in life will keep you centered, preparing you *in advance* to successfully navigate obstacles and do the next right thing. Ask God to sink your core principles deeper in you, helping you yield to His Son living His life in and through you. Summarize below what you learned about yourself and your core principles.

God's solution [to living a principled life] is His
Singular Solution, His Son living His life in and through me.

Chapter 9

Annual Main Thrusts

A Lifestyle Taking Ground

Roller coasters ascend, descend, twist, and turn—but end up where they started. They expend incredible amounts of kinetic and potential energy getting nowhere. Sometimes I feel like that: a lot of energy expended, and no forward progress. I can find myself not advancing, even with all my advantages: a father of integrity, an authentic disciple-making mother, two loving sisters, phenomenal wife, and a lifelong commitment to Jesus starting at age three-and-a-half. I can find myself not making progress, even with the best intentions—deepening my surrender, sharpening my focus, and engaging in a centered lifestyle. Even in the best circumstances, I can find myself on a roller coaster.

Annual main thrusts tackle lack of progress head-on. They resemble a fully committed military surge to take ground, advance, and keep taking ground until the desired objective is achieved. A thrust can't sit still, which sets it apart from an ordinary objective. A thrust is an objective insistent upon forward progress. My Commander enlists me in a committed surge using main thrusts to advance a lifestyle taking ground. Main thrusts are so tractive that I ask Him for one each year.

Maximizing Vital Forward Progress

In business we have objectives, goals, milestones, and metrics. Yet even in the best circumstances—when every person's goals, in every department, in every division of the entire company align—maximizing vital forward progress requires more. Employers address this with a company-wide annual main thrust. The annual main thrust does not diminish anyone's individual goals. Rather, it infuses each individual's goal with a company-wide priority. Each employee senses closer alignment with the employer's direction. One year it may be improving quality (while doing everything mentioned in our goals). Another year it may be improving our cost position (without sacrificing quality, while doing everything mentioned in our goals). Another year it may be prioritizing resources on international expansion (without sacrificing quality, cost position, or individual goals). In this way, accomplishments of both the individual and the entire group are maximized in the intended direction.

The undeniable effectiveness of annual main thrusts in the workplace brought me once again to my perennial question: *If it works that well in business, why wouldn't I use it for what concerns me most—my own life?* Clearly I'd be a fool to not explore how I can apply them to myself. In fact, I intentionally used the question to break my inertia, take action, and cooperate with Jesus to take ground in me. He exceeded my expectations: I found that annual main thrusts worked brilliantly, even better in personal life than in corporate life. Ever since then, in the fourth quarter of each year, I have asked Jesus to identify the main thrust He wants to actualize in me in the coming year. Vital forward progress actually happens.

25 Years, and Counting

For a quarter century now, my Commander has been taking ground in me through annual main thrusts. Each one codifies intentional, focused thrust to take ground in me. Jesus responds in personally relevant ways each time I ask, *Where specifically do You want to take ground in me in the coming year?* For illustrative purposes, my annual main thrusts are listed in figure 9.1. As I pray through past main thrusts, I recall the physical, spiritual, and emotional context. This facilitates our discussion, which focuses on how we can keep taking new ground.

Annual Main Thrusts

1990 Humbly walk with You, obediently by faith, faithfully. *St. Louis*

1991 Follow Your leading and guidance in everything so that in everything You might be glorified. *Tram on the way to work in Brussels*

1992 Simply do what I know is right; balanced priorities. *Brussels*

1993 Pray, plan, diligently do and trust. *Managing director's office, Norway*

1994 Quit seeking my own glory. *St. Louis*

1995 Be transformed by the renewing of my mind. *Shanghai*

1996 Consider it pure joy. *Shanghai*

1997 Live the life Christ wants me to live, not the one I desire. *Allentown*

1998 Serve the Lord. *Bethlehem*

1999 Shepherd those entrusted to me with integrity, love. *Bethlehem*

2000 Purify myself from everything that contaminates. *Bethlehem*

2001 Enjoy the Giver's presence; end preoccupation with His gifts. *Route 22*

2002 Do not lose heart; undertake the task by faith. *Allentown*

2003 Be thankful and so worship God with reverence and awe. *Allentown*

2004 Selflessly, humbly become the lowest servant. *Allentown*

2005 Seek a balanced life from an eternal perspective; re-balance. *Allentown*

2006 Wait for God's help to do the impossible. *New York City*

2007 The only thing that matters is faith expressed by love. *Allentown*

2008 Unity with Janet. *Allentown*

2009 Totally consecrated to God: zero tolerance for sin. *Allentown*

2010 One with Christ: eradicate anything contrary to God's will. *Allentown*

2011 Return to a communal life with Christ. *Back porch*

2012 Be as self-conscious as a rock. *Red chair, Prescott*

2013 Lock in multidimensional humility: accept God's providence, never elevate myself, never allow pride, and glory in Christ alone. *Prescott*

2014 Be diligent. (Rom. 12:11) *Prescott*

2015 Diligently, aggressively reallocate resources of this L.I.F.E.[1] *Prescott*

2016 Co-seize the moment for eternity. *Prescott*

2017 Finish the book. Sacrifice temporal for higher, eternal priorities. *Prescott*

Figure 9.1. Mark's Annual Main Thrusts

My annual main thrusts affirm God's love for me, exemplifying that He cares about taking ground in me so I accurately align with Him to fit in His grand plan. Like everything in *Truventure*, annual main thrusts are first and foremost a vehicle for spending time with my First Love, journeying with my Confidant. Like everything in *Truventure*, annual main thrusts are strategic and tractive. For a quarter century, my Commander has attacked the lack of forward progress in my life with personalized annual main thrusts, vital and essential for taking ground in me to walk out the victory He has already won.

An Epic Tale

Living a life strategically aligned with my Creator is like finding myself in an epic tale. Sometimes the Author foreshadows a twist in the tale with annual main thrusts, setting the stage for upcoming challenges and opportunities.

Upon reflection, God's focus for 1991 was like that—foreshadowing upcoming events. While riding the tram to work in Brussels, I felt the Holy Spirit pray through me: *Help me follow Your leading and guidance in everything, so that in everything You might be glorified.* It so profoundly resonated, that I knew it was my main thrust for the upcoming year. I didn't know it yet, but the upcoming year turned out to be pivotal: a new parent company, a dramatically different corporate culture, and an entirely new set of challenges. In His wisdom, God directed my focus on a higher level—above all the changes, before any of them occurred. When the changes came, I was inwardly prepared to follow my Sovereign CEO's *leading and guidance in everything, so that in everything He might be glorified.* This higher calling became an invaluable, useful maxim for daily decisions. I directly attribute the favor I received with the new parent company to the higher-level mindset that flowed from praying through this main thrust.

As every good tale contains conflict, so did my own epic tale. Later in the decade, on the other side of the world, my life took a turn for the worse. Invaluably, the Lover of my soul gave me the correct perspective through my annual main thrust: *Live the life Christ wants me to live, not the one I desire.* I would never have thought that up, yet I cannot think of a better main thrust for 1997. As the year progressed, I fell from favor in my corporate environment. Once an executive with over a thousand sub-ordinates, I became a lone contributor with an office dangerously close to the exit sign. I needed a clarion call that cut through the me-centric loss. God provided that in my main thrust. That year, I needed to focus on the life Christ wanted me to live instead of the one I desired.

The Author of my tale chose 2004 for strategic foreshadowing, pre-paring me to accept and embrace my life calling years later. His main thrust for me that year was: *Selflessly, humbly become the lowest servant to everyone for their edification and God's glory.* Initially, it made me squirm. I felt like Moses saying, "Here I am Lord; send Aaron." At first I hoped to get through the year quickly, but then I decided to dig in and pray it into my visceral knower, into my lifestyle, to obediently walk it out. My mind—so quick to say, *I know that*, yet so slow to apply it—finally realized that being the lowest servant was actually a really, really good position. After years of praying through this main thrust, I realize it is the *best* place to be.

Years later, when I asked Jesus, *What is my calling?* Instantly and deci-sively, God answered. While totally unexpected, it rang true: *Selflessly, humbly become the lowest servant to everyone for their edification and God's glory.* It was the main thrust He gave me for 2004. Jesus and I had already discussed its meaning and implications in great depth. In the years since, we revisited its benefits, how to make it a vital priority, and how to gain traction in it. The truths of 2004's main thrust were imbedded deeper into the fabric of my being. When the time came, I was ready to hear His voice and embrace it as my life calling. In retrospect, I could not be more pleased with His choice.

My main thrusts all have one thing in common; each is God's response to my request for where He wants to take significant ground in me next. He enjoys answering this request—I can sense it. Never vague, never con-demning, He has my best at heart with the end clearly in mind. I simply want to align with His direction in this epic tale.

Lifelong Traction

I start anticipating the coming year's main thrust in the fourth quarter of the current year. As October 1st approaches, I give myself permission to start asking God what main thrust He has for the next year. He typically answers during my quiet times, but I have learned to be alert at all times. He has revealed my main thrust while riding a tram in Brussels, while driving home from work, while sitting with Him in my den, and while overlooking a forest of rhododendrons and hemlocks from my back porch.

I write down my main thrust for the coming year in my annual main thrust document of my quiet time folder. I begin praying through it on a daily basis, asking Him to unwrap it, clarify and refine it, and use it to refine me. He invariably edits and unpacks each one. We share the quest of Him taking ground in me. My annual main thrusts are a vehicle for getting alone with Jesus, for Him to gain traction in me, a vehicle to get on the Spirit's escalator of deepening surrender and sidestep roller coasters.

For years, I prayed through my entire list of annual main thrusts daily. I wanted *lifelong* traction in *each* one. But as the list grew, this took more time. The time is worthwhile, but I don't have that much time every day. This is a *Truventure* dilemma that needs to be addressed, because each essential lifelong vehicle grows over the years. So no matter how succinct I am, more time is required to pray through them. *Truventure* should result in tractive alignment with Jesus, but not require an excessive amount of time. So I started implementing *one plus one* when praying through my main thrusts. I pray through my current main thrust, *plus one* from a previous year, stepping through the entire list in less than a month. This is simply one of many ways I balance commitment and time constraints.

Focus

If you are tempted to have more than one main thrust each year, please don't. It will sabotage your *Truventure*. Genuine traction, sustained progress, and a lifestyle taking ground require relentless focus. *Truventure* applies strategy to intentionally align our lives with the Creator. Every successful strategist knows less is more, and the key is focus, focus, *focus*. One main thrust per year, personally selected by the One who relentlessly contends for our highest good, allows for that focus.

Some may have difficulty picking only one priority objective for the year. I respectfully ask, *Do you clearly understand the most important thing*

God wants to accomplish in you this year? Once you understand *the* most important thing God wants to accomplish, there is tremendous liberty, which affords you freedom to focus on it. Some feel obligated to work on everything all the time. Having worked all over the world, in many industries and cultures, I have never seen that work. Of course there is a thrill at first, just like the roller coaster, but the end is ineffective. *Truventure* is about gaining significant sustained traction—an escape from the status quo. This requires courage to reject the need to fix everything at once and trust God's leadership, guidance, divine focus, and timing. My True Manager never impressed me to have multiple annual main thrusts. So if you feel compelled to work on everything all at once, try something different and ask Him what is *the* most important thing He wants to accomplish in you this year.

A number of my main thrusts highly correlate with an interesting twist, and what He teaches me through my annual main thrust is never boring; it actually gets more interesting as the year goes on. It is like scuba diving an underwater paradise: the slower I inch along, the more intriguing the scenery. As the second half of the year approaches, I find myself anxious to ensure full traction on this year's main thrust. I intensify my focus, asking Him for more clarity and specificity, and the journey becomes even more exciting. As the annual journey draws to an end, there is a bittersweet closure of this year's main thrust and unveiling of where my True Quest leads in the coming year's main thrust. Even the one who likes to work on lots of things at once will soon be satisfied, without sabotaging forward momentum, as annual main thrusts accumulate through the years of His faithfulness.

A Lifetime Taking Ground

The more I see God as He truly is, the more becoming Christ-like looks infinitely farther off. Happily, this need not discourage us, because our only progress is Christ Himself being tractive in us. We trust God, for whom nothing is impossible,[2] and growth comes from the Vine, not the branch itself.[3] But this does not give me license to squander time and energy riding roller coasters. If something is not working, I get off the roller coaster and find traction in Him. The One who has given us everything we need for life and godliness in Christ Jesus is sending Him back soon.[4] With Him comes the Day of Judgment, when each one's works will be obvious.[5] I want to rejoice in the gold He has refined in me on that day. Therefore, I hold myself accountable to get off every roller coaster for a lifestyle taking ground.

As I reflect on each of my annual main thrusts, they do resemble a fully committed military surge to take ground, advance, and keep taking ground until the desired objective has been achieved. Each main thrust is a visionary objective requiring an initial one-year surge to find sustained traction in a lifestyle of *Connected Integrity*. This is *Truventure*.

Annual Main Thrusts: *A Lifestyle Taking Ground*

My Commander enlists me in a committed surge using main thrusts to advance a lifestyle taking ground.

Genuine traction, sustained progress, and a lifestyle taking ground require relentless focus.

Once you understand the most important thing God wants to accomplish, there is tremendous liberty, which affords you freedom to focus on it.

Ask & Listen: Talk it over with the Commander

Your Commander stands ready to help you take ground that He might accomplish all that He wants to do in and through you. Pen a prayer asking Him to make your feet strong and steady for the trek ahead

Today's book involves the adventure found within the pages of your life. Ask God this question, *"Where specifically do You want to take ground in me?"* Make note of what you hear Him say.

Study what you have just written. Ask God to help you refine each word to reveal the essence He wants to communicate, leaving only the main thrust of what He wants to do in and through you in the coming season. Record below your refined statement as your annual main thrust.

Traction ⟶

"I press on toward the goal for the prize of the upward call of God in Christ Jesus." (Philippians 3:14)

* In light of your annual main thrust, what stands out to you from this passage?

* What question does this verse bring to mind?

* What do you sense God impressing onto your heart from this verse today?

Good work, valiant warrior! Ask your Commander to help you have relentless focus in gaining ground in this area. Record the insights you hear.

Essence

A lifestyle taking ground is how we *truventure*. As you press forward taking ground, ask God to help you make lifelong traction in this annual main thrust. Recap below what you've learned in this chapter.

⟳

**As I reflect on each of my annual main thrusts,
they do resemble a fully committed military surge
to take ground, advance, and keep taking ground until
the desired objective has been achieved.**

Chapter 10

Select Lessons

A Lifestyle of Solid Evidence

When I served as lead juror for a criminal trial, I was surprised at how subjective we jurors were at evaluating evidence. It was a valuable reminder of the intrinsic value of God's objectivity. It made me appreciate how He objectively points out evidence of my attitudes and actions that are not aligned with Him, pursuits of my agenda instead of His, fear instead of trust, hubris instead of humility. He forgives, but I want more—I want to truly change. I want a lifestyle of solid evidence that I am aligned with Truth Himself. To this end, I enlist Jesus on a daily basis to imbed select lessons into the fabric of my being.

Select lessons are lessons my Designer *selects* for me personally, which *resonate* with my soul, to the degree that I am *desperate* to learn them to the *fullest* extent, in the *deepest* way possible, as a *lifelong* endeavor. They are God's vehicle to substantively move me from evidence that I am not aligned with Jesus, to solid evidence that His character is imbedded in the fabric of my being. Select lessons are a powerful, personalized, on-going set of lessons, succinctly captured in a strategic prayer document that is easy to pray through. As I pray through my select lessons, He reveals even more truth. The current that runs through each select lesson is the revelation of Himself as my Singular Solution for a lifestyle of *Connected Integrity* with Him.

My First Select Lesson

My prime motivation for my first select lesson was that I wanted to never have to learn it again. I had recently crashed and burned on an assignment in Shanghai. Since it was not the first time God had used corporate conflict to get my attention, I sensed my difficulties were more about what He wanted to root out of me than they were about corporate circumstance.

My return stateside initiated a self-imposed postmortem in which I tried to succinctly capture my lessons learned. Driving home from work one evening, I was gripped with an unrelenting desperation to fully learn the lesson God wanted to teach me. That first select lesson is recorded below:

Post-Shanghai circa 1997

God provides mellow peace when I come through adversity in the following ways:

- Quit striving for self: Lean into Christ to be broken by Him and learn from Him.
- Rest in Him alone: Seek Him alone as my Singular Portion and Singular Hope.
- Completely submit to *His* will, plan, agenda, and timing.

My *Truventure* Guide reveals more within these truths as we journey through life together; they are more meaningful today than the day I wrote them. I love returning to my first select lesson, praying it deeper and deeper into the fabric of my being, listening to the Holy Spirit and how He wants to apply my first select lesson today.

My desire for this select lesson to become evidenced in me never wanes; it only increases. You could not pay me enough to discard this lesson; it is more vital than life. This highlights a key criterion for what distinguishes a select lesson—the lesson is so *vital* I become *desperate* for Jesus to imbed it into the fabric of my being. I care more about seeing proof of its existence in me than my next breath. This desperation *intensifies* with time; it never diminishes.

Aqua Elevator Shafts And Other Starting Points

As a teenager working the summer in northern Wisconsin, with a competitive swimmer's confidence around water, I didn't think twice before leaping into rushing river rapids. In fact, I didn't think at all; it was not an intelligent move. I was sucked down like an elevator. I remember thinking,

How can I be descending so far so fast? I may not make it! Downstream propulsion eventually ejected me from the current way downstream. Some of my select lessons start this way: overconfidence descending into desperation.

Desperate circumstances make me desperate for God's perspective; I want to see through the fog. I run to be alone with Jesus, closing the door on distractions. I approach Him in contrite humility and listen. He reveals the truth about my situation internally and externally, temporally and eternally. He cuts through the fog. We juxtapose His way with mine as we discuss what it looks like to apply His truth. I ask Him to imbed His truths in me. He graciously accomplishes this, like ejecting me from fatal rapids.

Some select lessons start in an aqua elevator shaft. Some feel like a bucket of cold water. Others feel more like a door opening, a light being turned on, an epiphany. Others feel like we are walking along a secluded path, just being together. God can use anything; once He used a movie line to make His point to me. No matter how they arrive, He delivers an essential truth of His Word articulated in the most visceral way. He, too, wants to imbed the select lesson into the fabric of my being.

How We Venture Together

God commits Himself to teach and accomplish His lessons in us. This affords us great faith, confidence, and rest in Him. We simply yield our mind to the mind of Christ and our spirit to His Spirit, waiting on Him to lead so we can follow. When I want to capture a lesson, I ask Him the most basic questions: *You got my attention, what do You want me to learn? You exposed a gap between Your character and mine, how can I cooperate so you can close it? What do You want to rule my decisions if this issue comes up again?* I write down God's answers to these questions as my select lessons.

I give my select lessons a quirky title to grab my attention and make me want to camp out on them again so Jesus can further illuminate. I include the date and location, which transport me back to the point of revelation. The title, date, and location for my select lessons create a storyline of God's work in me. My select lessons are evidence of Jesus's tenacity for me, and I feel loved.

God always has more to teach; therefore I consider select lessons to be evergreen, always a work in progress. I frequently edit them as 1) I gain more insight from the Holy Spirit, 2) He provides perspective from His Word and from my ongoing experiences, and 3) I am more honest with God and myself.

I do not obsess over words, because I know the Editor will improve them. I do obsess about being candid and objective. I try accurately describing where I am and what I am learning, rather than quote a platitude or sound like I have arrived. I find it useful to be succinct, because it is hard to consistently pray through loquacious lessons. At the same time, I dare not be so succinct that I lose the key points Jesus reveals.

I do not presuppose that what works for me will work for you. However, I do know my True Quest will draw near to you, as you draw near to Him. One great way to draw near to Jesus is by asking the ultimate select lesson question: *What truth do You want to imbed in me so I correctly align with You in every aspect of life?* Faithful and True answers faithfully and truthfully—true to Himself and true to His design of me—for significant traction in my *Truventure.*

Critical Success Factors

God keeps things interesting. No matter the lesson or the way He brings it up, select lessons reflect Jesus's most deep-soil[1] work in me. *Jesus's most deep-soil work in me* is such a significant experience that I want to understand how to cooperate with Him to this end, so I focus on several critical success factors.

#1: Complete Candor

Let's start with the pointy end of the spear. *Complete candor* with God and myself is critical for extracting lessons that transform. When I find myself resisting, I remember three things: 1) God already knows the things I want to hide, 2) He promises super-abounding grace, and 3) Everything hidden will be exposed. What do I want exposed—evidence of my insidious self behaving foolishly, or evidence of His character imbedded in me for a lifestyle of *Connected Integrity*? Choosing *Connected Integrity*, I race with contrite humility to my Singular Hope. I push past self-preservation—the hiding, sugar coating, rationalizing, and spin—and choose to be brutally honest, candid, and completely transparent with my Confidant. He is my Safety Zone, the One who knows me, yet loves me still. I endeavor to cooperate fully with Jesus so what is eventually exposed is His character in me, refined in the practicum of life.

Being candid with Jesus is worth doing poorly until it is done well. It takes practice, and the practice pays off. God knows everything, yet my reflexive inclination is to gloss over what self wants to hide, to divert attention from what He wants exposed. I have to consciously reject my insidious self's desire to rationalize. When this is difficult, I assertively lean into Him, to be broken by His grace, to be honest. There is no need to hide anything from God, and we have every reason to be candid with the One who already knows all about it. By venturing candidly with Truth Himself, truth is revealed—and not necessarily new truth—a lot of truth I already "know" but need to genuinely learn. Being candid with God and myself[2] is the pointy end of the spear that eventually, ultimately, yields solid evidence of *Connected Integrity* with Jesus.

#2: Desperate Determination

Inherent in the effectiveness of the first critical success factor, yet worthy of explicitly stating as the second, is *desperate determination*. Learning the lesson Jesus wants imbedded in me requires *desperate* dependence on Him. Accurately aligning with His lordship requires undeterred *determination*. As one who knows that only the bitter medicine will save his life, I must embrace being weaned[3] of my own agenda so I may submit to God's. After learning this lesson more deeply, more viscerally, the once-bitter medicine gradually becomes sweet. I become desperate to be weaned of my own agenda to learn, really learn, His truths.

#3: Prayer

Frequent venturing with Jesus—praying through my select lessons—is required for Him to imbed truths of the lesson into the fabric of my being. A lifelong commitment to learn each lesson more deeply is required because I have never learned everything or fully arrived.

This success factor ceases to be one if it degrades into a task; it is wind beneath my wings as long as it is fresh and vital. Each heartfelt prayer is another step in my lifelong adventure, vital to the voyage as we migrate to better practicing the presence of God. When my prayers start feeling like drudgery, I stop and refocus on my True Quest. With my eyes afresh on Him, each heartfelt prayer carries me closer to the heart of God.

When I am too busy to pray through all my select lessons, intimacy with Jesus causes me to reconsider the clock and say to myself, *Let me take a minute to pray through at least one of my select lessons.* Over the decades I have learned that I need to consistently process my select lessons with Jesus. Some days I cannot be deterred from eagerly opening my select lessons document; other days I open it on faith more than feeling. My feelings do not limit Him. Even when I do not feel like it, if I take the initiative to get alone with Him, He draws near. He responds to faith. In fact, He ambushes me with deeper insights when I brush past innate apathy, reorient myself to humbly receive, and expectantly engage Him in my select lessons. For me it is critically important to get alone with Jesus to review His selected lessons on a daily basis, despite time constraints or feelings, even if I only have time to pray through a portion and not the entire list. Even one step venturing with Jesus is invaluable.

#4: God's Perspective

The best part of journeying with Jesus is the opportunity to see things from *God's perspective.* By definition, seeing things from God's perspective is seeing them as they really are, seeing truth.[4] This critical success factor is proactively, intentionally, desperately seeking to see everything from God's perspective. He reveals in my spirit how He sees things when I wait on Him. Part of seeing things from God's perspective includes how He sees Himself, and with this He ushers in the pièce de résistance: becoming like Him because I see Him as He is.[5] Seeing, processing, walking out everything from God's perspective is the essence of *Truventure.* It is imperative. Without it, everything is vanity, but it's magical when He reveals His perspective.

His insights compel me to eagerly, humbly, ruthlessly, and objectively expose every gap between my lifestyle and His righteousness. I have to admit the evidence of specific gaps He exposes. I have to embrace the fact that God does not grade on the curve. I have to abandon excuses and flee rationalizations. I coined the term "proactive objectivity" to insistently hold myself accountable to be aggressively unbiased, without spin, desperate to see every thing in my life from God's perspective. Unfortunately, seeing does not guarantee doing. The wicked virus of self-preservation mutates to resist any truth that threatens its existence. Self[6] ambushes and undermines objectivity. I can protect self or disgrace it. I must proactively embrace objective truth, which humiliates self. It is ludicrous for me to say self is vile one minute, and polish it into acceptability the next. For example, very recently God admonished me this way: *This pursuit of an aligned relationship with Me is only words if it does not happen where the rubber meets the road, in difficult situations like this where you choose to follow Me instead of rationalizing your own way.* I had a choice to merely receive this as an important reminder, or embrace it as the kick-in-the-pants I needed to apologize to my wife. My truth adventure, my *Truventure*, must be fatal to self so I might be vital in Truth and He in me.

Indeed

One of my favorite select lessons is titled, *Indeed, Barcelona, April 26, 2007.* This select lesson illustrates each critical success factor. The lesson came during a long season when God was not delivering me the way I wanted. He allowed corporate rivals to run roughshod over me. Even those obligated to ask my side of the story never did. I became accustomed to feeling my Protection had stepped aside.

I was in Barcelona on business, up early having my quiet time, being *candid* with Jesus (critical success factor #1). That morning He gave me a healthy dissatisfaction with how I was feeling. I became *desperate* (critical success factor #2) to stand in decisive disagreement with the status quo of my feeling-based, self-centered, pseudo reality. I consciously chose to see things from *His perspective* (critical success factor #4) instead of continuing to look at everything from mine. God orchestrated these factors to create the right environment in my heart for His truth to penetrate. God uncensored, God unapologetic, spoke clearly to my heart: *Your feelings are quite right: I am not helping you in the way you want, period.* He emphasized the period. *In perfect love, complete wisdom, and absolute sovereignty, I have said no to your request for victory over your rivals and vindication with senior management. In fact, I'm tired of having to repeat Myself. Would you rather have your yes or My no?* He emphasized the question mark.

He moved me to insist by faith in the truth of His faithfulness, even though I didn't feel it. He moved me to insert the word *indeed* everywhere I could in order to personalize Psalm 30. "I will *indeed* exalt You, Lord, because You *indeed* have lifted me up and have *indeed* not allowed my enemies to triumph over me." I was yielding my spirit to the Spirit of Truth by choosing to believe His Word, even if it did not agree with my feeling-based, self-centered, pseudo reality. I was yielding my mind to the mind of Christ by claiming truths of His Word over discouragement cycling through my mind. He stretched my faith as I emphatically acknowledged God's Word was *indeed* true for me, despite feeling quite the opposite.

In those moments, I could actually feel truth soak into my mind, from my head into my heart, and I capitulated. I was no longer interested in the "woe is me" part of my saga, but I became infatuated with a desire to never deviate from the truth of His response. Over time, we dug deeper into His response, *praying* on a daily basis (critical success factor #3) for Him to imbed His truth in my being. We discussed what it looks like to walk it out. Over time, I practiced rejoicing in God's no answers more than pining for His yes answers, trusting in His highest good for me. I love that He does not patronize me, clearly speaks unfiltered truth, and provides grace for me to submit. He creates new, solid evidence of *Connected Integrity* in me.

Indeed, Barcelona, April 26, 2007, reminds me to stand on His truth uncensored, despite my feelings. It reminds me to not suppress my feelings, but to candidly share them with Him. It reminds me to look to Him to clarify truth and reveal how I am to think. This select lesson makes me want to venture together with Him, praying cooperatively, yielding my mind to the mind of Christ and my spirit to His Holy Spirit. *Indeed* has become a priceless truth marker in my *Truventure*.

Singular Solution

Few things deliver better results than a teachable spirit, but it can get even better! God strategically directs with select lessons, lessons He causes to resonate so powerfully within my soul that I am desperate to learn them to the fullest extent. As I pursue Him and the truths He wants to take deeper in me, with heavy use my select lessons receive a rich patina, a luster that reflects His image. Upon reflection I sense the tractive, reoccurring theme, the need to simply yield to Christ living His life in and through me. Of course I never "arrive," but I see evidence of attitudes and actions aligning with Him, of pursuing His agenda instead of mine. I take another step in my pursuit of a strategically aligned life with my Creator, another step in my quest for a lifestyle of solid evidence of *Connected Integrity* with Him.

Select Lessons: *A Lifestyle of Solid Evidence*

Select lessons are lessons my Designer selects for me personally, which resonate with my soul, to the degree that I am desperate to learn them to the fullest extent, in the deepest way possible, as a lifelong endeavor.

The title, date, and location for my select lessons create a storyline of God's work in me.

When my prayers start feeling like drudgery, I stop and refocus on my True Quest.

Ask & Listen: Talk it over with the Teacher

Jesus, the Master Teacher, has prepared your classroom uniquely for you. He knows not only what you need to learn but also how you best learn. Write a prayer asking the Teacher for understanding to receive all that He wants to teach.

Think about lessons that God causes to resonate so powerfully within your soul that you are desperate to learn them to the fullest extent. Ask God which one of these select lessons He wants you to focus on today. Write it down.

Ask Him what He wants you to learn about this lesson. Record your insights.

Traction ⌒→

Ask Him how He wants you to cooperate with Him in the future should a circumstance or issue arise to challenge the lesson God wants sunk deep within you. Record His answer.

Ask Him what He wants to rule your decisions should a circumstance or issue arise to challenge this select lesson. Write what you hear.

What truth does God want to imbed in you so you correctly align with Him in every aspect of life? Explore this question with God and write down His revelations.

Essence

A *lifestyle solid evidence* is how we *truventure*. God's storyline of work in you, as evidenced in your select lessons, reflects His character being imbedded into the fabric of your being. Ask Him to sink your select lesson ever deeper in you to strengthen your resolve to align with Him in your trek ahead.

⌐

God strategically directs with select lessons,
lessons He causes to resonate so powerfully within my soul
that I am desperate to learn them to the fullest extent.

Chapter 11

Quiet Times

A Lifestyle Processing Everything With Jesus

Everything in *Truventure* flows from my quiet times, which have evolved into a lifestyle processing everything with my Confidant. During quiet times, He imbeds in me the *Prerequisite Principles* from part 1 and the tractive vehicles from part 2. During our quiet times, my Gracious Lord deepens my surrender using my covenant with Him, aligns my motivation through core principles, takes ground in me with annual main thrusts, and harnesses my focus through my strategic intent. In the intimate climate of our quiet times, God sows select lessons to cultivate His most deep-soil work in me. I intentionally place all of me under the light of God's Word; His light dispels darkness and nourishes growth. He reveals truth, exposes lies, and accurately aligns me with Himself. I receive guidance for the next right thing to do and counsel on how to yield to Christ living His life in and through me. I relax and rest in Him, anxious to process everything with Him.

Everything

Quiet times are my vehicle to process everything with Jesus, so let's consider what *everything* means to me in this context. First and foremost, quiet times are about refocusing on Jesus as my *Everything*. Each and every thing must shift from being about me to being about Him, from orbiting around me to orbiting around Him. Setting aside every distraction, I get alone with Him to truly see Him, to clearly hear His thoughts, to authentically experience Him, and to genuinely honor Him. I anticipate hearing His voice and receiving fresh revelation as I look into His Word. He draws near to me as I draw near to Him. We discuss whatever He wants to talk about, and I get to ask Him whatever is on my mind. He orchestrates the flow; it is flexible not rigid, intentional not prescribed. Unrestricted, everything flows within a safe relationship.

Everything is on the table for discussion during our quiet times. Over time we discuss *everything* relevant, pertinent, practical, and fundamental to life. We intentionally discuss His providential work in life's "random" circumstances, taking time to explore what I need to understand and do in the current events of life. He unwraps, enriches, further develops, and refines my covenant, strategic intent, core principles, main thrusts, and select lessons during our quiet times. I wait expectantly; He reveals more and goes deeper. But whether it feels intentional or random, *everything* happens as I actively listen, having set aside the time to process *everything* with my Confidant.

Everything, in the context of *Connected Integrity,* means each and every thing I think, say, and do lines up perfectly with God's nature. *Everything* means everything at my current level of understanding. I cannot perceive my own depths, but He can. As God exposes more of me to His light, *everything* today includes more than it did yesterday. It is a process of progressive, ever-deepening surrender with the Lover of my soul.

Everything and a Triple-A Personality

Having been called a "triple-A" personality, I get that many of us can become hyper when God commands us to "Be holy, because I am holy."[1] We can become anxious for a tool kit when told *Connected Integrity* means everything about us aligns with God. Our pact comes into play here—everything is by grace alone, through faith alone, in Christ alone. This triple-A personality chooses the Solution Himself for everything. I have no interest in a mere tool kit to become Christ-like. Instead, I am desperate for Christ to live in and through me. My Everything Himself is my Singular Solution for everything in me to align with Him, 24/7, 365 days of the year, eternally. Jesus alone is the source of inner transformation that produces *Connected Integrity.* Only His work survives the fire. I rest in Him, so He can accomplish what He wants in me. Submissively at rest, I pray that I volitionally, genuinely, fully, and faithfully yield, cooperatively with Him, in everything He chooses. Where once my triple-A personality charged ahead, now I wait for His call.

Everything is never overwhelming. My gentle, unhurried, all-powerful Paragon Parent knows how to go deeper in me at just the right time. Sometimes it feels like He is going too slowly, sometimes too fast, but my Omniscient knows best. My responsibility is to submissively have my yes ready. *Everything* is not burdensome because He lets me process everything with Him to progressively yield to Him living His life in and through me. There is no striving, there is only yielding. *Truventure* is simply my way to embrace my Singular Solution with Strategic Intentionality. This simplicity calms my triple-A personality.

Incubator and Birthplace

The most current versions of anything I am developing—strategies, agreements, and ruminations—reside in my quiet times folder. Consequently, my quiet times have become the incubator of everything in my *Truventure*. I look to God Omniscient, not my own understanding, to advance things to the next level. As I prayerfully discuss each with Him, He provides fresh insights. I update, save, and re-file the most current version of whatever God and I work on, what we co-develop by His grace. He is a generous collaborator.

For example, one morning I tackled the business model, remuneration, roles, and responsibilities for a strategic alliance agreement at the end of my quiet time. It would have been futile to do it on my own. My most tractive advancements, my most significant learnings, my most strategic directions, are birthed in my quiet times. I strategize with partners and friends, but I am worthless without strategizing first with God—making quiet times the birthplace of everything in my *Truventure*.

Draw Near to God

My quiet times have evolved from "doing devotions" to "hanging out" with Jesus. I have always had meaningful, life-directing, life-giving devotions, but sometimes, especially when rushed by schedule or selfish ambition, I inadvertently degrade them into a task. When I am more concerned with

progressing through my Bible reading plan and prayer list than about getting alone with my Genuine Friend, I wither. I need to see the Son.

As I realized Jesus is my True Confidant, I became more intentional
about bringing Him into my confidence. I recalled how my college roommate and I talked about and shared everything from spending money
to the swim record we traded. This became a model for the relationship
I wanted with Jesus. The conversations Jesus and I had became more
authentic, more in-depth, more meaningful, and our relationship became
increasingly personal and progressively intimate.

I am in awe that the Almighty listens, clearly speaks truth, is never
wishy-washy, and fully understands. He holds me accountable to yield
to Him while He does for me what I am incapable of doing—everything
by grace alone, through faith alone, in Christ alone. In this life-long
journey I find myself asking more and more questions of the Answer
Himself. I embrace the journey of processing *everything* with Him. Processing everything with my True Confidant. Now that is a life worth
living!

The God Most High called Abraham His friend. The God of Israel
spoke to Moses face to face. Likewise, my Sovereign Lord speaks personally to *me* and identifies *me* as His friend. He draws near to me as I draw
near to Him. I throw in my lot with the psalmist who wrote, "I told You
about my life, and You listened to me; teach me Your statutes."[2] I intentionally hang out with Jesus. We each share, ask questions, listen, respond;
and meaningful intimacy grows.

Deep calls to deep:[3] quality time alone with Jesus heightens my commitment to carve out more ongoing, uninterrupted time with Him.[4] I
wait expectantly, and lean into Him with growing intentionality. I invite
Jesus to talk about what concerns Him, and invite His response to what
concerns me. I further explore what it means for Jesus to be my closest
Confidant, and our friendship unfolds.

His Supremacy Exalted

One might falsely assume hanging out with Jesus lessens His status. For
me, nothing could be further from the truth. The more I hang out with
Jesus, the more I perceive His supremacy—that His ways are higher than
my ways, and His thoughts are higher than my thoughts. He is exalted

and yet close, transcendent, and immanent. I envision Jesus as John saw Him in Revelation 1:13-18.

> and among the lampstands was One like the Son of Man, dressed in a long robe and with a gold sash wrapped around His chest. His head and hair were white like wool—white as snow—and His eyes like a fiery flame. His feet were like fine bronze as it is fired in a furnace, and His voice like the sound of cascading waters. He had seven stars in His right hand; a sharp double-edged sword came from His mouth, and His face was shining like the sun at midday.
>
> When I saw Him, I fell at His feet like a dead man. He laid His right hand on me and said, "Don't be afraid! I am the First and the Last, and the Living One. I was dead, but look—I am alive forever and ever, and I hold the keys of death and Hades."

Even with these words inspired by God Himself, none can fully grasp His supremacy. His love, mercy, and grace keep me from being left dead in His presence. His exalted nature creates in me a greater desire to more accurately see Him, to more dearly love Him, to more attentively dwell on His character. I am desperate to see Him—unfiltered, without domesticating attempts to make the Holy One palatable. I want to be a "quaker" in the spirit of George Fox's model of trembling at God's Word.[5] I want to experience the untamed Lion of Judah; I want Him unleashed on me that I might see Him as He really is, and so become like Him.

Hanging out with Jesus finds me prostrate before Him—trying to fathom His unfathomable supremacy. Hanging out with Jesus enhances my reverence for the One who is personal and supreme.

How My *Truventure* Advances

While I describe what hanging out with my Confidant is like for me, I am not providing a formula and I have no intention of telling you what to do or how to do it. I simply want to share how it works for me. In doing so, I hope you see relationship rather than ritual. I hope you see revelation that leads to grace-based integrity and restful truth walking, rather than striving. But I only really care that you are enticed by the Lover of your soul to pursue your own personal *Truventure* in a Spirit-led quest that works for you.

I approach my quiet time assured of God's love, and thankful for His loving kindness. At the same time, I enter my time with Jesus in a posture of repentance, confession, worship, and consecration. This is essential because I cannot align with Truth if there is active or latent rebellion[6] in me. When I approach Him in contrite humility I feel Him rush to me, wrap His arms around me and say, "Welcome home, son. Your repentance, confession, worship and consecration always lead you to Me. I love it when you ask Me to reveal every gap between us."

I do not presume that even after half a century I know how to repent, confess, worship, and consecrate myself as well as I desire. So I ask Him to help me more authentically repent, more genuinely confess, more lovingly worship, and more fully consecrate myself to Him. A posture of humility, gratitude, and deep desire to see whatever He wants me to see is the starting point for every quiet time with Him.

Fresh Insight: Bible Reading and Marking

Our time together revolves around His Word,[7,8,9] processing what He says to me each day. I document my quiet times in a "Bible Reading and Marking" document entitled "BRM," plus the date.[10] My BRM document includes Scriptures read, a selected passage, impressions, and a letter to my Confidant.

When I read portions of Scripture,[11] I typically start where I left off yesterday. I highlight each passage He causes to resonate within me. I review the highlighted passages and select the one that resonates most today. I copy the selected verse into today's BRM document. This initiates today's direction. It need not feel profound—it may be just a word—but it is what He wants to unpack for me today. One morning it was simply the word *copper*, but He had a special message from the unlikely word. Next, I write how the select portion of Scripture impresses me. As I write how it impresses me, the Author adds His own impressions. Together we edit, refine, and focus on what He wants to impress upon me today. This is what I call the Editor editing. He often begins editing before I even complete the first sentence. Other times He waits for me to prayerfully review each word and then shares His perspective. Sometimes He takes the conversation in a different direction from where I thought we were going—these are rich; I forget where I thought we were going as I embrace where He is going with the conversation. In every case, I gain fresh insight into where Christ wants truer alignment and where He wants to lead.

Sometimes He impresses upon me a fresh truth, other times He further unwraps a truth we explored yesterday. Sometimes He elaborates, other times He simplifies. He emphasizes varying words and phrases. No matter how great, no matter how Scriptural, if anything is not vibrating off the page I do not include it. As a result, today's BRM document contains my freshest insight from my Father.

Fresh Intimacy: Letter to God

Fresh insight from the Master of the Universe, while priceless, gets better! I continue intentionally drawing near to Him by writing Him a letter. I call mine a "Paraclete Letter to God," because I deliberately trust the Holy Spirit (Paraclete) to align my spirit with His, and my mind with the mind of Christ as I write a letter responding to His Word. I have written over 10,000 letters to God, and cannot imagine discontinuing this source of deepening intimacy with Him.

I love to see how my *Truventure* evolves. A simple example is the salutation in my letter to God. I evolved from starting *Dear Father* each time, to whatever seems most appropriate. Sometimes it is *Dear Lover of My Soul*, or *Dear Exalted Holiness,* or *Dear Beloved Redeemer*, or *Dear Creator, Savior, Sovereign and Judge*. The options are endless. Sometimes I link how I address Him with what He revealed about Himself in today's reading. In my letter, I ask Him to actualize in me what He revealed from His Word. This is key: as I write, I intentionally seek to become more aware of what He cares about, causing His will to go deeper into the fabric of my being.

But wait—there's more! In my letter I also address whatever is top of mind for either one of us. One day I am troubled by a family matter, another day conflicted over a business relationship. No matter what the topic, I explain my concern to Him in writing. He shares His view, and I include what I hear from Him in my letter. He continues to reveal, elaborate, and refine. We both ask questions during the process, and the Editor continues editing. I begin to see things from His perspective. Complex issues are simplified, root causes are revealed, and direction becomes clearer. By proactively processing everything with Him, our intimacy is refreshed and our *Truventure* advances.

Fresh Strategy: Strategic Prayer Documents

Decades of Bible reading and marking documents and letters to God have taken me on an exploration of various truths. Some of these are further developed and refined in my strategic prayer documents. Strategic prayer documents include my covenant, core principles, annual main thrusts, select lessons, and additional documents. As I pray through my strategic documents, God has me park on a phrase. I camp out on the phrase and ask Him to help me volitionally, genuinely, fully, and faithfully yield so the truth becomes ingrained in my character. I am intentional about it because when I tell Him that I love Him I want my actions to confirm what I tell Him. When I tell Him I love Him, I don't want Him to have to turn a blind eye to my lifestyle for my words to be believable. I want to pray through each document daily, but I avoid being legalistic. When time is limited, I bookmark where I stop and continue the exploration there the next day.

Fresh Processing: Everything Else

My quiet time folder contains my Bible reading and marking documents (each of which includes that day's letter to God), and all of my strategic prayer documents. Also residing in my quiet time folder are incubator versions of things Jesus and I are co-developing. It is not limited to "spiritual" things. I do not want to spend time on *anything* without inviting Him to collaborate. He and I both want to do everything together.

Sometimes I simply pray over the current version of what we are working on, sometimes He edits a bit, and sometimes He significantly advances the current version with substantive improvements, deletions, and refinements. Other times He births a whole new initiative. These new-birth versions may be about a new opportunity, business concept, killer app, value stream, book concept, spiritual insight, or personal correspondence not to be sent until Jesus and I are convinced it is ready. We co-develop, co-edit, and co-refine all things important to us, and they remain in my quiet time folder until ready for release. Even then, those things I want to continue praying into my life remain there.

I wish this had been my practice earlier in life. If every sticky correspondence I received and every fiery correspondence I wanted to launch back had been processed in my quiet time and discussed with Jesus before sending, then I would have made fewer enemies. If I had done the same with every vital presentation and important proposal, then I would have represented Jesus in the marketplace better than I did.

Vital and Fresh: Remaining at Rest

This may seem like a lot, and although I am committed to daily quiet times, my time constraints are different each day. Sometimes I am interrupted and other times not. Either way, I try not to get derailed. I try to remain at rest, processing all Jesus and I need to co-process together before concluding my quiet time with Him. There is no room for legalism, and lifeless rote is waste. The key is to remain vital, fresh, unhurried, in Him, and in the moment.

This is vitally important: even if I have only five minutes, I discipline myself to be in the moment, to rest, and to behave as if I have all day. The One who transcends time and can reveal what He wants in an instant, the One who works in me to will and do His good pleasure, does not need me to hurry through a procedure. Quiet times end at a different point each day, but always with a sense of tranquility in Him, and usually a step further in my *Truventure*. See Quiet Time Diagrams (figure 11.1).

Cold Coffee

Quiet times are by far the most enjoyable, fruitful, relaxed, and strategic time of my day—a protracted sunrise. Calm camaraderie with my Confidant stabilizes and centers me. My blood pressure mellows as I enter His rest. The clarity of His light dissipates the fog that surrounds me. We process everything together. He provides daily direction and draws me into *His* plan. He reminds me His plans for me are the very best providence can offer. Quiet times with the One who knows me and knows all the answers are so meaningful, significant, and tractive that time ceases to exist. My coffee gets cold.

Truth Himself uses the tractive vehicles—riding on the truth rails of *Prerequisite Principles*—to live His life in and through me for a lifestyle of *Connected Integrity* in Him. Having practiced hearing His voice, aligning with Him, and applying truth in every aspect of life, we are ready to investigate many more strategic questions, define being wildly successful, co-strategize and cooperate with Him to land that vision.

Quiet Time

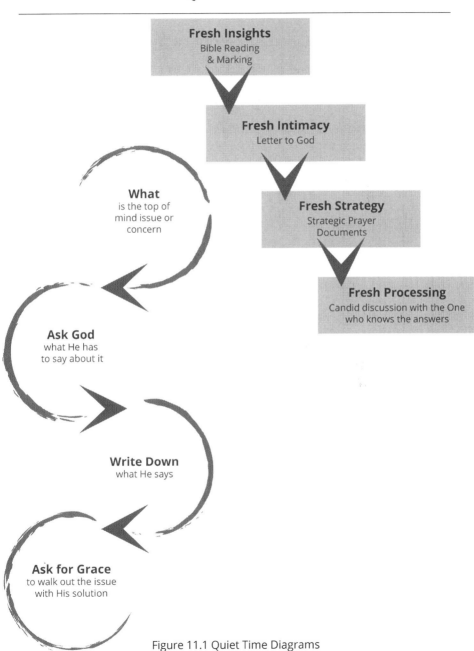

Figure 11.1 Quiet Time Diagrams

Quiet Times: *A Lifestyle Processing Everything with Jesus*

First and foremost, quiet times are about refocusing on Jesus as my Everything. Each and every thing must shift from being about me to being about Him, from orbiting around me to orbiting around Him.

My gentle, unhurried, all-powerful Paragon Parent knows how to go deeper in me at just the right time.

I want to experience the untamed Lion of Judah; I want Him unleashed on me that I might see Him as He really is, and so become like Him.

Ask & Listen: Talk it over with your Confidant

Imagine your Confidant sitting nearby. Contemplate His beauty, wonder, and power. Pen a few words thanking God for who He is.

Fresh Insights: Bible Reading & Marking

"Deep calls to deep in the roar of Your waterfalls; all Your breakers and Your billows have swept over me." (Psalm 42:7)

- Slowly read each word. Underline what stands out to you. What impressions do you have upon reading this verse?

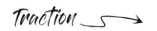

- What do you sense God impressing onto your heart from this verse today?

Fresh Intimacy: Letter to God

Imagine writing a letter to a trusted friend and pen a letter to God, the Friend who sticks closer than a brother.*

Fresh Strategy: Strategic Prayer Documents

Pull out your covenant with God (*reference chapter 6*) and select a phrase for today's focus. Ask God what He has to say about the selected passage. Write down what He says.

---

* Proverbs 18:24

Fresh Processing: Candid Discussion with the One who Knows the Answer

Top of mind for me is usually something challenging my peace or something important that is urgent. What is top of mind for you today? Talk to God about it and record insights you receive.

Essence

A lifestyle processing everything with Jesus is how we *truventure*. Fresh truths and revelations await as you hang out with Jesus, processing things together. If you let His truths transform you, you will progress even when the road is treacherous and discover breathtaking views along the way. Make a few notes to summarize your learnings.

⌐

Calm camaraderie with my Confidant
stabilizes and centers me.

Strategic Intentionality

11. Quiet Times:
A Lifestyle Processing
Everything With Jesus

10. Select Lessons:
A Lifestyle of Solid
Evidence

9. Annual Main Thrusts:
A Lifestyle Taking Ground

8. Core Principles:
A Centered Lifestyle

7. Strategic Intent:
A Lifestyle Doing the
Next Right Thing

6. Personal Covenant with God:
A Lifestyle of Deepening
Surrender

Personalized Truth Markers

For each chapter, write a *personal application* of the recorded truth:

◖▶ *6.* **Personal Covenant with God**—*A Lifestyle of Deepening Surrender*

I want the gaps between us exposed so I can yield to a lifestyle of Connected Integrity with Jesus, where every thought, belief, word, and action align with Truth Himself.

For me, it means _____

_____

_____

_____

_____

◖▶ *7.* **Strategic Intent**—*A Lifestyle of Doing the Next Right Thing*

Strategic intent helps me make intelligent choices and quiet the cacophony of oughts.

For me, it means _____

_____

_____

_____

◖▶ *8.* **Core Principles**—*A Centered Lifestyle*

I need to cooperate with Jesus now to imbed core principles into the fabric of my being in advance of upcoming tests.

For me, it means _____

_____

_____

_____

◐ 9. **Annual Main Thrusts**—*A Lifestyle Taking Ground*

My Commander enlists me in a committed surge using main thrusts to advance a lifestyle of Connected Integrity with Him.

For me, it means _____

_____

_____

_____

_____

◐ 10. **Select Lessons**—*A Lifestyle of Solid Evidence*

God strategically directs with select lessons, lessons He causes to resonate so powerfully within my soul that I am desperate to learn them to the fullest extent.

For me, it means _____

_____

_____

_____

_____

◐ 11. **Quiet Times**—*A Lifestyle Processing Everything With Jesus*

First and foremost, quiet times are about refocusing on Jesus as my Everything. Each and every thing must shift from being about me to being about Him, from orbiting around me to orbiting around Him.

For me, it means _____

_____

_____

_____

_____

PART THREE

Strategic Pyramid

In contrast to parts 1 and 2, where each chapter investigates a bite-sized principle or vehicle, the chapters in part 3 collectively build one vehicle: the *Strategic Pyramid*. It captures everything essential to land a vision of the true me being wildly successful per His grand plan—on one page. My *Strategic Pyramid* was birthed when I decided to apply to my own life what had already worked brilliantly for me in business. It is the most comprehensive strategic vehicle of my pursuit to strategically align with my Creator. My True Quest first uses my *Strategic Pyramid* to unveil His picture of me being wildly successful, then to provide a clear path for me to land that vision, and also to keep me on track as we implement it.

Chapter 12

Strategy on One Page
A Lifestyle for the Millennia

The Egyptian pyramids at Giza are one of the Seven Wonders of the Ancient World, and the only one still standing.[1] Though constructed 4500 years ago, their true means of construction remains a mystery, making them a marvel of their makers. They are well designed, carefully honed, and expertly assembled. Simple, powerful, and evocative; they stand the test of millennia.

My *Strategic Pyramid*[2] is well designed, carefully honed, and expertly assembled, in the form of a time-tested document for a life that glorifies my Creator. The *Strategic Pyramid* is strategy on one page. The pinnacle of the pyramid is a vision of the true me being wildly successful per His grand plan. The objective of the pyramid is landing the vision. Strategy on one page draws upon Wisdom Himself, for whom even the most complex is simple, in order to land one's vision—making it more likely to be realized and less likely to be shelved.

My Strategic Swiss Army Knife

My *Strategic Pyramid* is my Swiss Army knife for strategy. It serves multiple purposes in one by containing a strategic compass, strategic map, and dashboard. My strategic compass includes my vision, opportunity, and compelling imperative. My strategic map includes essential strategies to land my vision and required supporting blocks to land each strategy. My *Strategic Pyramid,* after I make it smart with metrics and color coding, serves as the dashboard and quick assessment.

My vision is the pinnacle of the pyramid. With it I envision a picture of the true me being wildly successful per God's grand plan. The row below vision provides my compelling imperative that tethers me to the mind of Christ, and an opportunity that He designed for my life so I can seize His dream for me. Known as the strategic compass, these three (vision, compelling imperative, and opportunity) provide strategic direction and decision-making guidance for life, ministry, business, and career decisions. The Strategic Compass aligns and realigns the true me with my True North for a lifestyle that withstands the millennia.

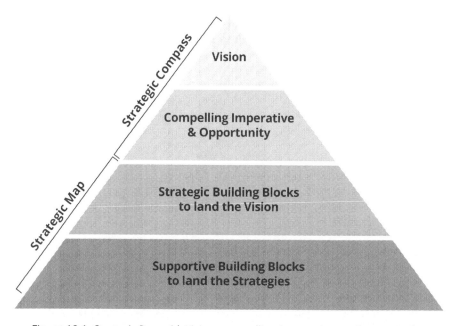

Figure 12.1. *Strategic Pyramid*. Vision, compelling imperative, and opportunity, serve as a strategic compass pointing in the right direction (chapter 17). Strategies and supporting blocks identify the clearest path, or strategic map, of what is needed to land the vision (chapter 18). The strategic compass, supported by the strategic map, provides strategy on one page.

The bulk of my *Strategic Pyramid* is a strategic map, comprised of a layer of strategic blocks and multiple layers of supporting blocks. Each strategy block must be essential to land the vision; collectively they are everything I need to land the vision. Likewise, each supporting block must be essential to land one or more of the strategies; collectively they are everything I need to land the strategies, which in turn land the vision.

My *Strategic Pyramid* employs a compass to point the right direction, and a map to identify the essential steps to get there—nothing more, nothing less. In this way it de-complicates life. To de-complicate, we need effective solutions to complex problems; for this we look to Wisdom Himself. He cuts through complexity to deliver strategy on one page, which makes it more likely to be realized and less likely to be shelved.

Like a Swiss Army knife, which contains several essential tools in one pocket-sized mechanism, my *Strategic Pyramid* contains vision and success measures, passion and opportunity, strategy and definitive steps on one simple page. I do not feel the need to get another strategic plan, any more than I feel the need to get another Swiss Army knife. Just as I sharpen the tools of my Swiss Army knife, the Holy Spirit sharpens each component of my *Strategic Pyramid*. He clarifies direction and makes steps more definitive toward our shared vision for my life. I use each component of my *Strategic Pyramid* in my pursuit of a strategically aligned life with my Creator and to co-invest it with Him for eternity.

Eliminating the Dross

Blaise Pascal, one of the brilliant minds of the seventeenth century, astutely quipped, "I would have written a shorter letter, but I did not have the time."[3] Likewise, many of us do not take the time required to condense our thoughts and communiqués to their most productive essence. Those who eliminate the dross to reveal the essence of the essentials receive a huge return for their effort and find the result more effectively achieves their target. This relates directly to strategy, where value tends to be inversely proportional to its length. Clearly articulated essentials reveal gravitas, something worthy of life's investment.

One page is a powerful constraint. There is no room for not really knowing, ambiguity, fluff, and jargon. By focusing on the essence of the essentials to land the vision of the true me being wildly successful per God's grand plan, I eliminate everything that is *not* the essence, everything that is *not* essential, everything that is *not* about the true me, everything that is *not* required to land the vision, and everything that is *not* per God's grand plan. What remains is a clear picture of what God wants to accomplish in my life.

Cooperating with God to eliminate the dross takes concentrated effort, but when I do it I feel lighter, leaner, more alive, and more agile in His hands. Just as eliminating dross removes unwanted impurities in metallurgy, eliminating the dross is essential to the *Strategic Pyramid* process, resulting in the essence of my life strategy on one page—making it more likely to be realized and less likely to be shelved.

My Dilemma

While I had the privilege to work for Fortune 400 companies committed to excellence, eliminating the dross to succinctly articulate the essentials was not universally applied, and I do not recall it being applied to planning. Corporate requirements were mind-numbingly endless. *Send us your vision, send us your opportunity case, send us your strategic plan, send us your operating plan, send us your capital plan, send us your— yada, yada, yada.* Each request made sense, but it made no sense to me that they were dealt with in silo fashion, each one totally independent of the others. No one seemed concerned whether the plans were consistent with each other. It seemed evident to me, however, that plans should be harmonized so if one aspect changed, there would be a ripple effect in other plans as well.

So I started wondering, *What if one could simplify everything to its essence and see the essentials needed to run a company—from one page?* This ignited my desire to develop an exceedingly simple, harmonized, strategic process focused exclusively on the essence of the essentials. My goal was one page from which I could run the company; any company. One page, but it had to have everything essential to landing the vision, without cheating by using a micro font.

While conceptualizing strategy on one page, I received a timely opportunity to radically transform a self-limiting business division into a wildly successful one. I decided to try out the concept, and my *Strategic Pyramid* process was birthed. I was told that an attempt at transforming the company had a 90% chance of failure. Undaunted, I identified a wildly successful vision and the essentials to land it. From one page, everyone in every division could see where the company was going, and understand how and why their contribution mattered. Positive results gathered momentum for all to see; a high-performance culture replaced self-limiting dysfunction. Earnings exceeded prior record earnings by 60%, and then by another 60%. Implementing radical strategies to land the vision in my first *Strategic Pyramid* proved the concept despite the odds, and the business division was transformed.

The *Strategic Pyramid* process went on to prove successful in start-ups, turnarounds, fledgling, and mature businesses. It resonated nationally and internationally. It proved successful in the market place, in ministries, and non-profits to define their success, their objectives, and radically transform their cultures. Parties that had been swimming their own way turned to swim a new direction, united.

But this created a personal crisis. I was plagued with the daunting question *If the marketplace is worthy of strategic excellence, isn't my life?* The crisis intensified as I considered how demanding it is to apply strategy effectively. Putting my head in the sand didn't work because there is no good reason to invest in the temporal and not the eternal. Didn't I owe Christ, my propitiation, the relentless pursuit of a strategically aligned life?[4] I capitulated and started developing my personal *Strategic Pyramid* by tackling the question, *What is the picture of the true me being wildly successful, and how do I land that vision?*

This led me to spend protracted periods of time with my Savior, asking related questions and developing straightforward answers. I was surprised at how engaged He was. From the beginning, He caused certain questions and answers to resonate unmistakably in me. Large or small, every day God had more to reveal and refine. Our first draft illustrated a joint effort, each of us engaging our mind and spirit with the other.

As I engaged God to develop and refine my *Strategic Pyramid*, I realized it was an exceptionally tractive way to live with *Strategic Intentionality*. This caused me to engage Him even more. Daily listening for what He wanted to further reveal and refine became my modus operandi for strategizing with God. I experienced ever-clearer direction while maintaining the course He originally provided in our first draft. What I received applying the *Strategic Pyramid* to my own life was even more radical than what I experienced at work—the true me wildly successful per God's grand plan—a shot at personalizing John 17:4, "I have glorified You on the earth by completing the work You gave me to do."

Essence of the Strategic Pyramid

My *Strategic Pyramid*—complete with my vision, compelling imperative, opportunity, and everything required to land the vision—explicitly articulates where I am going and specifically how to get there. Not only that, it also employs straightforward terminology, meaningful metrics, and milestones to see where I am vis-à-vis landing the vision. Landing the vision of being wildly successful in His grand plan is much more strategic than a brainstorming exercise, and much less pedantic than a list of sequential steps. The well designed, carefully honed, expertly assembled *Strategic Pyramid* has proved to work exceedingly well, providing clear direction with the flexibility required to land my vision. An effective *Strategic Pyramid* never remains stagnant, but always receives further enlightened unwrapping by the Holy Spirit. I anxiously await when He edits more than words. The essence of the *Strategic Pyramid* is not in the questions, process, or form. It is however, in the ongoing engagement and alignment with the Holy Spirit.

The simple, intuitive form of a pyramid serves me well, but a form can mean different things to different people. Alternatives already in use include cairn and flowing wind, and I look forward to the first strategic doughnut. The form is strictly utilitarian, a matter of personal preference. What matters is the substance of strategy on one page, with Whom I develop it, and how I walk it out.

A Lifestyle for the Millennia

Egyptians built their pyramids in celestial alignment;[5] I build my *Strategic Pyramid* to align with my Creator. Ancients looked to the stars for guidance; I look to the One who made the stars for guidance. He illuminates a simple, powerful, and compelling vision for my life. I find strategy on one page easy to use, easy to discuss with Wisdom Himself, and hard to put down because I want a lifestyle for the millennia.

Strategy on One Page: *A Lifestyle For the Millennia*

My Strategic Pyramid is well designed, carefully honed, and expertly assembled, in the form of a time-tested document for a life that glorifies my Creator.

Those who eliminate the dross to reveal the essence of the essentials receive a huge return for their effort and find the result more effectively achieves their target.

My Strategic Pyramid employs a compass to point the right direction, and map to identify the essential steps to get there—nothing more, nothing less.

Ask & Listen: Talk it over with God

Your Creator is eager to watch you unwrap the essentials to land the vision of you being wildly successful per His grand plan. Pen a prayer of thanksgiving for the lessons learned on the journey thus far.

Do you have a strategy on one page? ☐ Yes ☐ No

Do you know what opportunity is worthy of your life? ☐ Yes ☐ No

How many people do you know that can identify what wildly successful is for *their* life?

Reference the Prerequisite Principles map and personalized truth markers at the end of Part 1. What roles do each of the five prerequisite principles listed below play as you build your strategy on one page? Relax and take up this question with the One who knows and loves you best.

1 - Grace:

2 - Lordship:

3 - Truth & Lies:

4 - Mind & Spirit:

5 - The True You:

Ask God how the five prerequisite principles can help you withstand the sand storms of time to indeed become wildly successful. Record what you hear Him say.

Ask God to confirm that He created you to live a lifestyle for the millennia. Write down what you hear Him say.

Essence

A lifestyle for the millennia is how we *truventure*. God has a compelling plan for your life and will help you unwrap it step by step. Ask Jesus, Expedition Leader Extraordinaire, to lead you as you move forward to design and hone your own Strategic Pyramid.

I find strategy on one page easy to use, easy to discuss
with Wisdom Himself, and hard to put down because
I want a lifestyle for the millennia.

Chapter 13

The Essentials

A Lifestyle Distilling Discovery

There is nothing extraneous about the Egyptian pyramids. There is elegance in design and simplicity in the form, fit, and function of each block. I want the same elegance and simplicity for my *Strategic Pyramid*. To this end I pursue the truth about what God says about me, and His plan for my life. First, I quarry blocks for my *Strategic Pyramid* by asking numerous questions about the true me being wildly successful per my Creator's grand plan. The answers He causes to resonate within me result in a list of what I call my *essentials*. We distill the list of essentials to a *gleaned* list of essentials. Then we distill each essential on the gleaned list to its *essence*. The essence of each essential becomes quality building material for my *Strategic Pyramid*. The vehicles from part 2 may lend material to my list of essentials, and more essentials may be uncovered in this chapter, as the process goes beyond discovery to a lifestyle of distilling discovery (figure 13.1).

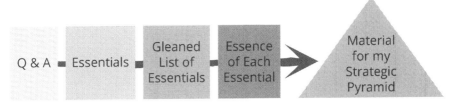

Figure 13.1. The process for a lifestyle of distilling discovery.

Mindset Shift

I felt apprehensive when I decided to apply strategy outside my career into my personal life. I knew from the marketplace how difficult it is to get strategy right, and how much work it is to land a vision. But then I realized my Designer had been strategizing for my success since before my conception.[1] Furthermore, He had been interacting strategically with me my entire life.[2] So I flipped my mindset from *beginning* to *continuing*. It felt less daunting.

Flipping my mindset to join what He planned and has been doing all my life, freed me up for the classic Chinese approach: I looked back to see ahead.[3] I asked Jesus to illuminate patterns He wanted to leverage going forward. Midwesterners liken this to looking back over the fence posts of life to see how they line up (figure 13.2). When I looked back over the fence posts of my life that lined me up with success, the most significant were when I took God at His Word, when I was brutally honest with myself and Him, and when I was in iron-sharpening-iron relationships with godly men. I shifted from producing my vision to cooperating with what He has been doing and wants to do in me.

Figure 13.2. Fence posts [4]

Discovering the Essentials

Most of my strategy work happens in my quiet time, when I am alone speaking candidly with the Lover of my soul. Candid intimacy with the One who knows everything naturally leads to questions. This section is about the questions I ask God to discover my essentials, which become building blocks quarried for my *Strategic Pyramid*. Following are three things I do to quarry my essentials: I engage in my own Q&A with God, ask Him follow-on questions, and listen to His questions for me. He causes some answers to resonate so powerfully with the true me that I identify them as essentials.

Q & A with God

The peak number of questions a child asks occurs around four years of age; apparently I am a four-year-old at heart. As I engage in Q & A with God, I become insanely curious about His perspective on every question. Sometimes He is quite poignant, and other times He seems to enjoy fostering my curiosity. So if my list of questions becomes a burden, just skim ahead. Even at four years of age I was programmed to organize before beginning, so characteristically I group questions. In the following case, I group them based on where I am looking.[5]

A. Looking up, my relationship with God.
  > For example, *What are God's personal dreams for me?*
B. Looking in, my relationship with myself.
  > For example, *What consistently compels me to do the next right thing?*
C. Looking out, my relationship with others.
  > For example, *With whom do I want to do life and why?*
D. Looking forward, my relationship with the future.
  > For example, *Where would it ultimately take me if I truly lived out my beliefs, values, and priorities?*[6]

More questions are listed for each category in appendix C.

I find it useful to answer each question four different ways, so I use four additional columns with the following headings.[7]

1. Where am I vis-à-vis the question at hand?
2. Where am I called to be?
3. What is stopping me?
4. What will close the gap?

An illustrative Q & A worksheet is provided in figure 13.3 with additional questions in Appendix C.

Looking Up (My Relationship with God)

What are God's dreams for me, personally?

What door has the Spirit opened for me personally and said: *"Come?"*

In what areas am I fully alive in Christ?

In what areas am I not fully alive in Christ?

Which goals are aligned with Jesus's goals for me? Which are not?

Looking In (My Relationship with Myself)

What core values & principles are important to me?

What makes me feel fully alive?

What do I need to learn in order to get where I want to go?

What might disqualify me from maximizing my life for Christ?

Looking Out (My Relationship with Others)

What iron-sharpening-iron relationships will help me get to where I want to go?

What elements of a support team will help me get where I want to go?

Who do I want to do life with?

Looking Forward (My Relationship with the Future)

What does wildly successful look like for my life?

What always draws me irresistibly to where I want to go with my life?

What opportunity is worth my life?

What has to happen for my life to be wildly successful?

If I had a clean slate & could design my life, what would it look like?

What do I need to do differently vis-à-vis my priorities so that I can maximize the investment in this life for eternity?

Where am I?	Where am I called to be?	What is stopping me?	What will close the gap?

Figure 13.3. Q & A worksheet.

I love asking God questions, but even I am easily overwhelmed perusing another person's list. It is more productive and less stressful to ask God my own questions. Two questions lower my stress when overwhelmed by another's list:

Which am I drawn to answer?[8]
Which am I afraid to answer?[9]

Many of my essentials have come from processing strategic vehicles from part 2. Several things on my list of essentials were derived from my personal covenant with God, strategic intent, core principles, annual main thrusts, and select lessons.

Follow-on Questions

Jesus's responsive insights to my questions indicate a deep well of wisdom and foresight. Knowing further insights exist compels me to draw them out with follow-on questions. I use various follow-on approaches, three of which are described below.

1. Sakichi Toyoda, inventor, industrialist, and founder of Toyota Industries, is credited with "The 5 Whys Technique."[10] For example, if I am exploring the question, *What might disqualify me from maximizing my life for Christ?* my response is often, "Squandering too much time." Toyoda-san's method seeks understanding by using five successive why's. Why am I squandering too much time? "Because I watch too much television." Why? "Because I am too tired." Why? "Because I do not have anything left after swim workouts." Why? "Because I swim mid-morning." Why? "Because I am placing my temporal priority—becoming an All-American in swimming—higher than my eternal priority—finishing the book." Oops, I've uncovered my root issue: I am not walking according to my priorities!

2. Phil Davis of Tungsten Branding invokes a similar approach, asking five successive times, *So you can what?* For example, if I am exploring the question, *If I had a clean slate and could design my life, what would it look like?* my response is often, "It would have less self-inflicted catastrophes." *So you can what?* "Be more effective." *So you can what?* "Get on with God's design for my life." *So you can what?* "Reciprocate His love." *So you can* what? "Be faithful." *So you can what?* "Invest this brief life for eternity." Oh, I've uncovered that my core priority is eternal investing!

3. Another sequence which works well for me, is asking three different follow-on questions: a) *How does that get walked out?*, b) *How can I be more specific?*, and c) *Can You reveal what this looks like from Your perspective?*

For example, if I am exploring *What do I need to do differently to maximize this life for eternity?* then, my response might be, "I need to postpone what gets in the way of eternal investing."

How does this get walked out?
　"I need to work on the book before I swim."

How can I be more specific?
　"I need five hours on the book while I am fresh and find a time to swim later, even if this jeopardizes becoming an All-American in swimming."

Can You reveal what this looks like from Your perspective?
　"A step in the pursuit of a strategically aligned life with Me, Connected Integrity, a worthwhile cost benefit ratio."

Oh, I get to more authentically invest this life for eternity!

As I ask questions, I envision God contending for my highest good. I receive His answers as invitations to flourish in ways that resonate with His design of me.

God's Questions

Truventure connects with the Godhead in personal dialogue and truth-walking. Not only does He answer, He also asks great questions. I'll share three examples.

My Confidant and I were co-editing answers to the existential question, *Why am I here?* when He suddenly flipped the question to, *Why am I not here?* Visceral answers flowed faster than I could copy them down: I am *not* here for self-satisfaction, self-gratification, indulgence, promotion, pontification, ambition, or accumulation. I am *not* here to waste time, energy, resources, opportunity, adversity, or any other learning experience. I am *not* here to escape, to watch as much television as I do. God added one three-letter word (not) to radically change my life.

God flipped the question on a friend of mine, who asked God what

He wanted him to do in the next stage of life. When the Father responded, *What would* you *like to do?* my friend felt the Father's eagerness to help His son do what he enjoyed. I recall this story to maximize my Q & A time with God by consciously resting in my Father's heart to work out what He designed His son to enjoy and thereby fit in His grand plan.

The final example is what I call a seismic question, one of which came to me when my career was descending to lower lows. I was sitting in my office one day when, out of nowhere, the question came to me: *What if I quit trying to create an impression that I am better than I am?* This was an inflection point, catapulting me into a quest to become ever more authentic with God, myself, and others. This happened after I had developed the *Strategic Pyramid* process, but before I considered applying it to my life. This seismic question drew me into a lifestyle of Q & A with Him.

A lifestyle of Q & A with God helps me quarry essential building blocks of my *Strategic Pyramid*. This two-way conversation with God is the modus operandi of *Truventure* strategy. Consequently, keeping an open mind and an open ear to God's questions during my Q & A process is part of a lifestyle of discovery and discovering my essentials.

A Gleaned List of Essentials

Now I have a plethora of answers to existential and strategic questions. Next, I sift through them as though the Master Archeologist is leading me on an archeological expedition. He is the expert at distinguishing between essentials and nonessentials. He causes certain answers to powerfully resonate within me. These powerfully resonating answers are copied onto a separate list I call my *gleaned list of essentials*, which will become potential building blocks in my *Strategic Pyramid* (figure 13.4).

Completing the archeological expedition with a gleaned list of essentials in hand is a monumental achievement. We order pizza!

The next step is equally important; we *distill* each gleaned essential to its *essence*. This critical step requires a clear head. So I make it a priority to get a good night's sleep. Afterwards, I will return to my gleaned list of essentials, rested and refueled with a fresh cup of coffee.

Essentials	Gleaned List of Essentials
☐ Truly believe everything God says & walk like it.	☑ Truly believe everything God says & walk like it.
☐ Be one who says what I mean & means what I say.	☐ Be one who says what I mean & means what I say.
☐ Be a finisher, like Jesus, doing all God commands.	☑ Be a finisher, like Jesus, doing all God commands.
☐ Choose what is eternal, not what will burn.	☑ Choose what is eternal, not what will burn.
☐ Integrity is very important.	☐ Integrity is very important.
☐ Do everything with God.	☑ Do everything with God.
☐ Focus on living for eternity instead of this life.	☑ Focus on living for eternity instead of this life.
☐ Lead worth following.	☐ Lead worth following.
☐ Be aligned with Christ.	☑ Be aligned with Christ.
☐ Abide in Christ, yielding to His Spirit.	☑ Abide in Christ, yielding to His Spirit.
☐ Wait on God to produce what He wants, His way, for His glory.	☐ Wait on God to produce what He wants, His way, for His glory.
☐ Engage in iron-sharpening-iron relationships.	☑ Engage in iron-sharpening-iron relationships.
☐ I want to be a man after God's heart	☐ I want to be a man after God's heart

Figure 13.4. My essentials distilled into my gleaned list of essentials.

Distilling Each Essential to its Essence

I needed to distill each gleaned essential to its essence to attain the powerful constraint of strategy on one page without using micro fonts. The essence of an essential has greater impact and versatility; it is easier to pray through, and it is more tractive in my pursuit of a strategically aligned life with my Creator.

To distill each essential to its essence, I eliminate unnecessary words and clarify the thought to make the essential increasingly succinct. Consider the example in figure 13.5.

A Gleaned Essential Began As:	The Essence Became:
People engaged & energized by God, within multiplying movements of niche communities, which impact their spheres of influence with an eternally significant lifestyle.	All our people engaged & energized by God, experiencing life together to make an eternal difference.

Figure 13.5. An example of distilling an essential to its essence.

The conciseness of the essence in this example is more memorable, and delivers stronger impact and inspiration. We are going for clear revelation, not self-pontification; premium-grade pure maple syrup, not sap; refined gold, not gold ore; French perfume, not eau de toilette—the essence of the essence.

Next, I replace generalized statements with specificity. Generalities tend to be generally followed, if at all. Strategic alignment with my Creator demands far more than generally following generalities. I ask for insight and wisdom to be specific yet succinct to hit the nail on the head, as in figure 13.6. The sequence from essentials, to a gleaned list, to the essence of the essentials is illustrated in figure 13.7.

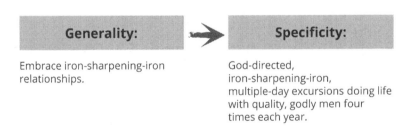

Generality:	Specificity:
Embrace iron-sharpening-iron relationships.	God-directed, iron-sharpening-iron, multiple-day excursions doing life with quality, godly men four times each year.

Figure 13.6. Converting a generality to be specific.

Essentials	Gleaned List of Essentials	Essence of Essentials
☐ Truly believe everything God says & walk like it.	☑ Truly believe everything God says & walk like it.	☆ Believe God & all that entails.
☐ Be one who says what I mean & means what I say.	☐ Be one who says what I mean & means what I say.	
☐ Be a finisher, like Jesus, doing all God commands.	☑ Be a finisher, like Jesus, doing all God commands.	☆ Complete all God commanded.
☐ Choose what is eternal, not what will burn.	☑ Choose what is eternal, not what will burn.	☆ Only what is eternally significant matters.
☐ Integrity is very important.	☐ Integrity is very important.	
☐ Do everything with God.	☑ Do everything with God.	☆ Co-invest with God.
☐ Focus on living for eternity instead of this life.	☑ Focus on living for eternity instead of this life.	☆ I can squander my life or invest it for eternity.
☐ Lead worth following.	☐ Lead worth following.	
☐ Be aligned with Christ.	☑ Be aligned with Christ.	☆ Align with Christ.
☐ Abide in Christ, yielding to His Spirit.	☑ Abide in Christ, yielding to His Spirit.	☆ Remain in Christ.
☐ Wait on God to produce what He wants, His way, for His glory.	☐ Wait on God to produce what He wants, His way, for His glory.	
☐ Engage in iron-sharpening-iron relationships.	☑ Engage in iron-sharpening-iron relationships.	☆ Engage in iron-sharpening-iron relationships.
☐ I want to be a man after God's heart.	☐ I want to be a man after God's heart.	

Figure 13.7. The essentials, to a gleaned list, to the essence of the essentials,

So far I have focused on each gleaned essential as its own island. Now I want to consider each vis-à-vis the others. I look for natural groupings or alliances that might increase the synergistic impact. For example, "remaining in Him," "resting in Him for Him to produce His fruit for His glory," and "aligning with Christ" are more potent for me when grouped together: "Align with Christ by remaining in Him, resting in Him to produce His fruit for His glory."[11] This process is illustrated in figure 13.8.

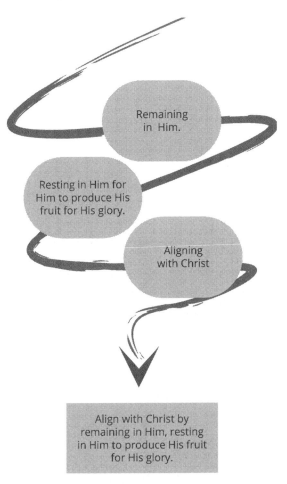

Figure 13.8. Grouping three essentials that naturally reinforce each other.

A Lifestyle of Distilling Discovery

In my pursuit for the truth about God and His plan for my life, I quarry essential truths and distill them to their essence. This lifestyle of distilling discovery helps achieve the elegance and simplicity I need for strategy on one page. I build my *Strategic Pyramid* with quality materials, the essence of the essentials, which Truth Himself uses to refine my understanding of the true me, His vision of me being wildly successful per His grand plan, and a path to walk it out.

The Essentials: *A Lifestyle Distilling Discovery*

But then I realized that my Designer had been strategizing for my success since before my conception.

He is the expert at distinguishing between essentials and nonessentials.

I needed to distill each gleaned essential to its essence to attain the powerful constraint of strategy on one page without using micro fonts.

Ask & Listen: Talk it over with the Master Archeologist

Your Heavenly Father has the answer to every question even before you ask. It is His delight to hear your questions, savor your curiosity, and lead you higher still. Write a prayer of preparation for your time of distilling discovery with Him.

Pull out your childlike curiosity; order an extra dash of persistent interrogation, followed by a four-course meal of patient listening. Take a few minutes to look back to see ahead. Think about the fence posts of your life and ask Jesus to show you patterns He wants to highlight moving forward. Jot down the fence posts in the space below.

Pause, quiet your mind, and free yourself from all self-imposed stress to get the right answer or even to answer every question. Turn to Appendix C.1 Master Questions List and ask yourself:

1) Which questions am I *drawn* to answer? List each one in the left column of the table below.

Question	Answer

2) Which questions am I *afraid* to answer? List each one in the left column of the table below.

Question	Answer

Traction ⟿

Ask God which question He would like to use to begin the archeology process. Use the follow-up questions below to carefully unpack this question. In the above tables, record your insights in the column to the right of the respective question. Repeat this process for additional questions on your list.

1) Where am I vis-à-vis the question at hand?

2) Where am I called to be?

3) What is stopping me?

4) What will close the gap?

5) Why? Why?

6) So you can what?

There is no pressure to answer a certain number of questions within a given amount of time. The Father has much to say. Ask Him to help you distinguish between essentials and nonessentials.

Now ask Him to lead you in selecting which answers are essential to the true you being wildly successful per His grand plan. Highlight these selected essentials.

Essence

A lifestyle distilling discovery is how we *truventure*. Praise the Master Archeologist for the discovery thus far and ask Him to lead you further still. Your journey has the makings of building blocks for a *Strategic Pyramid* built especially for you. Take time to extract the highlighted essentials from your answers and record them in a summary for use in the ensuing chapters.

Gleaned List of Essentials

I build my *Strategic Pyramid* with quality materials,
the essence of the essentials, which Truth Himself uses to
refine my understanding of the true me, His vision of me being
wildly successful per His grand plan, and a path to walk it out.

Chapter 14

Wildly Successful

A Lifestyle Envisioning the Master's Rendering

When I strategize with God I begin with first principles, which in this case means truths God declares about Himself and about me. Once grounded in these, I begin to wonder how He pictures the true me being wildly successful per His grand plan. I position this picture at the pinnacle of my *Strategic Pyramid*, where it defines what success looks like and determines what else belongs on my *Strategic Pyramid*.

When I undertook to discover His picture of the true me being wildly successful, I mistakenly envisioned myself in front of a blank canvas. Then I realized the Master Artist had already painted a masterpiece of me;[1] I simply needed to ask Him to reveal His rendering of the true me being wildly successful per His grand plan,[2] a work He promised to complete.[3] Now, instead of envisioning myself in front of a blank canvas, I pursue a lifestyle envisioning the Master's rendering in order to understand His vision for my life.

Leveraging Bad Examples for Good

Observing bad manners motivates me to have good manners; experiencing poor management motivates me to learn good management; hearing uninspired vision statements motivates me to pursue heartfelt vision statements. Most vision statements feel like a burial ground for every pop corporate term, leaving me lethargic and uninspired. I get the feeling their authors rely too heavily on management-endorsed buzzwords and corporate speak, rather than courageously describing what success looks like for their business.

Even companies I admire illustrate dependence on corporate speak, as in the following example.

The strategy includes a vision of the future where:

- *We are recognized as the leader everywhere we do business.*
- *Our products, services and solutions help our customers succeed.*
- *Our distribution system is a competitive advantage.*
- *Our supply chain is world class.*
- *Our business model drives superior results.*
- *Our people are talented and live* Our Values in Action.
- *Our work today helps our customers create a more sustainable world.*
- *Our financial performance consistently rewards our stockholders."*[4]

Each item listed identifies an initiative worthy of company focus and resource; I admire management's thoroughness and commitment to address each initiative. But in my opinion, describing "a vision of the future" by listing corporate initiatives fails to paint an inspiring picture, and such heavy dependence on corporate speak fails to rally the organization to the cause.

By contrast, consider a vision that successfully inspired me and rallied me to their cause: "Wildly successful churches throughout every needy area of NYC who enfold the needy into the local body of Christ."[5] This vision delivers a compelling picture of hope and how to get there. It replaces the perception of the inner city as a bottomless pit with a picture of wildly successful inner city churches breaking the cycle of poverty with transformed lives, transformed neighborhoods, and a transformed city. This vision statement dares two important things: it dares to envision what wildly successful looks like, and dares to describe it with clarity. Consequently, it paints a vivid picture that compels us to reach for something we would never aspire to otherwise.

Starting Point: God's Goodness

I mentioned when I undertook to discover His picture of the true me being wildly successful, I mistakenly envisioned myself in front of a blank canvas. That was not my biggest mistake. My biggest mistake was that I did not yet know to begin each step of the strategic process by saturating my mind with the goodness of God.

I can inadvertently allow life's disappointments to covertly handicap my perception of God's complete goodness. To counteract this I recall what God says about His goodness, reflect upon biblical examples, and link these to examples from my life.[6] In this way I consciously reject a calibrated version of God's goodness, and reassert unvarnished truths such as, *God cannot lie,*[7] *He is good,*[8] and *His love is eternal.*[9] As I soak in these truths—renouncing conscious and subconscious thoughts that disbelieve His innate goodness—disappointments fade and obstacles become irrelevant.[10] In light of God's goodness I see true reality. The portrait of a wildly successful me moves from a poorly lit room into the sunlight. Getting into the light of the immutable goodness of God is the first step, and must accompany every step in the development and execution of vision and strategy.

Likewise, the success of strategy sessions flows from focusing first and foremost on God's goodness. This point was powerfully demonstrated in two strategic summits where the Master Artist unveiled His heart and vision. In each case we intentionally focused on God's goodness and submitted to what He wanted to reveal.

In one case, God gave the founders of a startup in China the vision of "People fully activated and unleashed to thrive in life." God's goodness is inherent in their vision, so that through business cycle ups and downs clients and members of the company personally experience the goodness of God as He activates and unleashes them to thrive in life. In the other case, the founder of a formerly successful business was in dire straights; the bank had canceled its line of credit. During our worship interludes we kept returning to our "Good Good Father,"[11] who gave this man a total restart to his business and life.

In both summits we preemptively focused on the goodness of God, and in each case He revealed the picture He had painted of their business and of them wildly successful per His grand plan. Limitations became irrelevant as we rested in the goodness of God, for whom nothing is impossible. God's goodness is jugular to a lifestyle envisioning the Master's rendering.

Pulling Back the Curtain

Now that my starting point is God's goodness and the knowledge that my Good, Good Father already painted His masterpiece rendering of a wildly successful me, I simply ask the Master Artist to pull back the curtain. When He unveils His masterpiece, He illuminates aspects that resonate powerfully within me. I ask Him to pull back the curtain even more, and He reveals even more. With each successive peek, I see His design of me— including my quirky interests, relentless intentionality, and investor's compulsion—but even more, He causes aspects to resonate so powerfully within me that I spontaneously chuckle, *That's me! That's me!*

Primer and Paint

Parts of my vision statement are the primer applied to the canvas, and other parts are the Master Artist's paint-soaked brush strokes applied to the primer. My vision is: "Believing God and all that entails, Mark genuinely surrendered and aggressively co-invested his life for eternity and completed all God commanded him." The punch line, *completed all God commanded him*, could be as broad as everything Christ commands all His followers. This is primer.[12] It begs the question, *Did Mark complete the Mark-specific body of work his Sovereign gave him to do?* Every instance in my life where I complete God's *personal* commands for me is paint applied to the primer—in colors as vibrant and varied as God's creative plans for me. Every aspect of both primer and paint requires Christ living His life in and through me to land the vision and pursue a lifestyle envisioning the Master's rendering.

Process to Develop a Vision

I start the process to develop vision by perusing the gleaned list of essentials from chapter 13. I wonder, *If I could pick just one from my list of essentials what would that be?* One essential on my list captivates me—"complete what God gives me to do"—because I have always been irresistibly drawn to any verse in the Bible where God declares someone finished the work He gave him to do.[13] I aspired to do the same, but it felt beyond my reach. Then I realized nothing is beyond God's reach;[14] the Almighty sensed no such limitation when He painted His rendering of me. So I began to envision what that might look like. I began to wonder what it would be like to truly know the Mark-specific work God created me to do. I resisted undermining God's infinite goodness, and He reminded me of His promises to accomplish the work, so I courageously adopted the vision, "Mark completed all God commanded him." I was also especially drawn to another essential, "This man believed God and all that entails." I debated which one should be my vision, then realized the former is *what* and the latter *how*. I smiled as I wrote, "Believing God and all that entails, Mark completed all God commanded him." I reviewed my list of essentials again and looked back at some of the questions:[15]

1. If the true me fully lived out my true identity in Christ, what would that look like?
2. What deepest yearning in me fits hand-in-glove with His grand plan?
3. What does my Master's rendering of the true me being wildly successful look like?

Each question confirmed my vision and my conviction grew. Next I checked for authenticity and tractiveness, using questions such as those found in figure 14.1. If the answer is no, I reevaluate my vision in light of the question and revise it.

Does it resonate with my soul at the deepest level and His grand plan at the highest level?	☑
Is it ruthlessly authentic to His call on me?	☑
Is it defined well enough for me to know when I get there?	☑
Is this the best picture of the true me being wildly successful?	*Absolutely!*

Figure 14.1. Fidelity checklist.

Once my vision statement passed my fidelity checklist, I was confident that it reflected the true me and I claimed it as the pinnacle of what would become my *Strategic Pyramid* (figure 14.2).

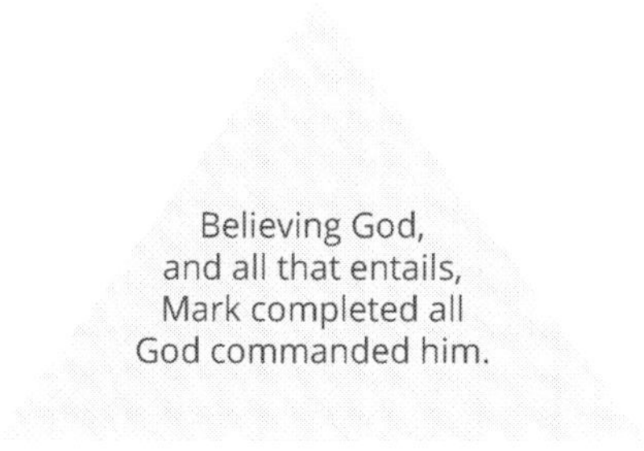

Believing God,
and all that entails,
Mark completed all
God commanded him.

Figure 14.2. My vision.

With the benefit of hindsight my process to develop and refine vision may appear clear and straightforward. However, my own path was more like bush whacking than following a clearly identified process. My trail meandered, but in retrospect my seemingly circuitous route was greatly used by God as I continually asked Him to reveal more.

Drawn to the Artist

The transcendent quality of great art highlights the artist more than the work itself. When I look at hand-painted reproductions of art in my office I think, *What a Van Gogh! What a Monet!* Similarly, the Master Artist's rendering of the true me being wildly successful draws me to Himself; it is never about me.

I never lose the wonder of how the consummate Maestro Artist reveals Himself in His brush strokes. He draws my attention to various aspects of His rendering of me: the background, foreground, what is happening, what I am becoming and the nuance or implication of each brush stroke. He uses core principles and select lessons to sketch my character. The more I meaningfully interact with Him, the more I experience the personal nature of God. When He adds the nuance *and all that entails* to my vision, He links it with one of my premier core principles, my deep desire for *Connected Integrity* with Him. We discuss these details of His rendering against my present reality, and further strategize to close the gaps between His rendering and my current lifestyle, so I progressively pursue a lifestyle envisioning the Master's rendering.

Whether we are discussing specific gaps of disconnected integrity, or the fullness of my vision, He points out that the size of my vision is not proportionate to my ability, but to the ability of God, who paints and executes His renaissance in my soul.[16] As I contemplate the gaps between the Master Artist's rendering and my current reality, He reminds me that I cannot close them, but He can.[17] As I contemplate the audacious challenge to complete *everything* He commands me, He reminds me that He has given me everything I need.[18] My job is to yield. The more I yield, like tilled soil, the more He prunes to produce more fruit.[19]

The more I yield, the more I want to hang out with Him. The more I hang out with Him, the more I realize He enjoys hanging out with me, never tiring of revealing His perspective, never tiring of connecting the dots between His truths and the place He designed for me in His grand mosaic. He becomes more personable and more profound as I spend time with Him. I ask the Master Artist to unveil more; the more He unveils, the more He reveals His true genius.

Nailing it

Jesus said to His Father, "I have glorified You on the earth by completing the work You gave Me to do."[20] Jesus knew the unique purpose of His unique life. He nailed it by remaining one with the Father. Jesus's example compels me to know the Creator's Mark-specific purposes, in this place at this time in history. I too want to nail the vision of my life. I do this by yielding to Jesus living His life in and through me as I pursue a lifestyle envisioning the Master's rendering. I trust God to complete the work He began—His rendering of the true me being wildly successful per His grand plan. Every block in my *Strategic Pyramid* is vital, none more than the pinnacle—the vision for my life.

Wildly Successful: *A Lifestyle Envisioning the Master's Rendering*

When I strategize with My Creator I begin with first principles, which in this case means truths God declares about Himself and about me.

Then I realized the Master Artist had already painted a masterpiece of me; I simply needed to ask Him to reveal His rendering of the true me being wildly successful per His grand plan, a work He promised to complete.

In light of God's goodness I see true reality.

Ask & Listen: Talk it over with the Master Artist

Your Creator paints in brilliant color with the finest brush strokes. Write a prayer asking Him to guide you as you unwrap His masterpiece rendering of you wildly successful.

Listen to these lyrics: "You're a good good Father. It's who you are. And I'm loved by you. It's who I am."* According to God's Word, He cannot lie and He is altogether good, so what does good good Father mean to you?

Ask the Master Artist to reveal any place in which your view of His goodness is clouded by lackluster lies or misconceptions about His purpose for you and your life. Record anything He reveals and then ask Him to roll back the clouds and reveal the bold colors of truth.

---

* Anthony Brown and Pat Barrett, of the band Housefires. "Good Good Father," *Housefires II*. Atlanta: 2014.

Traction ⌇→

Now firmly grounded in God's goodness, glance back at your gleaned list of essentials recorded in chapter 13 Traction. Slowly read through the list and record below the one that captivates you most.

With this essential in mind, ponder the following while engaging your mind and spirit with His:

1) If the true me fully lived out my true identity in Christ, what would that look like?

2) How would I describe my deepest yearning?

3) What would it look like if God used my deepest yearning in His grand plan?

4) Does this picture resonate with my soul at the deepest level and His grand plan at the highest level? ☐ Yes ☐ No

5) Is it ruthlessly authentic to His call on me? ☐ Yes ☐ No

6) Is it defined well enough for me to know when I get there? ☐ Yes ☐ No

7) Is this the best picture of the true me being wildly successful? ☐ Yes ☐ No

Keep asking the Master Artist what He thinks until you can answer with a resounding, "Yes! That's me!"

Essence

A lifestyle envisioning the Master's Rendering is how we *truventure*. His rendering of you is a one-of-a-kind masterpiece. In the space below, succinctly describe the vision of you being wildly successful. Ask Him to confirm in your spirit the twinkle in the corner of your good good Father's eyes.

Vision
Picture of you being wildly successful per His grand plan

Every block in my *Strategic Pyramid* is vital in my pursuit
of a strategically aligned life with my Creator, but none
are more than the pinnacle—the vision of my life.

Chapter 15

Opportunity

A Lifestyle Seizing the Dream

I n *Truventure,* the fundamental truth that my Creator made the true me to fit in His grand mosaic has three outflows. The first is His vision for the true me, which we explored in the prior chapter. The second is the opportunity He specifically designed for my life, which we explore in this chapter. The third outflow is what compels me to align with Him in each of these, which is in the following chapter. God paints His vision of the true me being wildly successful per His grand plan on a canvas that covers the whole of life. I believe when He designed me, He was thinking about opportunities specific to my time in history, or *era,* and my area of influence, or *arena.* This makes "opportunity" one of the most strategic areas for me to live out my vision.

Hope, Dreams, and Ice Cream

In a child's world hope thrives, dreams flow freely, and life is savored like ice cream with sprinkles. For grown-ups, however, life conspires that we expect less than our Creator intends. I counter this by imagining myself as a five-year-old with my hand in the hand of the King—free to hope, dream, and savor life with abandon because nothing is impossible for the One who holds my hand.[1] I smile up at Him as He strolls alongside me,[2] guiding me to an opportunity greater than I can grasp.[3] I look to the horizon with great anticipation because the Giver of every good and perfect gift[4] lavishly designed me with a purpose-built opportunity, sans limitations because He promises to fulfill it. With my perspective aligned with

His—escaping the grip of every hope-crushing, dream-sapping, life-sucking conspiracy—I anticipate living out the opportunity designed for me and a child-like lifestyle seizing the dream.

Contemplating my God-built opportunity inspires me to seize hope, capture dreams, and savor life. I previously settled for a collection of universally acceptable good things, but now I want more. I want to seize God's dream, pursuing the opportunity specifically designed for me: "God gives me specific talents and very limited time: I can intentionally co-invest for eternal grace-rewards[5] to lay at His feet, or I can squander my opportunity." As I dream about laying grace-rewards at my Savior's feet, the temporal self-indulgences I renounce to co-invest this life for eternity seem a small price to pay. Once I consider self-indulgences a small price to pay, I realize my life can indeed be significant, which fills me with hope. Renewed with hope, dreaming freely of the life I get to co-invest with God for eternal grace-rewards, I savor my God-given significance like a kaleidoscope of sprinkles.

My Opportunity

For a lifestyle seizing God's dream for me, I get alone with my Savior to hear His heart and discover the opportunity He specifically designed for my life in my era and arena "for such a time as this."[6] I unplug to fully plug into Him, because I cannot dream while multitasking or staying connected with others on my electronic device. I engage my mind with His mind and my spirit with His Spirit as I peruse the gleaned list of essentials from chapter 13 to identify the life opportunity God had in mind when He created me. I am especially drawn to the essence of my answers to the following questions:

1. Freed of all constraints, what opportunity is worthy of my life?
   Eternal grace-rewards.
2. What life calling maximizes His return on me?
   Co-investing with God.
3. What is the dream to which I feel called?
   Having grace-rewards to lay at Christ's feet.

As I reflect on the essence of the answers to questions like these, I try to envision what it would look like to fully live out the answer. A picture emerges, one worthy of my life's investment, one of eternal significance (figure 15.1). We refine that which resonates most powerfully with His call on me, personally.

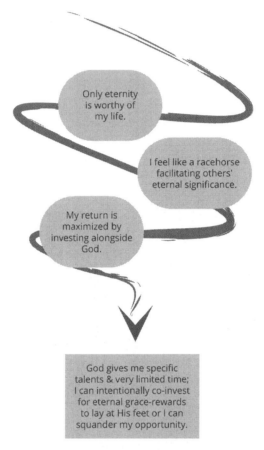

Figure 15.1. My opportunity.
A picture emerges after reflection on the essence of the essentials.

Era & Arena

Most of my opportunity statement relates to my era, not so much in terms of my specific time in history, but rather as an expression of my deep conviction that I indeed have extremely limited time to co-invest this vaporous life for eternity.[7] In my pursuit to see things from God's perspective, I asked Him to teach me to number my days.[8] I came to realize that even the 969-year life span of Methuselah is fleeting, relative to the next life.[9] The unknown duration of my remaining days (no matter how long or short) is the critical aspect of *my era*, which further heightens my opportunity to make it count.

My opportunity statement touches on my arena by acknowledging *God gives me specific talents,* but I use the rest of my *Strategic Pyramid* to highlight it. Arena is not limited to locales, but encompasses one's area of influence. My arena includes strategic areas of influence for which I was designed, namely expertise in the form of facilitating, coaching, mentoring, and befriending. Theodore Roosevelt's words inspire me:

> *[to be] the man who is **actually in the arena**, whose face is marred by dust and sweat and blood; **who strives valiantly**; [...] **who spends himself in a worthy cause**; who at the best knows in the end the triumph of high achievement, and who at the worst, if he fails, at least fails while **daring greatly**, so that his place shall never be with those cold and timid souls who know neither victory nor defeat.*[10]

I am called to *strive valiantly* in my arena, to *dare greatly*, and *spend myself in a worthy cause*. More than fearing failure, I fear the opportunity loss of missing my God-given dream. My era is the limited time I have to co-invest for others' eternal significance. My arena is strategic expertise. Opportunity, era, and arena intertwine to play a prominent role in a lifestyle seizing the dream.

Epic Examples

I want to highlight three historical examples of people who, as I see it, allowed their God-designed opportunity to play a leading role in how and where they walked out their vision. They are the Apostle Paul, who centered himself in hope in spite of setbacks; Daniel (of the Bible), who embraced the Sovereign's opportunity for him in exile; and William Wilberforce, who savored the impossible rather than allow "realistic limitations" to diminish a God-given dream. Each decided to "expect great things from God: attempt great things for God."[11]

Paul shouts: "I know mine! I have the opportunity to proclaim Christ where Christ has not been named!"[12] Despite his surprise at being sent to the Gentiles, this Hebrew of Hebrews[13] seized the Designer's opportunity for him—to proclaim Christ where He had not been named. As a result, vast regions were opened up for people to become Christ followers in Cyprus, Galatia, Macedonia, Achaia, Greece, and possibly Spain.[14,15] That is *what* he did, but *how* did he do it? The same way I want to execute my own designer opportunity—Christ living in me.[16] Furthermore, I want to live with Paul's irrepressible hope in the face of setbacks: "He has delivered us from such a terrible death, and He will deliver us. We have put our hope in Him that He will deliver us again."[17]

Exiled Daniel faced a predicament where most uprooted teenagers would ask, "What's the point? Where is God? Why shouldn't I just go with the flow?" When Daniel took huge risks, God allowed him to be thrown to the lions, literally. But for Daniel, not following the Lion of Judah was a far greater risk. Daniel's opportunity was to be the Sovereign's ambassador in the courts of godless sovereigns. That opportunity did not die in the lions' den. It transcended two great empires of the ancient world and reaches across the millennia as an epic example of a life well lived.[18]

William Wilberforce has been described as the greatest reformer in history.[19] His diary clearly articulates the opportunity to which he felt called—to be used of God to see slavery abolished and culture changed.[20] By the end of his life, British morals and sense of social responsibility increased in meaningfully significant ways. He died within days after the passage of the Slavery Abolition Act of 1833 was assured, abolishing slavery in most of the British Empire.[21] Among the heroes of the faith, Wilberforce stands tall as one who savored the impossible rather than taste defeat.

Figure 15.2 hypothesizes each man's vision and opportunity, to illustrate how opportunity and vision complement each other.

Individual	Opportunity Seized	Vision Embraced
Paul	I have the opportunity to proclaim Christ where He has not been named.	I see myself finishing the race, fully expended with no regrets.
Daniel	I have the opportunity to be the Sovereign's man in the courts of godless sovereigns.	I see myself remaining true to the One True, Living God.
Wilberforce	I have the opportunity to be used by God to see slavery abolished and culture changed in the British empire.	I see myself tenaciously standing for social justice on God's behalf.

Figure 15.2: Side-by-side illustration of opportunity and vision for three epic examples.

Mega-Truth

These men clearly expected great things from God and attempted great things for God. In doing so, they illustrate a mega-truth with compelling implications for me: *it is not about how big I am; it's about how big my God is.*[22] This mega-truth implies that limitations are irrelevant when I consider the opportunity God designed for my life. This eviscerates the lie, *Oh those are giants of the faith; I don't see something like that for me.* I cannot afford to diminish the power of the One, True, Living God; or my Savior's insatiable love for me, which means I do not have the right to limit the opportunity He chose for me. Furthermore, the mega-truth that *it is not about how big I am; it's about how big my God is* has serious implications on how I walk out my opportunity. I cannot afford to allow setbacks, obstacles, or degree of difficulty to dent my hope and perseverance. On the contrary, I am called to engage in the battle.[23,24]

Paul, Daniel, and Wilberforce each demonstrated the mega-truth that it was not about how big they were, but about how big their God is. They surrendered to God's—not man's—prevailing wisdom. Each seized the opportunity that resonated within him, without letting challenges limit them. Their God-given dreams resonated deeply enough that they fully invested their lives then, and the results reverberate through the millennia now. Each man challenges me to expect great things from God and attempt them by seizing the opportunity worthy of my life.

Two Modern Examples

Two women stand out to me as examples of strikingly different—yet equally valid—ways God's dream can be seized. The late Debbie Santiago[25] is an example of one who quickly identified her life opportunity—it was a no-brainer for her, with no complicating factors. Debbie, a former homeless drug addict, turned her life around after reading the Bible, which gave her deep empathy and compassion for all. I felt her sweet spirit while simply standing in the same room with her. Like heroes of the faith through the millennia, Debbie made every effort to remember the poor and invested her life to humbly serve them.[26] She seized her opportunity in her arena by focusing her influence on the less fortunate in Coney Island. She reciprocated her personal rescue by joining God to rescue others. At an event highlighting her partnership with Cru's inner city ministry, I recall Debbie wearing a big smile and clean second hand clothes, content to apply every resource toward rescuing others. Debbie quickly identified the life opportunity God had in mind when He created her and, like our three epic examples, Debbie went for it.

Angela Owen, on the other hand, exemplifies one who discovered her opportunity through thoughtful reflection, analysis, and insight. Angela, founder of TBL[27] Leadership Partners, makes a transformative difference in her arena, most recently North Carolina and China. Angela is one whose influence extends wherever she goes in whatever she is doing—whether it be professional consulting, community involvement, or leadership development. She left a successful career in a Fortune 100 company to help care for her parents and start her own business. In her new venture, Angela chose to work only with those committed to servant leadership—not a typical corporate priority, and not a typical choice for a startup where cash flow is never easy. These and other stepping stones led Angela to the opportunity God designed with her in mind: "God has anointed me with the skills, experience, influence, heart, and mind to help others discover and delight in the journeys of their own *Truventure*." God created

Angela with exceptional interpersonal skills and discernment, then gave her both corporate and entrepreneurial experience to prepare her to seize the opportunity of inviting others into their own Spirit-led quest.

Both Angela and Debbie seized their God-given opportunities, standing on the mega-truth that it is not about how big they are; it is about how big their God is. They chose to invest their life to seize their God-given dream in their arena, hope in the Almighty, and savor life with their Good, Good Father for such a time as this.

One Step at a Time

It's easy to see God fulfill the vision and opportunity He gave Paul, Daniel, and Wilberforce for their time in history. With the benefit of hindsight each man's opportunity looks brilliant, but it is doubtful these opportunities looked attractive when they needed to be embraced. Paul could have remained in Antioch, Daniel could have gone with the flow, and Wilberforce could have adopted incremental progress instead of radical cultural transformation. Instead, each seized the special opportunity God designed for his particular arena and era. They simply took the next right step—the next right step to walk out their entire lives with persistent faith in God.[28] They may not have perceived their time as special,[29] but we do. If I could see things from God's perspective, perhaps I would see each hour in history as poignant; perhaps I would see each hour as one to be seized. From across the millennia Paul, Daniel, and Wilberforce call me to seize the dream the Almighty Victor dreams for me.

Opportunity: *A Lifestyle Seizing the Dream*

I believe when He designed me, He was thinking about opportunities specific to my time in history, or era, and my area of influence, or arena.

God gives me specific talents and very limited time: I can intentionally co-invest for eternal grace-rewards to lay at His feet, or I can squander my opportunity.

It is not about how big I am; it's about how big my God is. This mega-truth implies that limitations are irrelevant when I consider the opportunity God designed for my life.

Ask & Listen: Talk it over with God

Imagine God's perspective on your life. He designed you with a unique purpose-built opportunity. Cast aside every limitation daring to dash the dreams God has for you. Remember...

it is *not* about how big the mountain is;
it is *not* about how big you are;
it's about *how big your God is*.

Peruse your gleaned list of essentials from Chapter 13 as you answer the questions below.

1) Freed of all constraints, what is worthy of my life?

2) What life calling maximizes His return on me?

3) What is the dream to which I feel called?

Discuss the questions with God, and His dream for you.

Ask God if there is anything else that He wants you to know. Continue to sharpen the picture until it resonates best with the opportunity worthy of your life. Record your Opportunity here:

> ## Opportunity
> *Description of the opportunity worthy of your life*

Essence

A lifestyle seizing the dream is how we *truventure*. Congratulations! It is a huge accomplishment to have discerned the dream God designed for you, the opportunity worthy of your life! Pause to soak in the magnificent landscape of opportunities specific to your time in history and thank your faithful Guide for showing you His perspective.

If I could see things from God's perspective,
perhaps I would see each hour in history as poignant;
perhaps, I would see each hour as one to be seized.

Chapter 16

Compelling Imperative
A Lifestyle Tethered to the Mind of Christ

A journal entry of Jim Elliot, martyred at age twenty-eight in Ecuador, transcends the ages: "He is no fool who gives up what he cannot keep to gain what he cannot lose." [1,2,3] This riveting, indisputable truth doubles down on the intrinsic wisdom of Christ's call to die daily to sin, self, and this world. [4,5]

This straightforward axiom never lets go; it points persistently to the mind of Christ and can be used to tether one's lifestyle to the mind of Christ. Jim's journal entry illustrates what a compelling imperative is and how it can so profoundly impact a life, even many lives, through the ages. A compelling imperative is an indisputable, axiomatic truth so riveting it doesn't leave you alone; it persistently points you to the next right thing for a lifestyle tethered to the mind of Christ. Consequently, it is an essential component of my *Strategic Pyramid* and vital to landing my vision.

More than Words

Like both strategic intent and annual main thrusts, compelling imperative is a business concept I began applying to my own life. These concepts attracted the attention of the business community for a year, but got my attention for a lifetime. Unlike the business community, I cannot treat tractive concepts as passing fads. They have become vital in my pursuit of a strategically aligned life with my Creator; I do not want to take a step without them. Because they are far more than words, I integrate them into my walk; they become increasingly ingrained in the fabric of my being. I want my compelling imperative to have a greater and greater grip on me, tenaciously compelling me to take the next right step for a lifestyle tethered to the mind of Christ.

The classic marketplace compelling imperative—*we exist to serve our customers*—focuses every employee on who ultimately pays their salaries, and gives license to eliminate work that does not ultimately add value to the customer. Sales revenue, morale, and profitability snowball if the manager walks the talk versus merely talking the talk.

Having observed its powerful force for good in the marketplace, I intuitively placed my compelling imperative prominently in my *Strategic Pyramid* (figure 16.1).

Vision
Mark completed everything God commanded him to do.

Compelling Imperative
Only what is eternally significant matters.

Opportunity
Co-invest this life for eternal grace-rewards.

Figure 16.1. Compelling imperative's position in my *Strategic Pyramid*.

My compelling imperative—*only what is eternally significant matters*—rivets me to the existential truth of where I am going and how I should then live.[6] It is the indisputable, axiomatic truth that cuts through what I should and should not be doing, and points to how I should be investing this life.

Emotively Evokes Desired Action

Strategy is primarily cognitive, but genuine passion gives it traction. The ideal compelling imperative is so cognitively profound that it emotively evokes the desired action. In its highest form a compelling imperative is pure transcendent essence, and thus has the power to evoke visceral, sustained passion. A compelling imperative is so rooted in truth, so cognitively sound that it reverberates and passionately compels implementation.

The entire person, emotions included, is invited into the entire *Strategic Pyramid* process. When I read my compelling imperative I hear the impassioned voice of the Lover of my soul, "You can run but you can't hide,[7] I want the very best for you,[8] come venture with Me." Mine need not evoke the same in you, but it must consistently, intrinsically motivate *me*. To this end, a well-chosen compelling imperative must innately become more evocative with use.

Emotion, passion, and the best intentions often meet their match in difficulties; yet I am promised difficulties.[9] In order to overcome, my passion must be inextricably grounded in Truth so I am persistently inspired to do the next right thing unto completion. If my passion is anchored in the Rock Himself, then it overcomes disappointment and affliction. Doing the next right thing unto completion is essential for landing one's vision. Therefore, I view my compelling imperative as a preloaded strategic weapon essential to make my strategy robust against all sorts of difficulties.

I regret when I do not persevere in the face of difficulties.[10] Therefore, I pursue a lifestyle tethered to the mind of Christ. As a kid, I played tetherball for hours. No matter how hard the ball was hit, no matter how many times it was hit in opposing directions, and no matter how long we played, that ball stayed tethered to the pole. My compelling imperative is essential because no matter how much I get knocked around, it keeps me connected to the mind of Christ.

A Triple Threat for Good

Whether I am experiencing promised trials or promised peace, my compelling imperative serves as a triple threat for good in all circumstances; it's like a lightning bolt, a compass needle, and jumper cables.

No matter what is going on in life, I receive clarity from my compelling imperative—like a lightning bolt that cannot be ignored. When I find myself pursuing my agenda instead of His, fighting for a fiefdom no citizen of heaven has reason to fight, consuming at the expense of sharing, my compelling imperative stops me in my tracks. *Only what is eternally significant matters* flashes like a lightning bolt and realigns me with the truth that "each one's work will become obvious, for the day will disclose it, because it will be revealed by fire; the fire will test the quality of each one's work."[11] My compelling imperative readies me for trial by fire each day, up to and including the day of judgment.[12]

Furthermore, no matter how I get myself turned in the wrong direction, my compelling imperative redirects me—like the needle of a compass pointing True North. I can be so engrossed in what I am doing that I become oblivious to self's subtle shift from what God wants to accomplish to what I think is important. I notice this in writing, competitive swimming, and even relationships—but no matter how I get myself turned in the wrong direction, my compelling imperative ceaselessly points back to my True North.[13]

Finally, no matter how I feel, my compelling imperative jumpstarts me to do the next right thing—like jumper cables properly connected. Newton's first law applies to me: "an object will remain at rest [...] unless acted upon by an external force."[14] I need jumper cables to get me off the couch. My compelling imperative electrifies my motivation to pursue what is eternally significant. I am prone to suboptimize this life, so I pray my compelling imperative into the fabric of my being. It helps prioritize life's opportunities and obligations, so my lifestyle aligns with my eternal priorities and I get off the couch.

Process

God knew when we developed my gleaned list of essentials in chapter 13 that we would come to this point. I am privileged to get alone with Him as a first step in discovering the axiomatic essential that will become my compelling imperative.

Usually I prefer espresso, but for this process I select chamomile tea for its soothing qualities. I need to be in a calm place, literally and metaphorically, to let that which is most compelling within me rise to the surface. As I engage my mind with the mind of Christ and my spirit with His, I look for the truth that irresistibly tethers me to the mind of Christ to draw me to where He wants me to go.

I try several. What I am looking for is a deep visceral response that irresistibly compels me to do the next right thing no matter the circumstance. I want what resonates most powerfully in the true me. I ask my God how to word it so He can powerfully use it in my life to land His rendering of the true me (figure 16.2).

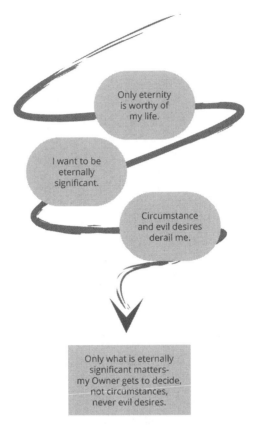

Figure 16.2. Funnel relevant essentials into a compelling imperative.

Priority, Action Required!

The term *compelling imperative* is dense in meaning; it feels preloaded. Like Jim Elliot's journal entry, my compelling imperative grabs my attention and justifiably demands action. It comes marked PRIORITY, IMPORTANT, ACTION REQUIRED. It rightly jumps to the front of the line, leapfrogs delays, and short circuits procrastination. It demands urgent, prolonged action toward completion. Like great art, it cannot be ignored; unlike great art, it will not let me stay seated. It thrusts me to seize life worth living, and tethers me to the mind of Christ so I am persistently pointed to the next right thing. My soul responds to my compelling imperative: *Yes!*

Compelling Imperative: *A Lifestyle Tethered to the Mind of Christ*

A compelling imperative is an indisputable, axiomatic truth so riveting it doesn't leave you alone; it persistently points you to the next right thing for a lifestyle tethered to the mind of Christ.

A compelling imperative is so rooted in truth, so cognitively sound that it reverberates and passionately compels implementation.

If my passion is anchored in the Rock Himself, then it overcomes disappointment and affliction.

Ask & Listen: Talk it over with Christ

For who has known or understood the mind (the counsels and purposes) of the Lord so as to guide and instruct Him and give Him knowledge? But we have the mind of Christ (the Messiah) and do hold the thoughts (feelings and purposes) of His heart. (1 Corinthians 2:16, AMP)

Christ stands as your True North, pointing the way before you. Ask Him to give you insight into the rich meaning in the words that lie just after the word "but". What does He bring to mind?

Use your gleaned list of essentials from Chapter 13 to answer the following:

1) What truth irresistibly tethers me to the mind of Christ? (For me it was, *God called me to be a warrior in His kingdom*)

2) What draws me irresistibly to where I want to go with my life? (For me it was, *Helping people discover who they truly are in God's eyes so that they might be free*)

3) What keeps me going when things get hard? (For me it was, *God gave me a unique role to play in His kingdom...He trusts me and others are counting on me*)

4) What compels me to overcome obstacles and do the next right thing? (For me it was, *I can do all things through Christ who strengthens me. - Philippians 4:13*)

Continue pondering until you discover that which triggers a deep visceral response, compelling you to do the next right thing regardless of circumstance. With this riveting truth in hand, record your Compelling Imperative here:

> ### Compelling Imperative
> *Truth that draws you where you want to go*

Essence

A lifestyle tethered to the mind of Christ is how we *truventure*. You now have a compelling imperative that tethers you to the mind of Christ and no matter what always moves you to take the next right step. Thank God for a compelling imperative that comes from heaven to you, marked Priority, Important, Action Required!

⌐

It [compelling imperative] comes marked
PRIORITY, IMPORTANT, ACTION REQUIRED.

Chapter 17

Strategic Compass
A Lifestyle Knowing the Right Direction

M y strategic compass—comprised of vision, opportunity, and compelling imperative—forms a minipyramid at the top of my *Strategic Pyramid*. God's rendering of the true me being wildly successful per His plan, the opportunity He designed for my life, and how He passionately compels me—my trio of strategic direction—collectively comprise my strategic compass. In this chapter, I fine-tune my drafted strategic compass (figure 17.1) into a *refined* strategic compass (figure 17.5) that reliably points to my True North for a lifestyle knowing the right direction. I need a fine-tuned strategic compass to remain on course in my lifelong *Truventure*. The more precisely my strategic compass points to my True North, and the more powerfully it resonates within me, the better my decisions are, and the easier it is to develop the rest of my *Strategic Pyramid*.

Decision-making and Truth-walking

The more I attentively listen to God, the more He can finely tune my strategic compass to His design of the true me being wildly successful per His plan. The more I yield to Him, the more He can direct my pursuit of a strategically aligned life with Him and maximize His return on investment in me.

My strategic compass maximizes me in two significant areas: decision-making and truth-walking. It increases the probability of making the right decisions and improves the quality of my decisions. It makes my walk more aligned with the truth and increases my consistency of walking in the truth. Clearly it does none of this in the drawer, but only if I use it to realign with my True North for a lifestyle knowing the right direction.

My strategic compass serves as a useful grid for decision-making. For example, when the pursuit of my dream isn't paying the bills, do I take an unrelated but well-paying job? Maybe yes, maybe no. With my strategic compass in hand, I ask God to appropriately position my circumstances within the transcendent context of the trio of strategic direction within my strategic compasss. He may tell me to trust His provision and, despite my lack of funds, go for the opportunity He designed for my brief life. Or He may point out I am to learn certain things from a seemingly unrelated job that will be part of the picture of me being wildly successful per His plan.

My strategic compass also helps in truth-walking. For example, my flesh is unrelenting: *What about me? What about me?!* By focusing on the precepts God placed in my strategic compass, I am better equipped to walk rightly in the right direction and consider others better than myself. For example, when I have a relational conflict, I find my struggle is actually with God, for He is using the corporate or interpersonal differences to penetrate the next level of immaturity in me. So when I pull out my strategic compass in times of conflict, I often realize I need to capitulate at a deeper level if I am to walk further in truth.

When I use my strategic compass, the probability of making the right decisions increases, the quality of my decisions improves, and I expend more effort aligning my direction with truth than wondering which way to go.

Deliberate vs. Rushed

As I helped others develop *Strategic Pyramids*, the strategic compass proved more powerful than I expected but less useful when rushed in its development. The value of a well-considered strategic compass increases throughout one's life, whereas a rushed strategic compass seems easily dictated by circumstances, making it less relevant over time. Careful deliberation is vital for quality construction of a strategic compass.

I once facilitated a business owner who chose to create two *Strategic Pyramids*, one for his business and another for his personal life. He carefully deliberated and correctly identified three components of the strategic compass for his business. Unfortunately, I was too inexperienced to notice at the time that he rushed through his personal strategic compass to get to his strategic map. We kept in touch, and I observed years later that his deliberate strategic compass remained reliable. In contrast, his rushed strategic compass was only vitally relevant for the crisis during which it was developed. This fails the purpose of the strategic compass, which equips a lifestyle of knowing the right direction throughout each and every stage of life.

Observing the results of the same individual deliberating on one strategic compass and rushing through the other led me to conclude that the strategic compass requires more time, rumination, and rethinking than I had expected. I went on to observe that those who make the investment[1] of careful deliberation receive substantive, sustainable, growing returns. The investment usually involves several iterations to identify the vision, which in turn is more stable when supported with a compelling imperative and opportunity that powerfully resonate. I suboptimize every portion of my *Strategic Pyramid* if I hurry through my strategic compass to get to the strategies and tactics.

My Strategy Game

Even visionaries require several iterations to accurately discern and validate their vision, compelling imperative, and opportunity—so I invest time and effort to develop a well-considered, finely tuned strategic compass through careful deliberation. I have fun taking apart my draft strategic compass, fine-tuning each element and reassembling them. This careful reconsideration of my *draft* strategic compass delivers a more accurate and precise *refined* strategic compass. I am drawn to three aspects of an ancient strategy game called "Go": simplicity, minimal rules, and maximum opportunities. Played with black and white pebbles on a grid, each player tries to encircle the opponent's pebbles. Despite its simplicity, this eldest board game has seemingly endless possibilities. My Chief Fun Officer and I play a game to refine my strategic compass, which also employs simplicity, minimal rules, and maximum opportunities.

To play the game well I need to be refreshed, alert to new perspectives, and anxious to explore new insights. I imagine myself with a self-made compass, in the presence of the Supreme Craftsman who wants to help transform it into a finely tuned compass. In my simple strategy game I use only three building blocks: vision, opportunity, and compelling imperative.[2] The play is simple: three consecutive rounds rephrasing one of the three blocks as if it were in each of the other two positions.

I begin by setting up the game board using my draft strategic compass as seen in figure 17.1.

Figure 17.1. Draft strategic compass.

Round 1: I rephrase my draft vision as an opportunity, then as a compelling imperative (figure 17.2).

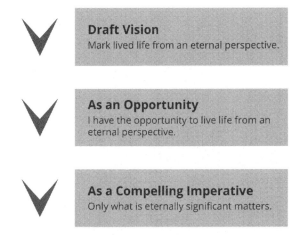

Figure 17.2. Round 1 revises my vision into an opportunity and a compelling imperative.

When I rephrased my vision as an opportunity I did little with the concept, but when I rephrased my vision as a compelling imperative the Holy Spirit pointed me to the heart of the issue—*only what is eternally significant matters*, which resonates much more powerfully within me than my draft vision.

Round 2: I rephrase my draft opportunity as a compelling imperative, then as a vision (figure 17.3).

Draft Opportunity
I have the opportunity to complete what God gave me.

As a Compelling Imperative
I am compelled to complete everything the Father commands me to do.

As a Vision
Mark completed everything God commanded him to do.

Figure 17.3. Round 2 revises my opportunity into a compelling imperative and a vision.

When my draft opportunity is rephrased as a vision statement, it grabs me. It cuts to the chase—*Mark completed everything God commanded him to do*. It draws me to live each moment with the ultimate end in view. My original opportunity resonates most powerfully in me when rephrased as a vision statement.

Round 3: I rephrase my draft compelling imperative as a vision, and then as an opportunity (figure 17.4).

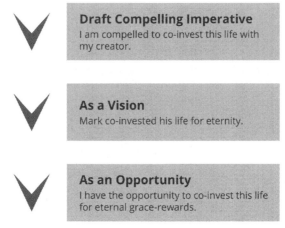

Figure 17.4. Round 3 revises my compelling imperative
as a vision and an opportunity.

When I rephrased my compelling imperative as a vision it popped;
it felt powerful. However, my concern was that it would not hold me
accountable enough for a vision statement. It lacked teeth regarding quality, quantity, and consistency. When I rephrased my compelling imperative
as an opportunity, my Expert Editor added "for eternal grace-rewards."
Rephrased as an opportunity, it solves many of the issues I had when
rephrased as a vision statement; when written as an opportunity, I am
immediately challenged to seize the day.

Round of reflection: I complete the game by selecting the best of each
round, yielding a refined strategic compass (figure 17.5).

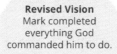

Figure 17.5. My refined strategic compass.

I allowed God maximum flexibility to reorient and edit at will. Time flies when I am in careful deliberation with Him. The game was successful: my strategic compass feels more finely tuned to the true me being wildly successful per God's plan, more robust for knowing the right direction through twists, turns, and seasons of life, and more worthy of my Investor's investment in me.

Game over: I get to celebrate with another favorite trio—brownie, vanilla, and chocolate (figure 17.6). I savor playing my strategy game with my Chief Fun Officer. He chose His moves well—each one a winner.

Figure 17.6. A delicious trio of a brownie, vanilla ice cream and chocolate fudge.

Useful for Navigating Life

A traditional compass is rendered worthless if the earth's magnetic field is cloaked; likewise my strategic compass is rendered worthless if left ignored in my pocket. A traditional compass is rendered worthless by magnetic interference; likewise my strategic compass is rendered worthless by self-centered interference instead of submitting to my Lord's perfect plan. A traditional compass is rendered worthless if its face isn't clear; likewise my strategic compass is rendered worthless if I don't live transparently, with a pure heart, to align with my True North. Cloaking, interference, and nontransparency keep me from correctly using my strategic compass in conjunction with my True North.

Creator of heaven and earth uses the elements of my trio of strategic direction like a constellation to navigate me through tumultuous and calm seas alike. He impresses upon me that He wants me to use my strategic compass more and more. I find the more I use my strategic compass for decision-making and truth-walking, the more I want my expert Craftsman to fine-tune the elements of my strategic compass for future seas. When I think about the future, I mentally check to make sure I have my strategic compass in hand for a lifestyle knowing the right direction.

Journey into the Wildness of God

Strategic Compass: *A Lifestyle Knowing the Right Direction*

The more precisely my strategic compass points to my True North, and the more powerfully it resonates within me, the better my decisions are, and the easier it is to develop the rest of my Strategic Pyramid.

My strategic compass maximizes me in two significant areas: decision-making and truth-walking.

When I use my strategic compass, the probability of making the right decisions increases, the quality of my decisions improves, and I expend more effort aligning my direction with truth than wondering which way to go.

Ask & Listen: Talk it over with your True North

The God of the Universe who holds every star in the sky wants to shine as your True North Star. Write a prayer asking him to help you calibrate your strategic compass in precise alignment with His heart and in clear resonance with your own.

It's time to play the Strategy Game! Grab a pen and a stack of index cards or post it notes. Write your Vision statement on an index card or post-it, your Compelling Imperative on another, and your Opportunity on a third. Arrange the three cards in pyramid form as shown in Figure 17.1

Round 1: Rephrase your draft vision as an opportunity, then as a compelling imperative. (reference Figure 17.2)

Round 2: Rephrase your draft opportunity as a compelling imperative, then as a vision (reference Figure 17.3)

Round 3: Rephrase your draft compelling imperative as a vision, and then as an opportunity (reference Figure 17.4)

Round of reflection: Select the best of each round. Record your revised vision, revised compelling imperative, and revised opportunity as shown in Figure 17.5

Essence

A lifestyle knowing the right direction is how we *truventure*. Congratulations! You carefully calibrated your strategic compass with your True North. Your strategic compass is a powerful tool to navigate you through tumultuous and calm seas alike. Write a prayer asking God to help you use it in decision-making and truth-walking.

‿

Creator of heaven and earth uses the elements
of my trio of strategic direction like a constellation to
navigate me through tumultuous and calm seas alike.

Chapter 18

Strategic Map

A Lifestyle Landing the Vision

Since a compass alone does not tell me where to cross the Himalayas or how to sidestep Death Valley, I compliment my strategic compass with a strategic map. Below the trio of blocks comprising my strategic compass are several rows of blocks that comprise my strategic map. The first row contains strategies to land the vision. The row of strategies is followed by rows of supporting blocks to land the strategies. Collectively, the strategy blocks and their supporting blocks provide tractive steps to land God's vision of me. Like my strategic compass, which informs my next right step for a lifestyle knowing the right direction, my strategic map informs my next right step for a lifestyle landing my vision. I place my strategic map beneath my strategic compass to form a robust *Strategic Pyramid* designed to land my vision under any circumstances.

Strategy Blocks

I determine the strategy blocks for my *Strategic Pyramid* by asking the simple question, *What lands my vision?* I wait for God to provide insight and miraculously deliver simplicity on the other side of complexity.[1] I ask the Omniscient for insight to identify the gaps between my current lifestyle and the true me being wildly successful; then I ask Him to identify the most effective strategies to close the gaps. I trust His desire to equip me to do His will,[2] and I claim His promises.[3] I wait expectantly, listen intently, and write down what He says. He often pulls from the gleaned list of essentials. I place each strategy in its own building block, assembled in a row.

I look for what is essential to land the vision—nothing more, nothing less. The guide I use is "less is more as long as it is sufficient." I am going for what mathematicians call elegance, simple yet powerful, co-developed with the Creator of an elegant universe. I believe He can and will bring to mind less than a handful of inspired strategies that jointly land His vision of a wildly successful true me. And He does, with just two in my *Strategic Pyramid*: an alignment strategy and an investment strategy (figure 18.1).

Figure 18.1. Two succinct strategies to land my vision.

Next I ask, *If each of the strategies is successfully landed, will the vision be landed?* If the answer is no, then the follow-on question is, *What additional strategy is necessary to land the vision?* Unless I identify everything essential, I will not possess a strategic map that lands my vision. When I am satisfied that my strategy blocks will land my vision, I move on to the supporting blocks.

Supporting Blocks

For a lifestyle that lands vision, I need more than strategies—I need another level of detail, which I call my *supporting blocks*. Just as I determined my strategies by asking, *What will land my vision?* I cascade the question by asking, *What will land each strategy?* I place His responses in supporting blocks and arrange them below the appropriate strategy. I give myself freedom to brainstorm, but ultimately I am not looking for an exhaustive list of what will land my vision—only what is essential. The Holy Spirit usually pulls from the gleaned list of essentials we refined in chapter 13.[5] I ask what needs to be true in order to land the particular strategy; I do not encumber myself with whether these are tactics or core competencies or areas of operational excellence.[6] The first draft of my strategic map includes essential strategies to land my vision, and essential supporting blocks to land each strategy (figure 18.2). It is definitely time for a Belgian praline—caramelized hazelnut encased in chocolate.

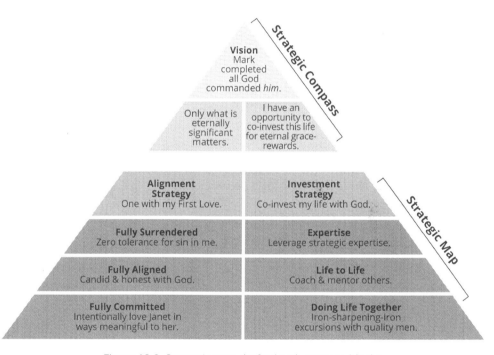

Figure 18.2. Strategic map drafted with strategy blocks and their respective supporting blocks.

Bare Essentials

It is tempting to throw as much as we can into our strategy in the hope that something in there qualifies. But this approach suffocates in its own verbosity and the bloated "strategy" ends up in a dead file. To avoid this trap, the only things allowed in my strategic map are those required to land the high-definition picture of the true me being wildly successful per His design. This section delineates some of what I call the bare essentials, a handful of criteria that help me narrow down the contents of my strategic map.

Less is More

Less is more reminds me to glean everything that is not essential. This sometimes applies to entire blocks. I remove any strategy or supporting block that is not absolutely essential to landing my vision. If I can fully land my vision without it, then it is not absolutely essential.[7] *Even less is even more* reminds me to further glean each remaining block to make my strategic map even more effective. My strategic map becomes more effective if everything is simplified and distilled to its essence, which makes it easier to execute and assess.[8]

Keep it simple is a close relative to *less is more*. The most poignant, direct, declarative statements clarify the strategy and increase my chances to reach the desired destination. I glean strategies of business speak and Christianese and, most importantly, I am careful not to use God's Word lightly in my *Strategic Pyramid*. I do not cast Scripture as a feint to avoid the heart of an issue. If a verse feels like the right answer to what will land my vision or strategy, then I ask myself, *What specific truth in this verse directly relates to landing my vision or strategy?* I dig deeper to link the core resonating truth within the verse to my vision. I want the content of my *Strategic Pyramid* to stand on its own, without crutches of business or Christian lingo, or even good crutches of entire Bible verses.

Not a Life Plan

Strategy on one page is audacious enough without trying to make it more than its intended purpose, which is to land the vision of a wildly successful me. So I resist the inclination to make it a life plan. A life plan is more comprehensive, addressing everything I deem important about my life. A strategic plan to land my vision is narrower and more precise than a life plan. It requires a high-definition target, undiluted clarity of essential steps, and undeterred focus.

A good example from my life plan, not on my strategic map, is competitive swimming. One of my life goals is to clock the fastest time in the nation for my age bracket. To this end, my life plan includes getting nine hours of sleep per night, working out at least one hour every day, staying injury free, and competing in three championship swim meets per year. Swimming competitively has been a huge priority in my life for six decades. It is undoubtedly part of the true me and plays a prominent role in my life plan, but it is not on my strategic map because it is not essential to landing my vision.

None of my Plans

Before proceeding further in my strategic map, I insist that none of my plans survive, only His. Additionally, I resist shoehorning my favorite concepts or institutionalizing my way of doing things in my strategic map. It is a fallacy to confuse a collection of favorite concepts as strategy to land a specific vision. For example, one of my lifelong favorite business concepts is decentralized authority and decision-making. But this concept is not in my business strategic map because it is not essential to land the vision of my business. I ask God the questions found in figure 18.3 to further glean the bare essentials.

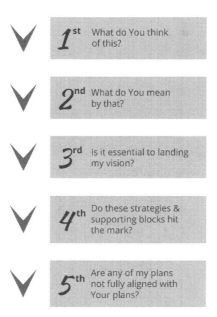

1st   What do You think of this?

2nd   What do You mean by that?

3rd   Is it essential to landing my vision?

4th   Do these strategies & supporting blocks hit the mark?

5th   Are any of my plans not fully aligned with Your plans?

Figure 18.3. Checklist to further glean the bare essentials for my strategic map.

Prototypical

An insightful way for me to keep to the bare essentials is to include everything *essential* without exhaustively including *everything*. There is often a prototypical member within a category of essentials that can represent the entire category without being general. In mathematical terms, by *prototypical* I mean if "x" were true then "y," "w," and "z" would most likely be true as well. Then I can confidently use "x" in my strategic map as a proxy for "y," "w," and "z," without having to list them all. For example, I do not have to list every aspect of being fully committed if I have one aspect of commitment that is prototypical, such as "fully committed: forsaking all others, intentionally love Janet seven ways each day that are meaningful to her." Marriage counselors can explain why this benefits my whole life, and neurobehavioral scientists can explain how and why prototypical works. I simply find it exceedingly effective.

Refining the Map

I enlist my Creator's insight to help me refine our draft of my strategic map. We use authenticity, wiggle room, gaps, God's fingerprints, arrangement, and honing iterations to arrive at a strategic map that resonates even more powerfully with the true me.

Authenticity

Authenticity is key to the refining process and my *Truventure*. So I eliminate everything that sounds like a lofty version of myself, oust over-spiritualizing, and delete superfluous words. In my strategic map—as in every aspect of my *Truventure*—I am going for the most authentic relationship possible between God uncensored and Mark uncontrived. He already knows everything about me, sees past my self-delusion yet loves me still. Therefore, I ask for grace to be authentic.

Wiggle Room

I desperately desire to align with Christ, but I reflexively cut myself slack. I have an incredible capacity for rationalization, personal biases, and rating myself higher than I should, so I enlist the Holy Eliminator of wiggle room to get in my face for tractive progress. We hunt for instances when I cut myself slack between my current reality and the given strategy or supporting block. My "fully surrendered" block initially read, "Zero tolerance for sin in me." But after a couple of years my Holy Eliminator pointed out how I was glossing over self's incessant longings. The block now reads: "Zero tolerance for sin and unsurrendered longing in me." There are realms where it is appropriate to cut myself slack, such as recuperation after a hectic schedule, but God grants no quarter[9] when it comes to the realm of self, whose desires are contrary to the Spirit.[10] And neither should I; therefore, I embrace eliminating wiggle room and the required brutal honesty.

Gaps

I ask God to reveal gaps between His rendering of me and my current reality to develop essential strategies, and I also use gaps to be more precise in my refined strategic map. There is a difference between "be a man of integrity," and "zero gaps between my every thought, word, action, and His righteousness." With the former, I inadvertently compare myself with past performance, an acceptable norm, or other people. But in the latter, the target is more precise: zero deviation from the Standard Himself.

I use gaps to hold myself accountable, too. If I simply state the desired outcome, "to be a man of integrity," then I easily read it and say to myself, *Yeah, I am doing that.* But when I read, "zero gaps between my lifestyle and Christ," then I better position myself for the Holy Spirit to identify specific gaps He wants to eliminate. Likewise I can write, "love my wife," or I can write, "zero gaps between how I love Janet and how she wants to be loved." With the former, I can easily think, *Yeah I am doing that,* but the latter stops me in my tracks with specific ways I need to change (figure 18.4).

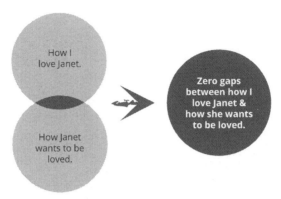

Figure 18.4. Application of Gaps for greater precision
and accountability in my strategic map.

The level of precision and accountability reached by using gaps makes them powerful and tractive in strategy development and implementation. Precision and accountability may require a few extra words, but the key is not less is *always* more; the key is less is more *as long as it is sufficient.*

God's Fingerprints

Sometimes as the Master Artist further unveils His rendering, I see His fingerprints in my strategic map. For example, my alignment strategy evolved when He focused on one block of my strategic map one day. I was mulling over my alignment strategy, "One with my First Love," when He identified what success looks like and how it is to occur—*resting in Him for Him to produce His fruit for His glory.* Later He added how to be proactively intentional—*volitionally, genuinely, fully, faithfully remain 'in Christ,' aligning with Him more and more.* My alignment strategy became: "One with my First Love: volitionally, genuinely, fully, faithfully remain in Christ, aligning with Him more and more, resting in Him for Him to produce His fruit for His glory." The result reveals God's fingerprints in the form of comprehensive, refined, divine wisdom in a tractive strategy for being one with Him.

Other times He reveals the same divine fingerprint on several blocks. I was praying through my *Strategic Pyramid*, when my Editor breezed through, ever so slightly editing each block. And yet He radically changed the perspective of each block from *me* to what He would accomplish for *others'* benefit (figure 18.5).

Figure 18.5. *Left*, the original supporting blocks for my investment strategy; *right*, the Editor's edits in italics—His fingerprints are evident in the change of focus from me to others.

The more I get alone with God and pray through my *Strategic Pyramid*, the more He reveals in His simple, powerful, evocative, and compelling roadmap for my life. Allowing the Holy Spirit free reign causes strategies to be included and rephrased that would not be if developed on my own. His fingerprint is identifiable: pristine, ancient, wise, and penetrating. The more I see God's fingerprints, the more I sense His heartbeat for His rendering of the true me being wildly successful per His grand plan.

Arrangement

Changing the arrangement of strategy and supporting blocks can often achieve greater impact in the strategic map. If a supporting block definitively applies to more than one strategy, then I make it wide enough to support each of them. An extreme example of this occurs when a supporting block is so fundamental it cries out to stretch across the entire base of the strategic map. Two American, unilingual friends left Southern California to start a business in China. At the base of their *Strategic Pyramid* is a supporting block essential to the entire venture: "Functional in Mandarin within 24 months." Seeing it across the bottom, supporting the entire *Strategic Pyramid*, reinforced time-critical resourcing of this foundational action needed to land their vision.

Figure 18.6. A special case with three foundational blocks supporting the entire strategic map.

In most cases, multiple supporting blocks spanning the entire strategic map indicate the map may be too general. Generality erodes traction, and without traction the map degrades into another useless strategic plan that dies in the drawer. Specificity and line of sight between the respective block and the vision translate into traction rather than abandonment. Notice the specificity in the three supporting blocks that span the entire strategic map in figure 18.6.

In business it is helpful to arrange external, or customer-facing, blocks to the right and internal enabling blocks on the left.[11] My strategic map migrates blocks primarily focused on *being* to the left, and *executing* to the right. Chrysalis founders chose three columns that flow left to right (figure 18.6). On the left they input external expertise; in the middle they developed internal expertise; and on the right they built an external consulting business. There are many ways to arrange the blocks in a strategic map to be more coherent, more powerful, and easier to pray through.

Honing Iterations

I further refine my strategic map with honing iterations, a series of questions I ask of each and every strategy and supporting block. My objective is God's perspective for more clarity, yielding blocks as well honed as the Egyptians'. To this end, I use the questions in figure 18.7 to apply insight and rigor to the process.[12]

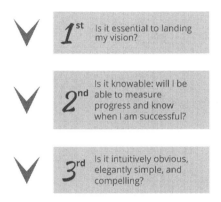

1st Is it essential to landing my vision?

2nd Is it knowable: will I be able to measure progress and know when I am successful?

3rd Is it intuitively obvious, elegantly simple, and compelling?

Figure 18.7. Honing iterations further refine my strategic map.

In conclusion, when I authentically engage with God, He responds by eliminating wiggle room, closing gaps, rearranging and honing my blocks—leaving His fingerprints throughout my refined strategic map.

Compass + Map = Pyramid

I fit my refined strategic map under my refined strategic compass (figure 18.8). Together they comprise my *Strategic Pyramid*, for strategy on one page. I celebrate this milestone with more ice cream—it beats anything the Egyptians had.

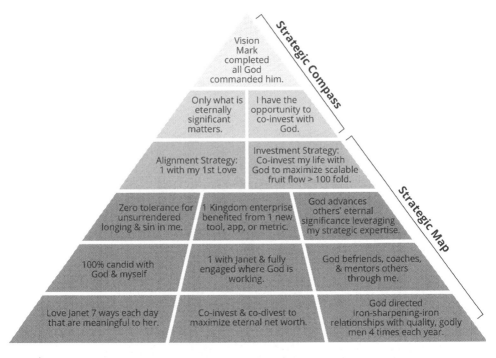

Figure 18.8. Strategic Pyramid incorporating
Strategic Compass & Strategic Map.

Fun

When my computer science professor, also an elder in my church, referred to God doing something "unbelievable," he used to say, "Incredible!" and then chuckle, "Not really." When I find how much fun developing my *Strategic Pyramid* is (not to mention walking it out), I feel it is both *unbelievable* and *incredible*—but I shouldn't be surprised.

Walking out my *Strategic Pyramid* with my wife is a great example of how unbelievably, incredibly, not-so-surprisingly fun strategy can be. The center block in my *Strategic Pyramid* reads, "One with Janet: fully engaged in life that is meaningful to her, and together in ministry where God is highly active." Since numbers speak to Janet, we analyzed data for Global Media Outreach, a ministry we both believe in.[13] Since nature is good medicine for Janet, we went on a learning vacation in the Canadian Rockies, where we tripped over trilobite fossils, studying the Cambrian Explosion with an organization called Reasons to Believe.[14]

I find it incredible that staying in a chateau on Lake Louise is a step in my *Truventure* to land my vision. I'm having fun in my pursuit to strategically align with my Creator! God designed each of us to enjoy things that resonate with our soul. It does not have to be what others call fun: Janet's college roommate diagramed sentences for fun. What is fun for the true you?

Figure 18.9. It's your life, isn't it worth having fun?
God is certainly having fun—have you seen a narwhal?

A Robust Map

In my true adventure, I find all I need in my True Quest. He takes *Prerequisite Principles* deeper in me, leverages vehicles of *Strategic Intentionality*, and unveils His vision of me. But wait—it gets even better! He delivers a robust strategic map, which in combination with my strategic compass navigates my Himalayas and Death Valleys to land His vision of the true me being wildly successful per His grand plan.

Strategic Map: *A Lifestyle Landing the Vision*

I look for what is essential to land the vision—nothing more, nothing less.

He already knows everything about me, sees past my self-delusion yet loves me still. Therefore, I ask for grace to be authentic.

The more I get alone with my Creator and pray through my Strategic Pyramid, the more He reveals in His simple, powerful, evocative , and compelling roadmap for my life.

Ask & Listen: Talk it over with God

Before starting to build your strategy and supporting blocks, go outside and take a walk with the One who knows you best and thank Him for:

1 - Having a *specific plan* for your life,

2 - Helping you identify *your essentials*,

3 - Envisioning *you wildly successful*,

4 - Designing an *opportunity worthy of your life*,

5 - Giving you a *personalized compelling imperative* to tether you to the mind of Christ, and

6 - Calibrating your *Strategic Compass* to more accurately align with Him and His plans for you.

Step 1: Strategy Development

Ask God what is required to land your vision and place each strategy on its own index card.

Review each strategy and ask, *Is it essential?* Remove or refine anything that is not essential to landing your vision. Elegance is key, simple, and powerful. Whatever is not essential, move to a "Parking Lot" for later consideration.

Next ask, *If each of the strategies is successfully landed, will the vision be landed?* ☐ Yes ☐ No

If no, then ask, *What additional strategy is necessary to land the vision?* Repeat this process until you've gleaned the essential strategies required to land the vision.

Place your strategy index cards in a row beneath your strategic compass.

Step 2: Supporting Block Development

It's time to craft your supporting blocks. Begin by picking one strategy and asking, *What will land this strategy?* Record each response on an index card and place it below the appropriate strategy. For each supporting block, ask *Is it essential?*

Next ask, *If each of the supporting blocks is successfully landed, will that particular strategy be landed?* ☐ Yes ☐ No

If no, then ask, *What additional supporting block is necessary to land the strategy?* Repeat this process until you've gleaned the essential supporting blocks for each strategy.

Place each supporting block index card in a column below its respective strategy.

Well done, faithful one! You now have your first draft of your strategic map! Take a break and celebrate with your favorite treat!

Step 3: Refining the Map

In strategy, specificity is often better than generality. Reach each block to God and ask Him to help you make it more precise. Ask Him to reveal His divine fingerprints on your blocks. Trust God to lead you in refining each block to its essence. Ask Him to hone each block so that collectively they land the vision of you wildly successful per His grand plan.

Traction ⟿

Essence

A lifestyle landing the vision is how we *truventure*. The Himalayas and Death Valleys of life can be tricky to navigate, but your Map Maker accounted for treacherous terrain when helping you build your Strategic Map. Write a thank you note to God for delivering a robust map to land the vision of you wildly successful per His grand plan.

⇁

He delivers a robust strategic map, which in combination
with my strategic compass navigates my Himalayas and
Death Valleys to land His vision of the true me
being wildly successful per His grand plan.

Chapter 19

Smart Pyramid

An Examined Lifestyle

G od and I developed my *Strategic Pyramid* for one purpose—to implement it. With my completed *Strategic Pyramid* in hand I asked Him, "How?" He said, "Follow Me," and provided two tractive ways to land my *Strategic Pyramid*. First, we make it smart with executive content. Second, we make my "Smart Pyramid" smarter with enlightened engagement. In the process of smart implementation of my *Strategic Pyramid*, I experience an examined life well lived. After all, as Socrates said, "The unexamined life is not worth living."[1]

Executive Content

The first way to make my *Strategic Pyramid* smart is by adding key executive content, which we do in the following progression: target metrics, actual metrics, relevant results, color coding, and finally a composite metric.

Target Metrics

Youngsters tell us how old they are before they can tell us much more about themselves. We use numbers to convey precise information with clarity and impact. We check numbers on nutrition labels and emphasize our point using numbers, as in "zero tolerance for drugs." For clarity we say, "sales dropped 20%" rather than "sales dropped a lot—well, not a huge amount—but not that little either." Consequently, numbers play an essential role in strategy.

I use all sorts of metrics in my smart *Strategic Pyramid*: classic metrics, numbers in place of words, and words in place of numbers. Classic metrics include numbers, percentages, ratios, and frequency. I use a number in place of a word if it registers faster in my mind and spirit. Alternatively, I use a word as metric if it is knowable and quantifiable, for example, *all, each, fully, every, never,* and *zero.* Figure 19.1 provides various metrics, styles, and examples. I identify metrics by underlining them or using a bold font.[2] I choose the style of metric based on what most tractively motivates me toward the desired target.

Metric	Style	Example
Number	Simple Number	Love Janet **7** ways
	Frequency	**each** day, or **4x/yr**.
	Dollar amount	$**X** Lifetime giving goal
	Ratio	Exceed **10:1** eternal to current net worth
Number to represent a word	Number for impact or accountability	**1** with my 1st Love
Word to represent a number	Words that are knowable & quantifiable, Examples: *all, each, fully, every, never, zero*	**Zero** tolerance for unsurrendered longing & sin.

Figure 19.1. Different metric types, styles and examples.

It is vital I not limit God when co-developing target metrics. He is not resource limited,[3] and strives for my highest good with the express purpose of maximizing His glory for all eternity.

Actual vs. Target Metrics

Incorporating target metrics into my *Strategic Pyramid* is the first way to make it smart; the second is adding the current actual metric versus the desired target metric. For example, essential to landing my vision is *God advancing others' eternal significance.* He identified a lifetime goal for me to use strategic expertise one hundred times more than in my business career. For a lifetime goal I include plan-to-date (PTD) and year-to-date (YTD) actuals. These require little space within the block (figure 19.2), which supports the constraint and benefit of everything essential on one page.

> God advances others' eternal significance by leveraging my strategic expertise **>100x** my career.
>
> **57** PTD (**6** YTD)

Figure 19.2. Using plan-to-date and current year actual metrics.

Relevant Results

Executives want to know, *What is your target and are you hitting it?* Having delivered target and actual results, I give my Chief Executive Officer (CEO) relevant results. Relevant results back up the actual metric by briefly identifying how progress was achieved. God knew I needed iron-sharpening-iron relationships to land my vision. Knowing I am a strong introvert, He wasted no time inviting me into group of quality, godly men committed to journeying through life together to satisfy two of the four target times per year. These show up in my smart *Strategic Pyramid* as numbered relevant results: *accomplished* in standard black and *planned* in green or italic font. This easily fits within the pyramid block, providing relevant status versus my target metric (figure 19.3).

> God directed, iron-sharpening-iron, multiple-day excursions doing life with quality, godly men **4x/yr.**
>
> 1) Feb AZ Retreat,
> 2) Artists with CK,
> 3) Dar's Strategic Summit with AO & JH
> *4) Oct. CA Retreat*

Figure 19.3. Using relevant results: accomplished and planned.

Executive content such as target and actual metrics, accomplished and planned relevant results, make my *Strategic Pyramid* smart. I use these for ongoing discussions with God. Using different color fonts for accomplished and planned relevant results foreshadows the fourth way I add executive content to make my *Strategic Pyramid* smart.

Color Coding

The fourth way to make my *Strategic Pyramid* smart is color coding each block.[4] It is quick and easy because each block already includes metrics (target and actual), plus relevant results (accomplished and planned). After making sure the information is current, I ask God for His qualitative assessment and color commentary. Together we assign a color to each block using a simple color code, such as the one in figure 19.4. The result is a color-coded "Smart Pyramid."

At a glance, color coding reveals which blocks are working and which are not. Also, at a glance the color collage of the entire pyramid reveals how I am doing vis-à-vis landing my vision. In this way, my color-coded "Smart Pyramid" serves as a dashboard. The light indicator and pertinent information are readily apparent for each block. The overall color collage gives me a qualitative feel for landing my vision. A quantitative feel comes with a composite metric.[5]

Composite Metric: Percent Landed[6]

I calculate a simple composite metric, percent landed, for quantitative assessment. With each block already color coded, I assign a numerical grade to each color (figure 19.4).

Color	What It Indicates	Number
Red	No progress	1
Pink	Minimal progress	2
Yellow	Current pace will not achieve target	3
Light Green	On track to achieve target	4
Dark Green	Target achieved or exceeded	5

Figure 19.4. Color, indication, numerical value.

I total the grades for all of the blocks, divide by the number of blocks, divide by the maximum grade (in this case five), and multiply by 100 to calculate percent landed. This composite metric, percent landed, is the fifth way to make my *Strategic Pyramid* smart.[7]

Having identified target metrics, along the way I supplement them with actuals, relevant results, color coding, and percent landed. This summarizes the first way I implement my *Strategic Pyramid*—I keep both target and current progress in view for an examined life well lived.

Enlightened Engagement

The second way to successfully implement my *Strategic Pyramid* is engagement with my Chief Executive Officer and God-selected advisors. I discuss my "Smart Pyramid" (found in Appendix D.4) with God on a daily basis, where He unveils tractive insights. Periodically He invites me to evaluate what is working or not. During both daily and periodic sessions, He reveals how to more effectively implement my *Strategic Pyramid*. Additionally, He leverages the experience and wisdom of godly men twice a year, during which time He enlightens them to enlighten me.

CEO Review with my Confidant

I use daily and periodic reviews with my CEO. He delivers accurate assessments with grace and truth.[8] I experience zero condemnation,[9] no fear,[10] and am eager to seize the day. Theologically I knew there is no fear in love, but I did not viscerally know until He pointed out that in 40+ CEO reviews I had never experienced anything but love and acceptance from Him.

Sometimes the Lover of my soul draws my attention to red, pink, or yellow blocks since they obviously need attention. We discuss why I am falling behind, and His specific remedies to close the gaps.[11] Other times He draws my attention to where He is working in the green blocks so I can more intentionally join Him there.[12]

The most valuable use of my *Strategic Pyramid* is discussing it with my CEO. Some days I pray through it completely. When I am pressed for time, rather than miss an opportunity to enlist the Almighty about what is strategically vital, I pick one block and pray through it.

Quickly Going Deep in Community

In addition to discussing my "Smart Pyramid" with God on a daily basis, I discuss it with God-selected advisors twice a year. Time is our scarcest commodity; therefore, it is essential to quickly and accurately bring the group to a common, base-level understanding. We kick off our biannual retreat with dinner, then bring each other up-to-date using our "Smart Pyramids."

We use "Smart Pyramids" to deliver efficient, effective updates in order to maximize our time to adequately address important issues (and watch an epic movie each night). Despite being apart half a year, color coding quickly and accurately identifies success and problem areas. I no longer waste their time with "I am doing ok—not great, but not that bad either," followed by hours untangling what that means.

With "Smart Pyramids" we quickly realize what is working and not because color coding is grasped instantaneously; the color of each block is accurately supported with concise, relevant results. This quick assessment frees our time for relaxed discussion. With each of us on the same page, we lose no time arriving at relevant questions and thoughtful answers. An accurate, common, base-level understanding lets us quickly address jugular issues and deliver pertinent advice.

Long ago we exchanged the desire to earn one another's acceptance for the desire to receive heartfelt counsel. So I chuckle when the guys ask, "That block was red last time too—what gives?" I candidly explain, which leads to the best part—targeted Q&A with God-selected advisors who enlist the Almighty to break through obstacles and receive further direction on my behalf.[13] For quickly going deep in community, sharing "Smart Pyramids" has become an excellent means of quickly getting on the same page for what strategically matters and relevantly engaging one another and God.[14]

Never-ending Epic Venture

It would be interesting to show Socrates my "Smart Pyramid," rich with executive content such as desired and actual metrics, relevant results, color coding, and a composite metric for an examined life worth living. But I get to discuss my "Smart Pyramid" with God Omniscient and God-selected advisors, each of whom I respect more than Socrates. Implementing my *Strategic Pyramid* with God and godly men is essential to my *Truventure*.

I do not want my Truventure to end any more than I would want a vein of gold to end. Neither do I want your gold exploration—your adventure with Truth—to end. I am jealous to see the true you wildly successful, unleashed to thrive, tractively advancing. I am excited for your epic venture with your True Quest!

Smart Pyramid: *An Examined Lifestyle*

God and I developed my Strategic Pyramid for one purpose—to implement it.

Numbers play a huge role in strategy.

I use daily and periodic reviews with my CEO.

Ask & Listen: Talk it over with your True Quest

Your Good, Good Father is so proud of you. Pause to let Him affirm you personally and write down what He impresses upon you.

You use numbers every day, and you know how to quantify using words such as all, everything, or never. Ask God to lead you in identifying appropriate target metrics for each block of your Strategic Pyramid.

Step 1: Target Metrics for Strategies

Review each strategy block and ask, *What metric best defines success for this block?* Record a metric (number or word used in place of a number) at the bottom of the strategy block. *(Reference Appendix D.4)*

Continue this process until you have placed a metric within each strategy block.

Step 2: Target Metrics for Supporting Blocks

Review each supporting block and ask, *What metric best defines success for this block?* Record that metric at the bottom of the supporting block. *(Reference Appendix D.4)*

Continue this process until you have placed a metric within each supporting block.

Congratulations! You've reached another significant milestone. Take a celebratory victory lap. Come back tomorrow to complete the next part of traction.

Step 3: Progress Review

Draw close to God; trust Him to speak to you with grace and truth. Select a starting block on your Strategic Pyramid to review your current results. Ask yourself, *Where am I now as compared to my target results?* Record your actual results within the respective block, repeating the process for the remaining blocks. *(Reference Appendix D.4)* Explore color coding and refining metrics as you complete your review.

Step 4: Going Deep and Climbing Higher in Community

Listen to counsel and accept discipline, that you may be wise the rest of your days. (Proverbs 10:20, NASB) Prayerfully ask God who you should invite into an examined life using your Strategic Pyramid with you. Thank Him for the extraordinary community that He has and will bring into your life to help you land the true you being wildly successful, unleashed to thrive, reactively advancing.

Essence

An examined lifestyle is how we *truventure*. Transparency with God Omniscient and God-selected advisors unleashes you to advance ever further on your epic venture life replete with spectacular views. Write a prayer of thanksgiving and praise for the journey thus far. Well done!

⌐

I am jealous to see the true you wildly successful,
unleashed to thrive, tractively advancing.

Strategic Pyramid

19. Smart Pyramid:
An Examined Lifestyle

18. Strategic Map:
A Lifestyle Landing
the Vision

**17. Strategic
Compass:**
A Lifestyle Knowing the
Right Direction

**16. Compelling
Imperative:**
A Lifestyle Tethered to
the Mind of Christ

15. Opportunity:
A Lifestyle Seizing
the Dream

**14. Wildly
Successful:**
A Lifestyle
Envisioning the
Master's Rendering

13. The Essentials:
A Lifestyle Distilling
Discovery

12. Strategy on One Page:
A Lifestyle for the Millennia

Personalized Truth Markers

For each chapter, write a *personal application* of the recorded truth:

◐ *12.* **Strategy on One Page**—*A Lifestyle for the Millennia*

He continues to unwrap His simple, powerful, evocative, and compelling plan for my life—and I see the fingerprints and heartbeat of God.

For me, it means _____

_____

_____

_____

_____

◐ *13.* **The Essentials**—*A Lifestyle Distilling Discovery*

In my pursuit for the truth about God and His plan for my life, I quarry essential truths and distill them to their essence.

For me, it means _____

_____

_____

_____

_____

◐ *14.* **Wildly Successful**—*A Lifestyle Envisioning the Master's Rendering*

I trust [God] to complete the work He began—His rendering of the true me being wildly successful per His grand plan.

For me, it means _____

_____

_____

_____

❯ 15. **Opportunity**—*A Lifestyle Seizing the Dream*

I believe when He designed me, He was thinking about opportunities specific to my time in history, or era, and my area of influence, or arena.

For me, it means _____

_____

_____

_____

_____

❯ 16. **Compelling Imperative**—*A Lifestyle Tethered to the Mind of Christ*

My compelling imperative is the indisputable, axiomatic truth that cuts through what I should and should not be doing, and points to how I should be investing this life.

For me, it means _____

_____

_____

_____

_____

❯ 17. **Strategic Compass**—*A Lifestyle Knowing the Right Direction*

My strategic compass helps maximize my Investor's return on me in two significant areas: decision-making and truth-walking.

For me, it means _____

_____

_____

_____

_____

◐ 18. **Strategic Map**—*A Lifestyle Landing the Vision*

A strategic plan to land my vision is narrower and more precise than a life plan. It requires a high-definition target, undiluted clarity of essential steps and undeterred focus.

For me, it means _____

_____

_____

_____

_____

◐ 19. **Smart Pyramid**—*An Examined Lifestyle*

In the process of smart implementation of my *Strategic Pyramid*, I experience an examined life well lived.

For me, it means _____

_____

_____

_____

_____

_____

Epilogue
by Angela Owen

Pisgah National Forest

With a breathtaking view of the Blue Ridge Parkway before me, my *Truventure* journey began on the deck of my mountain home. It was exactly one year after my departure from a thriving career in corporate America. The prior summer, I returned to my childhood community, remotely nestled in the lush Pisgah National Forest, and worked alongside my trusted colleague and friend, John Hemken, to launch our new company, TBL Leadership Partners. Now we sat together with John's best friend, Mark, to build my first *Strategic Pyramid*. Since then, Mark Modjeska has become my beloved brother, trusted mentor, and co-author.

My first year as a small business owner routed me through exciting highs and depressing lows, great faith and intense doubt, audacious courage and paralyzing fear. Launching a new venture daunted me from the onset and grew more overwhelming as a national financial crisis unfolded. Facing the pressures of stifled cash flow and uncertainty in my client base, my business was on the edge and my nerves were frayed. Something had to change.

To help me begin my *Strategic Pyramid* process, Mark gently began asking me questions. I desperately tried to "get the right answers," repetitively seeking confirmation from him and John. I soon found they were adept at flipping the questions back to me, causing me to think and rethink, assuring me that God would inform me directly and that I was totally capable of hearing Him. My internal expectations to "get it right" slowly subsided, my muscles began to relax, and freedom to dream unleashed within my heart, mind, and spirit. A picture emerged of me being wildly successful, and I felt God's purposes for my life pressed ever more clearly within my being. The connection to my business venture surfaced in intricate yet brilliantly simple form. Dreams deep within me emerged to make their way onto my *Strategic Pyramid,* alongside practical strategies and focused tactics. Breakthrough began to displace despair. Clarity for my business unfolded, but the battle for my personal and professional identity had just begun.

A Warrior Princess Awakes

Identity crisis clashed within me. Doubt shadowed my most carefully laid plans. *Did I truly have what it takes to make my business successful? Would I truly believe God and all that I heard Him say as we crafted my Strategic Pyramid?* At this crossroads, would I entertain doubt and lies or would I anchor firmly into Truth Himself?

Praying through my *Strategic Pyramid* served as a platform to face the plethora of questions and worries that plagued me. In the midst of one such prayer time, God gave me a mental image that captivated me and marked my course in seismic proportions. The corner of my home office became a movie theatre where a revelation of my true identity in Christ was projected. As I saw the picture play out before me, I also heard the powerful yet tender voice of my King whisper to my heart, *You are my Warrior Princess.*

Rocked to my core by the revelation, the fire to fight suddenly flared within my heart. In the midst of my cries for help and solutions to practical matters, such as cash flow and finding clients, God adjusted my view to more fully see His picture of me being wildly successful. I knelt in prayer a woman oppressed by self-doubt and worry. I arose a woman compelled to stand on the battlefield of life.

Mark calls the vehicles he uses in *Truventure* a means to get alone with the Lover of his soul, for a strategically aligned life with his Creator. These vehicles have proven themselves faithful for me as well. Praying through my *Strategic Pyramid* empowers me to refute lies, grow in intimacy with God, and seize each day strategically.

An Unlikely Place of Covenant

I anchored deeper and deeper into God's clarion call on me as His Warrior Princess. I enjoyed my rhythmic time of praying through my *Strategic Pyramid*, asking Jesus what He thought about each block. While by no means perfect, my *Truventure* journey was exciting and full of life. It challenged me to tread further, deeper, and higher with the Lover of my soul. Additionally, Mark became a treasured business counselor with whom I interacted frequently via coaching calls. I loved listening to him share more of his *Truventure* journey as he coached me on my own *Truventure*. I found myself particularly intrigued by his covenant with God and I decided to write my own.

On multiple occasions, I sat in the quiet of my home office to pen my covenant. But not one word flowed from pen to paper. This stagnant cycle continued for weeks, completely stalling all development of my own covenant with God. I wondered if the words would ever come, and then the cork released in the most unlikely of places.

When my flight from Washington Dulles to Greenville, South Carolina, was delayed—again—the interruption to my plans threatened to swallow me into the frenzy of fatigued airline workers and stressed travelers. But the still, small voice of my King beckoned me to be still. Anxious to hear Him more, I found a remote corner of the airport and opened my laptop. My fingers typed a simple title at the top of the page: "A Warrior Princess's Covenant with her King." The words began flowing and my thoughts released to ride wave after wave of creative interaction with God. My covenant with God came to life as the One who created me and loves me best painted picture after picture within the pages of my covenant.

I share my story to demonstrate—as Mark often states—*Truventure* is not prescriptive. Every *Truventurer's* journey will be as unique as their DNA and carries the promise of an increasingly intimate and strategically aligned life with your Creator.

Pyramids, Cairns, and Ezer

The uniqueness of my own *Truventure* is also demonstrated in the shape of my *Strategic Pyramid,* which continued to be refined and eventually took shape as a cairn. Once completed, it looked more like a set of carefully balanced rocks than a precise stack of perfectly hewn stones. As I continued to pray through my covenant with God and my *Strategic Pyramid* (now cairn), a particular part of my covenant and one particular stone on my cairn arrested my heart for months of intense prayer and focus.

From my Covenant

> I trust my King with my marriage. I submit my marriage to the Lordship of my Miracle Maker and expectantly wait with biblical hope for my marriage to be exceedingly, abundantly beyond all that I could think or ask according to the power that works within my husband and me.

From my Strategic Cairn

> Unconditionally discover, delight, and be *ezer*[1] *kenegdo*[2] to my TBL man!

As anyone who has been married more than five minutes can attest—marriage is hard, and mine has been no exception. My husband, Todd, and I have walked many roads littered with pain and heartache. In the midst of our struggles, I've longed for him to experience his own clarion call of identity in Christ—just as I had when God called me His Warrior Princess. My longing grew deeper and my prayers grew louder, yet evidence of such revelation for Todd seemed to slip further out of reach. I resolved to stay in the battle alongside him, and sought my King for discernment and direction. Eventually, a radical shift did occur, and an extraordinary view was just around the *Truventure* bend.

God, the Master Storyteller, brought my friend John Hemken back into the plot to help unleash my husband into his own *Truventure*. This time we went to John's home in Wisconsin, where Todd experienced breakthrough, freedom, and truth. Few things are more thrilling than experiencing the ripple effects of my *Truventure* with the man of my dreams, my beloved Todd.

The Journey Continues

We've peeked at a few of the stops along the way of my *Truventure*. The journey of learning, unpacking, writing, and praying my covenant with God and my strategic cairn continues to thrill my heart, inform my plans, and direct my footsteps. The views from both the peaks and the valleys of communion with God still take my breath away. The depths plumbed, with my hand in His, draw me ever deeper into His heart and ever higher into the wilderness of the Untamed Lion of Judah.

I remember the day Mark asked for my help writing this book. Neither of us had a real clue what we were about to begin. This journey called *Truventure* continues to delight us, test us, and stir us further still. We pray that something within our ventures serves to stir you in your own.

———

The Undomesticated Lion of Judah awaits your pursuit...step into your journey for eternal significance.

Please take a minute to review *Truventure:
Strategy for Wildly Succussful Living* on Amazon.

Thank you!

**Learn more and join the journey at
WWW.TRUVENTURE.COM**

Mark's Contract with GOD

In Brief:

This contract confirms my unconditional, total surrender, full submission and irrevocable release of all aspects of this life to the love and Lordship of Jesus.

Ownership:

I am not my own, I have been bought with a price. I want to reciprocate Jesus's sacrifice by surrendering my life to Him, reciprocate God's love by doing what He commands.

This life belongs to my Owner who wants to experience and co-invest it with me, His way for eternity. For this I need to grow up to reality–the truth of His will and providence.

1. I consciously abandon all my preconceived notions of what this life ought to be so that I can become receptive to, submit to and embrace His providence however He chooses to unfold it.
2. I cannot afford longings that are not His plan for me. I want to be that man who has truly forsaken all to follow Jesus.
3. I choose to forget the past, be in the moment, press into Christ, fully yield to His plan and call on me.
4. He has given me life; seize each moment and every innumerable decision in order to maximally leverage each moment and decision for God's eternal glory. Each moment and every innumerable decision either
   a. Elapses worthless, or
   b. Worse because of sin, or is
   c. Co-invested for eternity or is
   d. Maximally co-invested for His eternal glory.

Roles & Responsibilities:

God is Owner means His will preempts everything. I am obliged to think about Him in all my ways, to always listen to Him, to always do what He says, to always be preoccupied with Him instead of desires that are not His highest good for me.

God assigned me the job of steward over this life. This means I am privileged with a fiduciary and sacred responsibility to always consider and diligently execute His best interests in every aspect of this L.I.F.E.[1]

God gifts me the privilege to experience Him, remain in Him, and with Him co-invest this vaporous L.I.F.E. for eternal grace-rewards to lie at His feet. This is an investor's dream! This is the high calling of steward-ship, co-investing all of me in Him.

Lifestyle of Reciprocal Love:

I want to align with the truth of God's genuine love for me, personally.

I want to reciprocate God's welcoming agape love for me as proper motivation for consecration and stewardship. I want to be compelled by His faithful love to remain in His love rather than depart His presence to indulge in the lust of the eyes, the lust of the flesh and the pride of life.

My exalted Creator, Sovereign, Judge, Lover of my soul desires fellow-ship with me. Unrestricted time alone with God: how priceless is that! I desire to habitually remain in Him, dwell on His nature, character, words and actions. I can be with Him during quiet times and all my waking hours by discussing everything with Him all the time.

Jesus already knows everything; holding anything back, leaving any stone unturned, only retards my progress. I commit myself to ever more complete candor with my Confidant.

Lifestyle of Faith in Practice:

To the pursuit of complete consecration, genuine stewardship and recip-rocal love for God, I add trusting Jesus, Creator of the universe, the Trustworthy who set His face like flint unto the cross for me, my Propiti-ation, the Rock of my salvation, my Confidant, the Lover of my soul, the One named Faithful and True.

First, I choose to trust Jesus to manage every aspect of this life and carry every one of my burdens. I choose to take every concern to Him, leave them in His care and return them to His care as often as necessary to truly remain in His rest.[2] I am crucified in Christ; I am resurrected a new creation in Christ. This life belongs to Jesus so all its problems are Jesus' problems. I simply want to do what He tells me to do by the grace He provides so that Jesus lives His life in and through me. I gladly commit myself to act upon His instructions and guidance.

- I anchor this by becoming a 5-year-old child holding the hand of the King, trusting the Almighty as I wait for the All Knowing to tell me the next right thing to do.

Second, despite how overwhelming temptation feels, I choose to trust the Almighty to completely, continually save me from the power of temptation and sin.

- I anchor this by choosing to follow the Holy Spirit's lead to take the way of escape (1 Cor. 10:13), instead of departing Jesus's Presence to engage in the
  - Lust of the eyes—no matter how desirable,
  - Lust of the flesh—no matter how compelling,
  - Pride of life—no matter how "right it might feel."

Third, I choose to trust God to fulfill all His promises and answer all my prayers in the way He, the Wise and Loving Sovereign, chooses. He may delay His answer, His answer may be different than my preconceived notion or desire and He may in His sovereignty say "no" to my request, thank God!

I only want what the All Wise, Sovereign, Lover of my soul wants for me-nothing more, nothing less. I strive to be weaned from everything except what the One who desires my highest good providentially wants for me.

- I anchor this by resting in God's providential will for this book. What and how He chooses to do with it is above my pay grade.

Fourth, I choose to not let thoughts of my own inadequacy, which are totally irrelevant under grace, deter me from praying and speaking in the power and authority of the name of Jesus, totally trusting Him (not me) as He leads.

- I choose to anchor this belief by expectantly waiting for apples of golden wisdom in settings of silver insight.

Fifth, I choose to totally trust in God's absolute sovereignty, complete wisdom and perfect love for me.[3] I trust that no matter how severe the trial, trivial or frequent the aggravation that everything is filtered through His hands before it comes to me.

- I anchor this by looking for God's perspective in every circumstance.

Sixth, In advance, I choose to be content in Jesus no matter what. I choose to totally trust that in whatever comes, for this I have Jesus.[4] I choose to trust that Jesus's promised presence is more than sufficient in any circumstance (even if I cannot feel it, I know He is present with me) and that He will provide grace to submit.

God is my Singular Possession. I choose to be content in my All in All, my Singular Possession wrapped with the promised presence of Jesus.

I choose to match every confiscation of temporal possession-which by the way has been sovereignly allowed-with the joy of eternal possessions secured in Jesus.

I choose not to love my life in the face of persecution—which by the way has been sovereignly allowed-and death but rather overcome by the blood of the Lamb and by the Word of His testimony.

Despite how inconvenient and painful, I choose to embrace tests and trials. Everything is a test, a test wherein He wants and can prove me faithful, which I can be if and only if I appropriate His grace to fully surrender and genuinely yield to Him.

My singular, universal prayer is "Father, Your will be done in 'my' life as it is in heaven, for Your ways are always best."

- I anchor this by claiming Jesus as my All in All in advance of upcoming disappointments, set backs, adversity, crisis, trials, prolonged sufferings, persecution, confiscation, tribulation and death.

Transcendent Choices: [5]

With everlasting gratitude I choose to humbly:

1. Lack what You withhold: If He withholds it, then it is something I do not want anyway!
    A. Items He has withheld: promotion, vindication, [...] and ___?
    B. Items He may choose to withhold: significant ministry, impactful book, [...] and _?

2. Relinquish what You take: He can never take what He has not previously graciously given; every good and perfect gift is from above.
    A. Items He has taken: favor, recognition, [...] and _?
    B. Items He may choose to take: finances, health, [...] and ___?

3. Suffer what You inflict and allow: He is entirely just to do whatever He chooses with His possession.
    A. Items He has allowed: self-inflicted problems, prolonged problems, false accusation, [...] and ___?
    B. Items He may choose to inflict or allow: pain, confiscation, [...] and ___?

4. Receive what You give: Whatever He gives I want to want - because He applies perfect love to me with complete wisdom absolute sovereignty.
    A. Items He has given: Minimal requirement job (shorn of prestige, position & authority) for a productive transition to retirement, which bridged the great recession and a generous severance package, [...] and ___?
    B. Items I felt promised to me: June 13, 2012, Aug. 5, 2012 promise of Abraham, Nov. 20, 2015 promise "'Do not be afraid, O worm Jacob, O little Israel, for I myself will help you," declares the Lord, your Redeemer, the Holy One of Israel. "See, I will make you into a threshing sledge, new and sharp, with many teeth. You will thresh the mountains and crush them, and reduce the hills to chaff."' (Is. 41:14-15)
    C. Items He continues to give: a balanced life with Janet, participation with lunar men, opportunity to co-invest this L.I.F.E. with the Almighty and Lover of my soul!

5. To be what You require: FEAR GOD AND KEEP HIS COMMANDS.[6,7,8]

Signed: Mark Modjeska
Date: 17 October 2003 and co-edited with my Editor on a daily basis for life!

Appendix: Inventory

Illustrative rather than exhaustive inventory to continually:

1. ASK, AM I HOLDING OR TAKING ANYTHING BACK?

2. REQUEST: SUPER ABOUNDING GRACE TO MORE FULLY AND COMPLETELY SURRENDER THEM

3. RECONSECRATE THEM AND ALL OF ME TO THE LOVER OF MY SOUL

    - Mind, heart, eyes, ears, tongue, hands, feet. All my inputs, processing and outputs.
    - Authority, rights, will, and decisions. I have no latitude to decide to yield to any temptation!
    - Beliefs, convictions, attitudes, thoughts. I have no latitude to think any thoughts, harbor any lies, resentments, or attitudes contrary to those of God.
    - Ambitions, hopes, dreams, desires, affections. I have no latitude to harbor any longings contrary to Christ.
    - How I spend my time, what I watch, what I listen to, and what I read. I have no latitude to squander time.
    - Health, eating, swimming, vacation, holidays, and skiing. I am a steward of this temple of the Holy Spirit; treat it accordingly!
    - Wife, family, friends. What will I wish I had invested in relationships?
    - Ministry, strategy, befriending, coaching, mentoring, book, website, eMBA, A2B, influence. I am to never steal glory for what God may accomplish despite me.
    - Wealth, finances, stock, options, pension, social security, insurance, retirement, inheritance, security. I have no latitude to depend upon anything but Christ alone for my security, protection ,and provision.
    - House, location, land, privacy, views, cars, electronics, et al. All these will burn; regard them accordingly.

APPENDIX A.2

A Warrior Princess's Covenant with Her King

This covenant validates my unconditional, total surrender, full submission and irrevocable release of all aspects of my life to the Lordship of Jesus Christ, my Savior, my Lord, and my King.

I choose to trust my King with all parts of my life both internally and externally. I give the whole of my life to the One who created me, sustains me, and blesses me. Only my King can give me the ZOE life, and He does so in and through all circumstances. I renounce all fear and worry as enemies of the Kingdom of God and fully trust that whatever storm may come my way, my King safely holds me in the palm of His hand.

My life is not my own...it is wholly His. As a daughter of the King, I am an ambassador of His Kingdom of Righteousness, and as such, I am called to represent my King with excellence in all that I think, say, and do. My thoughts belong to Him. My words belong to Him. My actions belong to Him. I renounce every thought, every word and every action that brings dishonor to my King.

My King has called me forth as His warrior princess and as such I release all desires and longings contrary to the heart of my King. I freely choose to accept His mission for my life, choosing to step forth with courage that is not my own to shine forth His light into this dark world. I choose to daily take up the full armor of God that I might stand firm against the attacks of the enemy, the world, and the flesh. I renounce all notions of self-seeking self-preservation, fear, anxiety, or selfishness that threaten to detract me from the battles at hand.

Wherever He calls me, I will go. Deep calls to deep, and my King calls me to do business on deep waters for His kingdom. I renounce all petty notions of "playing it safe" in the shallows and choose to embrace the life of adventure He has called me to live.

I commit my ways to Him and trust the desires of my heart wholly to Him. I renounce all selfish, fleshly desires and trust my King to stir within me desires that bring glory to Him and Him alone.

I TRUST MY KING…

I trust the heart of my King, the Lover of my soul to always, always, always be faithful. He will never leave me nor forsake me. He will never harm me in any way. His love for me is unconditional. His perfect love for me casts out all fear. Regardless of the circumstances that may surround me, I am forever safe in the arms of the Lover of my soul.

I trust my King with my marriage. I submit my marriage to the Lordship of my Miracle Maker and expectantly wait with biblical hope for my marriage to be exceedingly, abundantly beyond all that I could think or ask according to the power that works within my husband and me.

I trust the word of God which is quick and powerful and sharper than any two edged sword to cut away all parts of my life that in any way hinder my walk with my King and my witness for Him and His kingdom.

I trust my King with my children. I submit their growth as young warriors in His Kingdom to the One who formed them in my womb. They are not mine, but His. He sees every tear they shed, feels every hurt they experience, and gives them strength to walk through every challenge life may ever cast their way.

I trust my King, my Lord, my Leader, with my business. My King has blessed me, stretched me, and sustained me. All that I have was a gift from His hand. All that I need, He has promised to provide. This business is not mine but His, and I trust my King to lead me in the way of profit and to prosper me…not for my sake or glory but for the glory of His great name and for the advancement of His kingdom on earth as it is in heaven.

I trust my King, My Lord, and my Jehovah Rapha, with my physical health. I lay down my body as the temple of the Holy Spirit and pledge to care for my body as a vessel holy to my King.

APPENDIX INVENTORY

My heart belongs to Him—When yielded to the direction and authority of the Spirit, the attitude of my heart reflects that of my King.

My lips belong to Him—Every word is precious. Every word is powerful.

My time belongs to Him—Every minute is priceless.

My resources belong to Him—Every blessing and gift is from God…may I use them for your glory.

My dreams & desires belong to Him—He gives me the desires of my heart.

My name belongs to Him—who I am matters not unless ultimately glorifying to the name of Jesus and lifting His name on high.

My feelings belong to Him—I choose to surrender my feelings to my King and train them to line up with my faith.

Signed: Angela Owen

APPENDIX B

Quiet Time Diagrams

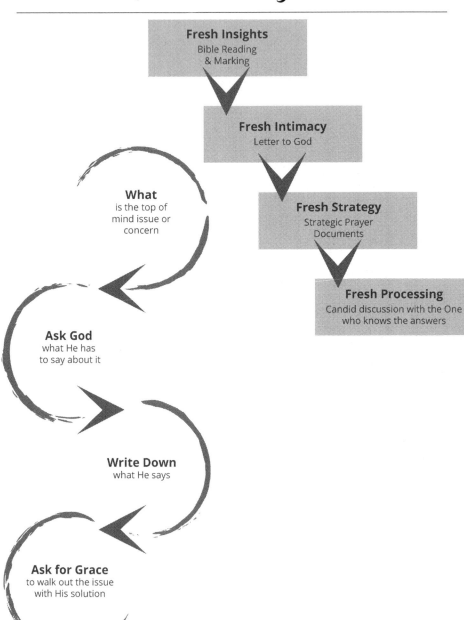

Fresh Insights
Bible Reading
& Marking

Fresh Intimacy
Letter to God

Fresh Strategy
Strategic Prayer
Documents

Fresh Processing
Candid discussion with the One
who knows the answers

What
is the top of
mind issue or
concern

Ask God
what He has
to say about it

Write Down
what He says

Ask for Grace
to walk out the issue
with His solution

APPENDIX C.1

Master Question List

LOOKING UP (my relationship with God)

What are the most significant things God has taught me?

What are God's dreams for me, personally?

Why did God make me the way I am?

What door has the Spirit opened for me personally and said "come"?

What are the most significant ways God has used me?

In what areas am I fully alive in Christ? In what areas am I not fully alive in Christ?

Which goals are aligned with Jesus's goals for me? Which are not?

Do I really believe God? How? How not?

Do I really trust God? How? How not?

Does my reality match my theology?

Do I harbor any unconfessed sin?

LOOKING IN (my relationship with me)

What are the most significant life lessons that get me to where I want to go in my life?

What drives me in a way consistent with where I want to go?

What core values and principles are important to me?

What do I fear?

Where am I getting stuck? What is blocking a fulfilled life?

What makes me feel fully alive?

What do I need to learn (or become more proficient in) to get where I want to go?

What strengths, talents, gifts, and personality traits do I have that can help me get to where I want to go?

How would I describe a job that is perfectly suited to strengths, my aspirations and me?

When am I the happiest?

Where am I the happiest? Where is the perfect place for me to live?

What are my most significant strengths, talents, gifts and personality traits?

What are the best aspects of me?

What steps should I take to close the gaps between what I believe and me?

In what ways does my life align with my what I believe? How? How not?

What unmet expectations do I have?

What behaviors and longings are not Christ-like?

LOOKING OUT (my relationship with others)

For a fulfilled life, what closure do I need and with whom? (Unresolved conflicts, broken relationships)

With whom do I need to be aligned so that the next stage of my life is meaningful?

What iron sharpening iron relationships will help me get where I want to go?

As specific as possible, what elements of a support team helps get me where I want to go?

Who do I want to do life with?

Have I "gone to school" on my spouse again, recently?

LOOKING FORWARD (my relationship with my future)

What does wildly successful look like for my life?

What is the best epitaph that I want written about me?

If I live out all of my values, beliefs, priorities, and goals where would that ultimately take me?

What always draws me irresistibly to where I want to go with my life?

What repeatedly hinders me from where I want to go with my life?

What opportunity is worth my life?

God created me personally to seize what opportunity?

What cause am I willing to give my life to?

What life calling maximizes my life for eternity?

What has to happen for my life to be wildly successful?

How do I maximize my life for eternity?

If I had a clean slate and could design my life, what would it look like?

What is one of the essential building blocks to land my strategy?

What is my eternal investment portfolio? What in it can be used to become wildly successful?

With whom do I have influence that I can leverage for the Kingdom?

What is the most strategic use of my finances?

What expertise do I have to leverage for the Kingdom?

How can I maximize my Eternal Net Worth?

How can I be more strategic about my eternal versus current net worth?

Do the most important fence posts of my life tell me something?

Who do I respect enough to be transparent and journey with?

APPENDIX C.2

Master Questions Current versus Desired

	Current *Where am I?*	Desired *Where do I want to be?*
LOOKING UP (my relationship with God)		
What are the most significant things God has taught me?		
What are God's dreams for me, personally?		
Why did God make me the way I am?		
What door has the Spirit opened for me personally and said "come"?		
What are the most significant ways God has used me?		
In what areas am I fully alive in Christ? In what areas am I not fully alive in Christ?		
Which goals are aligned with Jesus's goals for me? Which are not?		
Do I really believe God? How? How not?		
Do I really trust God? How? How not?		
Does my reality match my theology?		
Do I harbor any unconfessed sin?		

	Current *Where am I?*	Desired *Where do I want to be?*
LOOKING IN **(my relationship with me)**		
What are the most significant life lessons that get me to where I want to go in my life?		
What drives me in a way consistent with where I want to go?		
What core values and principles are important to me?		
What do I fear?		
Where am I getting stuck? What is blocking a fulfilled life?		
What makes me feel fully alive?		
What do I need to learn or become more proficient in order to get where I want to go?		
What strengths, talents, gifts, and personality traits do I have that can help me get to where I want to go?		
How would I describe a job that is perfectly suited to strengths, my aspirations and me?		
When am I the happiest?		
Where am I the happiest? Where is the perfect place for me to live?		
What are my most significant strengths, talents, gifts and personality traits?		
What are the best aspects of me?		
What steps should I take to close the gaps between what I believe and me?		
In what ways does my life align with my what I believe? How? How not?		

	Current *Where am I?*	Desired *Where do I want to be?*
What unmet expectations do I have?		
What behaviors and longings are not Christ-like?		
LOOKING OUT **(my relationship with others)**		
For a fulfilled life, what closure do I need and with whom? (Unresolved conflicts, broken relationships)		
With whom do I need to be aligned so that the next stage of my life is meaningful?		
What iron sharpening iron relationships will help me get where I want to go?		
As specific as possible, what elements of a support team helps get me where I want to go?		
Who do I want to do life with?		
Have I "gone to school" on my spouse again, recently?		
LOOKING FORWARD **(my relationship with my future)**		
What does wildly successful look like for my life?		
What is the best epitaph that I want written about me?		
If I live out all of my values, beliefs, priorities & goals where would that ultimately take me?		
What always draws me irresistibly to where I want to go with my life?		
What repeatedly hinders me from where I want to go with my life?		

	Current *Where am I?*	Desired *Where do I want to be?*
What opportunity is worth my life?		
God created me personally to seize what opportunity?		
What cause am I willing to give my life to?		
What life calling maximizes my life for eternity?		
What has to happen for my life to be wildly successful?		
How do I maximize my life for eternity?		
If I had a clean slate and could design my life, what would it look like?		
What is one of the essential building blocks to land my strategy?		
What is my eternal investment portfolio? What in it can be used to become wildly successful?		
With whom do I have influence that I can leverage for the Kingdom?		
What is the most strategic use of my finances?		
What expertise do I have to leverage for the Kingdom?		
How can I maximize my Eternal Net Worth?		
How can I be more strategic about my eternal versus current net worth?		
Do the most important fence posts of my life tell me something?		
Who do I respect enough to be transparent and journey with?		

Master Questions Barriers & Plans

	Barriers *What is stopping me?*	Plans *What will close the gap? How, when, with whom?*
LOOKING UP **(my relationship with God)**		
What are the most significant things God has taught me?		
What are God's dreams for me, personally?		
Why did God make me the way I am?		
What door has the Spirit opened for me personally and said "come"?		
What are the most significant ways God has used me?		
In what areas am I fully alive in Christ? In what areas am I not fully alive in Christ?		
Which goals are aligned with Jesus's goals for me? Which are not?		
Do I really believe God? How? How not?		
Do I really trust God? How? How not?		
Does my reality match my theology?		
Do I harbor any unconfessed sin?		

	Barriers *What is stopping me?*	Plans *What will close the gap? How, when, with whom?*
LOOKING IN (my relationship with me)		
What are the most significant life lessons that get me to where I want to go in my life?		
What drives me in a way consistent with where I want to go?		
What core values and principles are important to me?		
What do I fear?		
Where am I getting stuck? What is blocking a fulfilled life?		
What makes me feel fully alive?		
What do I need to learn or become more proficient in order to get where I want to go?		
What strengths, talents, gifts, and personality traits do I have that can help me get to where I want to go?		
How would I describe a job that is perfectly suited to strengths, my aspirations and me?		
When am I the happiest?		
Where am I the happiest? Where is the perfect place for me to live?		
What are my most significant strengths, talents, gifts and personality traits?		
What are the best aspects of me?		

	Barriers *What is stopping me?*	Plans *What will close the gap? How, when, with whom?*
What steps should I take to close the gaps between what I believe and me?		
In what ways does my life align with my what I believe? How? How not?		
What unmet expectations do I have?		
What behaviors and longings are not Christ-like?		
LOOKING OUT *(my relationship with others)*		
For a fulfilled life, what closure do I need and with whom? (Unresolved conflicts, broken relationships)		
With whom do I need to be aligned so that the next stage of my life is meaningful?		
What iron sharpening iron relationships will help me get where I want to go?		
As specific as possible, what elements of a support team helps get me where I want to go?		
Who do I want to do life with?		
Have I "gone to school" on my spouse again, recently?		
LOOKING FORWARD *(my relationship with my future)*		
What does wildly successful look like for my life?		

	Barriers *What is stop- ping me?*	Plans *What will close the gap? How, when, with whom?*
What is the best epitaph that I want written about me?		
If I live out all of my values, beliefs, priorities & goals where would that ultimately take me?		
What always draws me irresistibly to where I want to go with my life?		
What repeatedly hinders me from where I want to go with my life?		
What opportunity is worth my life?		
God created me personally to seize what opportunity?		
What cause am I willing to give my life to?		
What life calling maximizes my life for eternity?		
What has to happen for my life to be wildly successful?		
How do I maximize my life for eternity?		
If I had a clean slate and could design my life, what would it look like?		
What is one of the essential building blocks to land my strategy?		
What is my eternal investment portfolio? What in it can be used to become wildly successful?		
With whom do I have influence that I can leverage for the Kingdom?		

	Barriers *What is stop- ping me?*	Plans *What will close the gap? How, when, with whom?*
What is the most strategic use of my finances?		
What expertise do I have to leverage for the Kingdom?		
How can I maximize my Eternal Net Worth?		
How can I be more strategic about my eternal versus current net worth?		
Do the most important fence posts of my life tell me something?		
Who do I respect enough to be transparent and journey with?		

Strategic Pyramid Template

Vision
Picture
you being
wildly
successful.

**Compelling
Imperative**
Truth that
draws you
where you
want to go.

Describe the
opportunity
worth your life.
Opportunity

Strategy
To land
the vision

Strategy
To land
the vision

Strategy
To land
the vision

Strategy
To land
the vision

**An illustration of a block
that supports the 2
strategies above**

**A supporting
block** that
supports the
strategy above

**An illustration of a block
that supports the 2 support
blocks above**

An illustration of a block that supports all of the strategies

APPENDIX D.2

Mark's Strategic Pyramid

Mark
completed
all God
commanded *him*.

Only what is
eternally
significant
matters.

I have the
opportunity
to co-invest
with God.

Alignment Strategy:
1 with my 1st Love

Investment Strategy:
Co-invest my life with
God to maximize scalable
fruit flow > 100 fold.

Zero tolerance for
unsurrendered
longing & sin in me.

1 with Janet, fully
engaged in life
meaningful to her

God advances others
by using my strategic
expertise >100x my
career.

Zero gaps between my
lifestyle, believing God &
all that entails

Co-invest & co-divest to
maximize eternal net
worth > $X.

God befriends, coaches,
mentors through me 4x/yr

Love Janet 7 ways meaningful
to her each day

1 enterprise benefited by
1 new killer app / year.

Iron sharpening iron excursions
doing life with quality men 4x/yr

Angela's Strategic Cairn

Vision
Fully experience the
Truventure of Pursuing Truth,
the Untamed Lion of Judah,
the Great Adventurer Himself

Compelling Imperative
I am a valiant warrior for the
kingdom of God! I walk boldly
that others would be set free!

Opportunity Case
God has anointed me to help
others discover their own
Truventure journeys.

Strategy
Become a TBL Leader at
the DNA level through
my own Truventure

Strategy
Discover and support
Todd, Lexy & Tyler in
their Truventure
journeys with Jesus

Strategy
Multiply TBL DNA
in & through
Truventures near
and far

Strategy
Converge TBL
offerings into
confluence For
Truventure

Practice being fully aligned
with my King by fully
embracing my Truventure
Cairn Portfolio

Unconditionally
discover, delight & be
ezerkenegdo to my
husband!

Leverage TRUVENTURE to
change lives and change the
world as TBL leaders are
strategically intentional each day

Soar with my "eagle friend"
MC, as a visionary with bold,
radical faith that fights from
a place of rest

Purposefully
discover, develop &
delight in the TBL
Leader in my children

"Bounce back" to
strengthen TBL/Truventure
treks from TC to CH

APPENDIX D.4

Mark's Smart Pyramid

On track to achieve/ achieved
Current pace will not achieve target
No progress
Mark completed **all** God commanded *him*.
Only what is eternally significant matters.
I have the opportunity to co-invest with God.
Alignment Strategy: **1** with my 1st Love
Investment Strategy: Co-invest my life with God to maximize scalable fruit flow **> 100 fold.**
Zero tolerance for unsurrendered longing & sin in me. Current = **0**
1 with Janet, **fully** engaged in life meaningful to her **1, GMO Conference**
God advances others through my expertise >100x my career. **57** ptd, **10** ytd
Zero gaps between my lifestyle, believing God & all that entails Current = **0**
Co-invest & co-divest to maximize eternal net worth > **$X**. Current = **51%** of target
God befriends, coaches, mentors through me **4x/yr** 1) AO, 2) TM, 3) AO in Strategic Summit, 4) Doc Dar
Love Janet **7** ways meaningful to her each day **6**
1 Enterprise benefited by **1** new killer app / year. Current = **?** Wiring Diagrams
Iron sharpening iron excursions doing life with quality men **4x/yr** 1) Feb retreat, 2) Artists, 3) Dar Str. Summit, 4) Oct retreat

APPENDIX E

Truventure® Preferred Path

The *Truventure preferred path* seeks to maximize what matters most to you, your life, and life work by aligning with Truth Himself in every aspect of life, ministry and business. The benefits are hitting the target for which you were designed and maximizing the impact of your life, business, and ministry per His grand plan—which definitely includes *you!*

The *Truventure preferred path* answers to the question, "How do I get the most of *Truventure* and the *Strategic Pyramid*?"[1] The *Truventure* preferred path recommends that you:

1. Enlist in a Trek Group to process and walk out *Truventure* in community.
2. Schedule a facilitated Strategic Summit with an approved *Truventure* facilitator to develop a personalized Strategic Pyramid for you, your business and/or ministry.
3. Enlist in a *Truventure* Journeying Council to use your Strategic Pyramids in a community of members who each use their Strategic Pyramid to land the vision of their life, business and/ or ministry.

What is a Trek Group?

Trek groups leverage meaningful exchange of a book oriented mastermind group (a group of people who collectively help each other achieve success) to gain greater insight and better implement *Truventure*.

What is a facilitated Strategic Summit?

The Strategic Summit, a focused multi-day session, leverages the expertise of approved *Truventure* facilitators, breakthrough, business and ministry experts, and dedicated prayer warriors to develop a personalized Strategic Pyramid. The Strategic Pyramid may be developed for one's life, business, ministry, or any combination.

Additional time may be added to afford the client a chance to bring their biggest problems to experienced experts who are unified in their dedication to see the client's highest good fulfilled. Experts model how to wisely solve the client's problems by practicing hearing the voice of the One who knows the answers and wants to share it with *you*.

What is a *Truventure* Journeying Council?

Members of a *Truventure* Journeying Council collectively benefit by coming together to land their vision with the support of a like-minded, like-hearted community. The purpose for each member is to help hear and submit to the voice of the True Owner, think strategically, eliminate barriers, maximize his or her life, business, and/or ministry.

APPENDIX F

Glossary of Terms

Cairn: rocks assembled vertically as a memorial and / or mile marker.

Communiqué: an official statement

Compelling imperative: an irresistible, axiomatic truth so riveting it demands action unto completion

Connected integrity: every aspect of me aligned with every truth God requires of me

Core principles: character traits that strongly resonate with one's soul

Covenant: a binding agreement

Grace: God's favor given me based exclusively on Christ's merit, not mine

Quiet time: one-on-one time with God

Maestro: the consummate artist

Main thrust: an objective with the intensity and perseverance of a military surge

Modus operandi: standard way of operating

Rest: a place of complete trust in God

Pièce de résistance: the best and most important or exciting thing, often the last in a series

Prerequisite principles: principles that must be fully grasped to rightly understand subsequent subject matter

Select lessons: learnings I am desperate to ingrain in the fabric of my character and learn to the fullest extent possible

Sans: without

Self: part of me innately contrary to God

Smart pyramid: a *Strategic Pyramid* made smart with target metrics, actual metrics, and supporting data

Strategic cairn: a strategic plan that includes everything essential to land the vision on one page in the form of a pyramid

Strategic compass: a trio of strategic direction comprised of vision, opportunity and compelling imperative

Strategic intent: an overarching, umbrella objective

Strategic map: strategies and tactics to accomplish vision

Strategic Pyramid: a strategic plan that includes everything essential to land the vision on one page, prototypically but not necessarily in the form of a pyramid

Strategy: the path preferred over other paths to the desired destination

Surrender: capitulate, submit, yield

Tractive: describes significant progress toward a desired destination

True you: God's unique design of you

Truventure: short for true adventure

Vis-à-vis: in relation to, regarding

Wildly successful: success exceeding one's wildest dream

APPENDIX G

Alternative Names for God

In my attempt to bring God into each and every experience, I use contextually appropriate names for God. It is not original with me; God and the patriarchs did it all the time.

Advocate
Almighty
Answer Himself
Author
Author of Truth
Beloved Redeemer
Benevolent Boss
Brilliance Himself
Chief Executive Officer (CEO)
Chief Fun Officer
Christ
Co-editor
Co-_____ (fill in the blank)
Commander
Complete Protection
Confidant
Counselor
Counter Party
Craftsman
Creative Artist
Creator
Designer

Editor
Even Keel
Everything
Everything Himself
Exalted Holiness
Expert Editor
Faithful and True
Father
Full Provision
Gardener
Generous Landowner
Genuine Friend
Giver of every good and
    perfect gift
God
God All-wise
God Almighty
God Most High
God of Israel
Good, Good Father
Gracious Father
Great Artist

Holy Eliminator
Holy Spirit
Jesus
Judge
Liberator
Liege Lord
Light
Lion of Judah
Logos
Lord
Lover of my soul
King
Manager
Maestro Artist
Master Archeologist
Master Artist
Master Instructor
Master of the universe
Omniscient
One, True, Living God
One who cannot lie
One who knows
One who owns everything
One who relentlessly contends
    for our highest good
Only Way
Owner
Paragon Parent
Perfect Example
Potter
Promised Sufficiency
Protection

Rock
Redeemer
Safety Zone
Savior
Singular Hope
Singular Portion
Singular Possession
Singular Provision
Singular Solution
Singular True Quest
Solution
Son
Sovereign
Sovereign CEO
Sovereign Lord
Spirit of Truth
Standard Himself
Supreme Craftsman
True Owner
True Quest
True Manager
True North
Truth
Truth Himself
Truventure Guide
Ultimate Force Himself
Vine
Way Himself
Wisdom Himself

Add your favorite names for God
below:

About the Authors

Mark Modjeska

Mark spent over twenty years overseeing a variety of global high-tech businesses as an expat in Continental Europe and Scandinavia, as well as from the US. He was later appointed China President for a Fortune 400 Company, stationed in Hong Kong and Shanghai. Mark briefly retired prior to co-founding *Truventure®* Enterprises.

Swim championships and snow skiing still dominate Mark's calendar. He lives with the wife of his youth in the central highlands of Arizona.

Angela Owen

Angela Owen, a former executive with Procter & Gamble, has over twenty-five years of business experience with international corporations, small and medium enterprises, and entrepreneurs. She is founder and president of TBL Leadership Partners and co-founder of *Truventure®* Enterprises.

Angela enjoys reading, writing, hiking, basketball, music, spending time with her family, and pursuing Jesus. She lives in the mountains of North Carolina with her high school sweetheart and husband, Todd, and their two beautiful children, Lexy and Tyler.

Notes

Chapter 1: Grace—Resting as a Lifestyle

1. "I am the vine; you are the branches. The one who remains in Me and I in him produces much fruit, because you can do nothing without Me. If anyone does not remain in Me, he is thrown aside like a branch and he withers. They gather them, throw them into the fire, and they are burned." John 15:5-6.
2. "Are you so foolish? After beginning with the Spirit, are you now going to be made complete by the flesh?" Gal. 3:3.
3. "I have been crucified with Christ; and it is no longer I who live, but Christ lives in me; and the life, which I now live in the flesh I live by faith in the Son of God, who loved me and gave Himself up for me." Gal. 2:19b, 20.
4. Heb. 10:14 (The Living Bible).
5. Jerry Bridges, *Transforming Grace.* (Colorado Springs, CO: NavPress, 1994), page number unknown because I gave away my 4th edition and cannot find another. But I took notes, enjoy! *You do not understand grace when you:*
   * *Live with a vague sense of His disapproval.*
   * *Don't really believe that He likes you.*
   * *Cannot honestly say you see yourself as "blameless" in His eyes.*
   * *Feel more confident before Him if you've been "faithful" with your Christian disciplines.*
   * *Are not experiencing consistent peace & joy in your Christian life.*
   * *Shy away from asking Him for things because you think it annoys Him.*
   * *Assume you can do something to make Him love you more or less.*
   * *Feel sheepish bringing your needs before Him when you've just failed Him.*
   * *Fear that the day may not go as well as expected because you missed your quiet time.*
   * *Assume 1 John 1:9 no longer applies to you, that you have sinned so many times you've used up all your credit.*
   * *Feel you deserve an answer to prayer because of your hard work and sacrifice.*
   * *Think of His grace as something that makes up the difference between the best you can do and what He expects from you.*
   * *Can think of someone you look down upon.*
   * *Think of the Christian life as the cost of discipleship rather than the chance to experience an unending supply of His goodness toward you.*
   * *Believe you've been called into His service because of your worthiness or qualifications.*
6. John Lynch, Bruce McNicol, Bill Thrall, *The Cure* (San Clemente, CA: CrossSection, 2016).
7. "Jesus told him, 'I am the way, the truth, and the life. No one comes to the Father except through Me.'" John 14:6.
8. "Return to your rest, my soul, for the LORD has been good to you." Ps. 116:7.
9. "All of you, take up My yoke and learn from Me, because I am gentle and humble in heart, and you will find rest for yourselves." Mat. 11:29.

10. "But even if we or an angel from heaven should preach to you a gospel other than what we have preached to you, a curse be on him!" Gal. 1:8.

Chapter 2: Lordship—A Lifestyle Yielded to My True Owner

1. There are numerous books on lordship; this chapter does not attempt to teach but to simply share my journey as it relates to strategy and my *Truventure*.
2. "But who are you, a mere man, to talk back to God? Will what is formed say to the one who formed it, 'Why did you make me like this?' Or has the potter no right over the clay, to make from the same lump one piece of pottery for honor and another for dishonor?" Rom. 9:20-21.
3. Stephen Prothero, "Thomas Jefferson's Cut-and-Paste Bible," *Wall Street Journal*, March 25, 2011.
4. John 15:15.
5. "The Spirit Himself testifies together with our spirit that we are God's children, and if children, also heirs-heirs of God and coheirs with Christ—seeing that we suffer with Him so that we may also be glorified with Him." Rom. 8:16-17.
6. "So you are no longer a slave but a son, and if a son, then an heir through God." Gal. 4:7.
7. "Don't harm the earth or the sea or the trees until we seal the slaves of our God on their foreheads." Rev. 7:3.
8. "A voice came from the throne, saying: Praise our God, all His slaves, who fear Him, both small and great!" Rev. 19:5.
9. "and there will no longer be any curse. The throne of God and of the Lamb will be in the city, and His slaves will serve Him. […] Then he said to me, 'These words are faithful and true. And the Lord, the God of the spirits of the prophets, has sent His angel to show His slaves what must quickly take place.'" Rev. 22:3,6.
10. "Paul, a slave of Christ Jesus, called as an apostle and singled out for God's good news—" Rom. 1:1. See also Phil. 1:1, Titus 1:1.
11. "James, a slave of God and of the Lord Jesus Christ […]" James 1:1a.
12. "Simeon Peter, a slave and an apostle of Jesus Christ: […]" 2 Pet. 1:1a.
13. "The revelation of Jesus Christ that God gave Him to show His slaves what must quickly take place. He sent it and signified it through His angel to His slave John," Rev. 1:1.
14. Rev. 1:1.
15. "As God's slaves, live as free people, but don't use your freedom as a way to conceal evil." 1 Pet. 2:16.
16. Don't you know that if you offer yourselves to someone as obedient slaves, you are slaves of that one you obey—either of sin leading to death or of obedience leading to righteousness?" Rom. 6:16.
17. God partnering with man is a multifaceted thread through the entire Word of God. The partnership begins with His choice to make us in His image (Gen. 1:26). God partners with Abraham and his offspring to bless the nations (Gen. 12:2), culminating with Immanuel, God with us (Is. 7:14, Mt. 1:23). Even at our worst, He says "Come, let us discuss this" (Is. 1:18), and "My grace is sufficient for you, for power is made perfect in weakness" (2 Cor. 12:8-10). And for me the de crème del la crème: "His divine power has given us everything we need for a godly life through our knowledge of him who called us by his own glory and goodness. Through these he has given us his very great and precious promises, so that through them you may participate in the divine nature, having escaped the corruption in the world caused by evil desires" 2 Pet. 1:3-4 (New International Version).
18. "He is the blessed and only Sovereign, the King of kings, and the Lord of lords," 1 Tim. 6:15b.

19. "But I count my life of no value to myself, so that I may finish my course and the ministry I received from the Lord Jesus, to testify to the gospel of God's grace." Acts 20:24.

20 "The earth and everything in it, the world and its inhabitants, belong to the Lord;" Ps. 24:1.

21. "Don't you know that your body is a sanctuary of the Holy Spirit who is in you, whom you have from God? You are not your own, for you were bought at a price. Therefore glorify God in your body." 1 Cor. 6:19-20.

22. "But if the slave declares: 'I love my master, my wife, and my children; I do not want to leave as a free man,' his master is to bring him to the judges and then bring him to the door or doorpost. His master must pierce his ear with an awl, and he will serve his master for life." Exod. 21:5-6.

23. So God created man in His own image; He created him in the image of God; He created them male and female." Gen. 1:27.

24. I did not give up my job or striving to be the very best I could be in the marketplace. I would have accepted a corporate VP position if God gave it to me. But if that was His will for me, it needed to be on His terms, not mine. His terms require death to selfish ambition.

25. "With your help I can advance against a troop; with my God I can scale a wall." Ps. 18:29 (New International Version).

26. "Why do you call Me 'Lord, Lord,' and don't do the things I say?" Luke 6:46.

Chapter 3: Truth and Lies—A Lifestyle Clearing the Decks

1. "God is not a man who lies, or a son of man who changes His mind. Does He speak and not act, or promise and not fulfill?" Num. 23:19. God holds up this aspect of His nature—*that He cannot lie*—to rock my world, to cause me to rethink everything through this paradigm lens.

2. "For we walk by faith, not by sight." 2 Cor. 5:7.

3. In some espionage stories the evil side sets up a façade organization, which portrays itself as good guys fighting the evil side, to enlist the innocent unwittingly. The core of this façade organization is evil. Likewise, the root of every innocuous lie is evil.

4. "When the days were coming to a close for Him to be taken up, He *determined* to journey to Jerusalem" (emphasis mine). Luke 9:51.

5. "Call to Me and I will answer you and tell you great and incomprehensible things you do not know." Jer. 33:3.

6. "You are of your father the Devil, and you want to carry out your father's desires. He was a murderer from the beginning and has not stood in the truth, because there is no truth in him. When he tells a lie, he speaks from his own nature, because he is a liar and the father of liars." John 8:44.

7. Book of Job.

8. Judges 14:1-16:30.

9. Hezekiah is my go-to example when I feel knocked down and sense impending doom. Hezekiah took his nation's impending doom to his Promised Sufficiency, Full Provision and Complete Protection in 2 Kings 19:14. "Hezekiah took the letter from the hand of the messengers, read it, then went up to the Lord's temple, and spread it out before the Lord."

10. "I have been crucified with Christ and I no longer live, but Christ lives in me. The life I now live in the body, I live by faith in the Son of God, who loved me and gave Himself for me." Gal. 2:19b-20.

11. "Be serious! Be alert! Your adversary the Devil is prowling around like a roaring lion, looking for anyone he can devour." 1Peter 5:8.

12. Mat. 16:23.
13. "Then He said to them all, 'If anyone wants to come with Me, he must deny himself, take up his cross daily, and follow Me.'" Luke 9:23.
14. I say, *amoral*, meaning outside the sphere to which moral judgments apply. Money is a resource; it can be used morally or immorally, but is itself amoral. God talks about the use and attitude towards money in moral terms, but He does not attribute the actual size of one's bank balance as either morally good or immorally bad. The state itself is amoral. One can reach financial constraint morally, amorally or immorally. In each case, there is a risk of letting the stresses of the circumstance rival trust in the Singular Provision. Godly people may remain in the condition of financial constraint for life—some involuntarily and some voluntarily—and still feel rich in Christ. It is the heart issue of allowing oneself to continue *feeling* constrained that is the slippery slope—not the size of one's bank account. The slope itself is the transition zone between an amoral condition and an immoral internalization that defies the truth of God. Hopefully we jump off the slope onto the Rock.
15. The avalanche began when John was 49. Prolonged attacks went unabated. The story reached its climax when John was 57.
16. Basic chemistry tells us we cannot dilute something pure with something else and it remains pure. God does not dilute His truth to accommodate—to come to equilibrium with—circumstances.
17. This is a sampling of verses on being attentive to one's life (i.e., alert), and wise instead of self-deluded (i.e., self-aware):
   "Be serious! Be alert! Your adversary the Devil is prowling around like a roaring lion, looking for anyone he can devour." 1 Pet. 5:8.
   "Pay close attention to your life and your teaching; persevere in these things, for by doing this you will save both yourself and your hearers." 1 Tim. 4:16.
   "The sensible man's wisdom is to consider his way, but the stupidity of fools deceives them." Prov. 14:8.
   "Do you see a man who is wise in his own eyes? There is more hope for a fool than for him." Prov. 26:12.
18. "And he said to Him, 'I will give You all these things if You will fall down and worship me.' Then Jesus told him, 'Go away, Satan! For it is written: Worship the Lord your God, and serve only Him.'" Mat. 4:9-10.
19. "Shadrach, Meshach, and Abednego replied to the king, 'Nebuchadnezzar, we don't need to give you an answer to this question. If the God we serve exists, then He can rescue us from the furnace of blazing fire, and He can rescue us from the power of you, the king. But even if He does not rescue us, we want you as king to know that we will not serve your gods or worship the gold statue you set up.'" Dan. 3:16-18.
20. Jer. 29:11. John's name and emphasis added.
21. I imagine this scene based on Luke 15:11-32, "The Parable of the Lost Son." Although titled after the younger son, I think of it as a parable of the gracious father. Jesus, who came to reveal the Father, emphasizes that upon his son's return, the father gave him a) the truth of sonship, plus b) enviable gifts.
22. The sequence of steps in one's *Truventure* reminds hikers of multistage hikes, chemists of a sequence of chemical reactions that make complex enzymes, and electrical engineers of the many circuits in a microprocessor. The question for *Truventurers,* whether they relate to hikes, complex molecules or microprocessors, is the same: *What can catalyze the slowest (i.e. rate-determining) step?* The answer: genuine, wholehearted submission to the Holy Spirit.

Chapter 4: Mind and Spirit—A Lifestyle of a Branch in the Vine

1. "Trust in the Lord with all your heart and do not rely on your own understanding; think about Him in all your ways, and He will guide you on the right paths." Prov. 3:5,6.
2. "But without faith it is impossible to [walk with God and] please Him, for whoever comes [near] to God must [necessarily] believe that God exists and that He rewards those who [earnestly and diligently] seek Him." Heb. 11:6 (Amplified).
3. James 4:8a.
4. Jer. 33:3.
5. My top recommendation is *Hearing God's Voice,* by Henry and Richard Blackaby, (Nashville: Broadman & Holman, 2002). Key elements include: know how God speaks, God speaks directly to you, be equipped to hear, and how to respond in obedience to what He says.
6. Many from my generation are still waiting on the Spirit to tell them how to program their Video Cassette Recorder (VCR).
7. Jim Collins and Jerry Porras, *Built to Last* (New York: Harper Collins, 1994). Collins and Porras popularized the "Tyranny of the OR." In its place they advocated the "Genius of the AND."
8. Acts 17:28. We often read "in Him we live and move and exist," as a comforting thought, which of course it is. But it challenges me—I wonder how authentically am I living *in Christ* and *Christ living His life in and through* me?
9. The phrase "hanging out with Jesus" could be misinterpreted; I am not implying that we are peers; nothing could be further from the truth. He is exalted above me more than I can comprehend. And yet He desires a vital—not stilted—relationship with me. I expound more on this in chapter 11, "Quiet Times."
10. *NIV Study Bible* (Grand Rapids, MI: The Zondervan Corporation, 1985), map 1, "World of the Patriarchs." They set out for Canaan, went up the river in a northwest direction. Stopped in Harran. Then Abraham went south-by-southwest to Canaan. The ultimate destination, Canaan, is almost due west of original starting point, Ur.
11. "Do not intermarry with them. Do not give your daughters to their sons or take their daughters for your sons, because they will turn your sons away from Me to worship other gods. Then the Lord's anger will burn against you, and He will swiftly destroy you." Deut. 7:3-4.
12. "The Lord said to Gideon, 'I will deliver you with the 300 men who lapped and hand the Midianites over to you. But everyone else is to go home.'" Judges 7:7.
13. "When our enemies heard that we knew their scheme and that God had frustrated it, every one of us returned to his own work on the wall. From that day on, half of my men did the work while the other half held spears, shields, bows, and armor. The officers supported all the people of Judah, who were rebuilding the wall. The laborers who carried the loads worked with one hand and held a weapon with the other. Each of the builders had his sword strapped around his waist while he was building, and the trumpeter was beside me." Neh. 4:15-18.
14. "You yourselves know that these hands have provided for my needs and for those who were with me. In every way I've shown you that by laboring like this, it is necessary to help the weak and to keep in mind the words of the Lord Jesus, for He said, 'It is more blessed to give than to receive.'" Acts 20:34-35.

Chapter 5: The True You—A Lifestyle Embracing the Truth about You

1. The true you being wildly successful is the subject of chapter 14 in part 3. The rest of part 3 explores what it takes to see that become a reality.

2. This is just a sampling. Italics added.

> "Praise the God and Father of our Lord Jesus Christ, who has blessed us *in Christ* with every spiritual blessing in the heavens." Eph. 1:3.

> "But it is from Him that you are *in Christ Jesus*, who became God-given wisdom for us—our righteousness, sanctification, and redemption." 1 Cor. 1:30.

> "Therefore, if anyone is *in Christ*, he is a new creation; old things have passed away, and look, new things have come." 2 Cor. 5:17.

> "For we are His creation, created *in Christ Jesus* for good works, which God prepared ahead of time so that we should walk in them." Eph. 2:10.

> "But now *in Christ Jesus*, you who were far away have been brought near by the blood of the Messiah." Eph. 2:13.

> "and be found *in Him*, not having a righteousness of my own from the law, but one that is through faith in Christ—the righteousness from God based on faith." Phil. 3:9.

> "He has saved us and called us with a holy calling, not according to our works, but according to His own purpose and grace, which was given to us *in Christ Jesus* before time began." 2 Tim. 1:9.

> "Now the God of all grace, who called you to His eternal glory *in Christ Jesus*, will personally restore, establish, strengthen, and support you after you have suffered a little." 1 Peter 5:10.

> "And we know that the Son of God has come and has given us understanding so that we may know the true One. We are *in the true One*—that is, *in His Son Jesus Christ*. He is the true God and eternal life." 1 John 5:20.

3. Scene where Eric responds to his sister's plea to give up running and return to China missions, *Chariots of Fire*, written by Colin Welland, directed by Hugh Hudson. (Burbank, CA: Warner Home Video, 1981).

4. DC Talk. "Colored People." Song number two on the album *Jesus Freak*. ForeFront Records. Originally released Nov. 21, 1995.

5. "He didn't have an impressive form or majesty that we should look at Him, no appearance that we should desire Him. He was despised and rejected by men, a man of suffering who knew what sickness was. He was like someone people turned away from; He was despised, and we didn't value Him." Is. 53:2b-3.

6. "He was in the world, and the world was created through Him, yet the world did not recognize Him." John 1:10.

7. "The soldiers also twisted together a crown of thorns, put it on His head, and threw a purple robe around Him." John 19:2.

8. "It is never about me," is one of my favorite quotes, shared with me by an incredible friend, Steve Young. Heroes of the faith (e.g., Joseph, Daniel, David, and Paul), declared the same by their lifestyles. Paul put this lifestyle to words in Gal. 2:20.

9. If you prefer *illumination* to *revelation*, then you are in the good company of theologians; in this book I am focused on the interchangeable aspects of their meaning. Specifically, I agree with Paul, "that the God of our Lord Jesus Christ, the glorious Father, would give you a spirit of wisdom and revelation in the knowledge of Him." Eph. 1:17.

10. "He humbled you by letting you go hungry; then He gave you manna to eat, which you and your fathers had not known, so that you might learn that man does not live on bread alone but on every word that comes from the mouth of the Lord." Deut. 8:3.

11. "'For My thoughts are not your thoughts, and your ways are not My ways.' This is the Lord's declaration. 'For as heaven is higher than earth, so My ways are higher than your ways, and My thoughts than your thoughts.'" Is. 55:8-9.
12. 2 Cor. 3:5.
13. You may have noticed that "Truth & Lies" is strategically placed before "The True You" in *Prerequisite Principles*. If you feel the urge to re-read "Truth & Lies" to see what the Revealer will reveal concerning lies about your identity, I encourage you to do so.
14. "Dear friends, we are God's children now, and what we will be has not yet been revealed. We know that when He appears, we will be like Him because we will see Him as He is." 1 John 3:2.
15. Scene where "the prisoner wishes to say a word," *Braveheart*, directed by Mel Gibson. (Hollywood, CA: Paramount, 1995).
16. "You will know the truth, and the truth will set you free." John 8:32.

Chapter 6: Personal Covenant with God—A Lifestyle of Deepening Surrender

1. Dr. Bill Bright (1921-2003) founded Campus Crusade for Christ, now Cru. Bill was awarded the $1.1 million Templeton Prize for Progress in Religion, which he donated to promote the spiritual benefits of fasting and prayer. Bill received numerous lifetime awards and was inducted into the National Religious Broadcasters Hall of Fame.
2. "Don't you know that your body is a sanctuary of the Holy Spirit who is in you, whom you have from God? You are not your own, for you were bought at a price. Therefore glorify God in your body." 1 Cor. 6:19-20.
3. Jerry Bridges, *Transforming Grace* (Colorado Springs: NavPress, 1994), Page 226. Apparently this verse is from an ancient hymn provided to Jerry from a friend. I use the same verbs and intent but not the exact phraseology.
4. With God, there is no legalese.
5. "For it is God who is working in you, enabling you both to desire and to work out His good purpose." Phil. 2:13.
6. "His divine power has given us everything required for life and godliness through the knowledge of Him who called us by His own glory and goodness." 2 Peter 1:3.

Chapter 7: Strategic Intent—A Lifestyle Doing the Next Right Thing

1. Gary Hamel and C.K. Prahalad, *Strategic Intent* (Watertown: Harvard Business Press Books, 2010). Hamel and Prahalad popularized the concept of strategic intent in 1989. It quickly gained widespread traction in business.
2. INSEAD is one of the world's leading graduate business schools, with campuses in France, Singapore, and Abu Dhabi. The name INSEAD comes from the original name in French, "Institut Europeen d'Administration des Affaires" (European Institute of Business Administration). I attended the Advanced Management Program in France—an intense four weeks (felt more like twelve) with the goal of transforming senior executives into thoughtful business leaders. Several of the courses used the Harvard business cases in their material. Having taken strategy at both Harvard and INSEAD, I recommend INSEAD—and not just because of the cuisine.
3. My Japanese friends would say more on behalf of Komatsu. However, I was born and raised in Peoria, IL, where Caterpillar had its headquarters. Consequently, "formidable competitor" is high praise coming from a Peorian, and I will leave it at that.
4. "Daniel determined that he would not defile himself [...]" Dan. 1:8.
5. Dan. 1:20 and 2:27,28,48.

6. Daniel's long-lasting reputation is illustrated in Dan. 5:11a, "There is a man in your kingdom who has the spirit of the holy gods in him. In the days of your predecessor he was found to have insight, intelligence, and wisdom like the wisdom of the gods." As for Daniel's determination not to usurp God's glory, I see this evidenced in Daniel chapter 9.

Chapter 8: Core Principles—A Centered Lifestyle

1. "For those He foreknew He also predestined to be conformed to the image of His Son, so that He would be the firstborn among many brothers. And those He predestined, He also called; and those He called, He also justified; and those He justified, He also glorified." Rom. 8:29, 30.

2. "But the boat was already over a mile from land, battered by the waves, because the wind was against them. Around three in the morning, He came toward them walking on the sea. When the disciples saw Him walking on the sea, they were terrified. 'It's a ghost!' they said, and cried out in fear. Immediately Jesus spoke to them. 'Have courage! It is I. Don't be afraid.' 'Lord, if it's You,' Peter answered Him, 'command me to come to You on the water.' 'Come!' He said. And climbing out of the boat, Peter started walking on the water and came toward Jesus." Mat. 14:24-29.

Chapter 9: Annual Main Thrusts—A Lifestyle Taking Ground

1. Dave Hannah, founder and chairman of Lift Up America, owner of World Premiere Events, coined the acronym L.I.F.E. It stands for Labor (or one's time), Influence, Finance, and Expertise.

2. "For nothing will be impossible with God." Luke 1:37.

3. "Remain in Me, and I in you. Just as a branch is unable to produce fruit by itself unless it remains on the vine, so neither can you unless you remain in Me." John 15:4.

4. "Look! I am coming quickly, and My reward is with Me to repay each person according to what he has done." Rev. 22:12.

5. "If anyone builds on that foundation with gold, silver, costly stones, wood, hay, or straw, each one's work will become obvious, for the day will disclose it, because it will be revealed by fire; the fire will test the quality of each one's work. If anyone's work that he has built survives, he will receive a reward." 1 Cor. 3:12-14.

Chapter 10: Select Lessons—A Lifestyle of Solid Evidence

1. "But the ones sown on good ground are those who hear the word, welcome it, and produce a crop: 30, 60, and 100 times what was sown." Mark 4:20.

2. Being truly candid with God and oneself is as rare as genuine humility; these two rarities—humility and authenticity—are often found together.

3. "Instead, I have calmed and quieted myself like a little weaned child with its mother; I am like a little child." Ps. 131:2.

4. If I do not diligently choose to steadfastly see everything strictly through the lens of God's Truth, I forgo much of His good plan for me and make life much more difficult than it need be.

5. "We know that when He appears, we will be like Him because we will see Him as He is." 1 John 3:2b.

6. By *self* I mean that part of me that is contrary to God, that selfishly exercises it's own way in disobedience to God. It is not something to tame and sanctify, but to starve and reckon crucified with Christ.

Chapter 11: Quiet Times—A Lifestyle Processing Everything with Jesus

1. Lev. 11:44,45; 19:2.
2. Ps. 119:26.
3. "Deep calls to deep in the roar of Your waterfalls; all Your breakers and Your billows have swept over me." Ps. 42:7.
4. One of my favorite fields of mathematics is series equations. I like to learn what happens when an equation is taken to a certain value or limit (e.g., to zero or infinity). When I think about my quiet time mathematically, I imagine taking my hanging out with Jesus to 24/7, and it becomes intentional, strategic practicing of God's presence. What a life!
5. George Fox, founder of the Quakers, is known to have quaked (i.e., trembled at the Word of God) and admonished others to do so. This subject is also addressed in C.H. Spurgeon's sermon, "Trembling at the Word of the Lord." First delivered at the Metropolitan Tabernacle in London, England, on Thursday evening, May 1, 1884, it was intended for reading on the Lord's Day.
6. "May You forgive Your people who sinned against You and all their rebellions against You" 1 Kings 8:50a.
7. "I have treasured Your word in my heart so that I may not sin against You." Psalm 119:11.
8. "Sanctify them by the truth; Your word is truth." John 15:17.
9. "And now I commit you to God and to the message of His grace, which is able to build you up and to give you an inheritance among all who are sanctified." Acts 20:32.
10. I originally used a template produced by The Navigators, called "My Reading Highlights." It includes space for the disciple to enter the date, Bible passage, verse that impressed the disciple, and how that verse impressed him or her. I use these basic elements in an electronic Word document that I create each day. At the time of writing a pdf version is available at, http://www.2-7series.com/getattachment/badc52f2-ba93-4c19-a247-82d0db978133/Download-Name
11. I use my hard copy Bible when at home; if traveling I use online Bible software or mobile app.

Chapter 12: Strategy on One Page—A Lifestyle for the Millennia

1. Robert Bauval & Adrian Gilbert. *The Orion Mystery: Unlocking the Secrets of the Pyramids* (New York: Crown Publishers, Inc., 1994) pages 1-2.
2. Richard L. Lynch and Kelvin F. Cross, *Measure Up!* (Malden, MA: Blackwell Publishers, 1991). Lynch and Cross use a Performance Pyramid to organize a corporation's performance measures. Their book (*Measure Up!*) and *Truventure* both utilize a pyramid, have a healthy dissatisfaction with ineffectual status quo, and value appropriate corporate measures to more effectively improve performance. Whereas, *Measure Up!* focuses primarily on identifying appropriate measures, *Truventure* focuses primarily on the development of a strategic process, applying it to business, ministry, and life.
3. Blaise Pascal. *The Provincial Letters* (Eugene, OR: Wipf and Stock Publishers, 1997) pages 175-176.
4. "And He died for all so that those who live should no longer live for themselves, but for the One who died for them and was raised." 2 Cor. 5:15.
5. Robert Bauval & Adrian Gilbert. *The Orion Mystery: Unlocking the Secrets of the Pyramids* (New York: Crown Publishers, Inc., 1994) page 123.

Chapter 13: The Essentials—A Lifestyle Distilling Discovery

1. "Your eyes saw me when I was formless; all my days were written in Your book and planned before a single one of them began." Ps. 139:16.

2. "Lord my God, You have done many things—Your wonderful works and Your plans for us; none can compare with You. If I were to report and speak of them, they are more than can be told." Ps. 40:5.

3. "Looking back to see ahead" is an aspect of Chinese culture one picks up living in China, but a little research reveals that B.G. Dyck applies the principle in *Look Back to See Ahead: Discover how God Works in your Life, and How He Shapes Your Future* (Maitland, FL: Xulon Press, 2011). I include the book summary here: *Whether you are a declared Christian or not, God has already been working in your life! This book should lead you to see how that has already happened as you Look Back over your life. It should also help to See Ahead and determine how God's work in the past will strongly influence your future, and how it will help you to share God's love with others! Retrospection can, and will change your life! Thanks be to God!*

4. Photo courtesy of We·Do.

5. My friend Chris Kraiss provided these categories, which I find very helpful.

6. Chris Kraiss also provided this question. It is an excellent example of someone formulating his own question, one that resonated with him, after perusing several questions offered for his consideration.

7. My friend John Hemken is a master at maximizing an idea; John looked at my list of questions and quickly began asking them four different ways—brilliant!

8. Coauthor Angela Owen suggested this pertinent question while helping others not become overloaded with the long list.

9. A university student Angela knows in Nanjing, China, demonstrated wisdom beyond his years with this question.

10. Jeffrey K. Liker. *The Toyota Way: 14 Management Principles from the World's Greatest Manufacturer* (New York: McGraw-Hill, 2004) page 47.

11. On the other hand, while I considered grouping "aligning with Christ" with "co-investing this life," I chose to keep them as separate, parallel strategies, so I do not sacrifice focus and traction.

Chapter 14: Wildly Successful—A Lifestyle Envisioning the Master's Rendering

1. "Your eyes saw me when I was formless; all my days were written in Your book and planned before a single one of them began." Ps. 139:16.

2. "'For I know the plans I have for you'—this is the Lord's declaration—'plans for your welfare, not for disaster, to give you a future and a hope. You will call to Me and come and pray to Me, and I will listen to you. You will seek Me and find Me when you search for Me with all your heart.'" Jer. 29:11-13.

3. "I am sure of this, that He who started a good work in you will carry it on to completion until the day of Christ Jesus." Phil. 1:6.

4. Caterpillar's company strategy as stated on their website: http://www.caterpillar.com/en/company/strategy.html

5. Clint Owens, former director of the Cru (formerly Campus Crusade for Christ) NYC inner city ministry, 2008.

6. "Do not be conformed to this age, but be transformed by the renewing of your mind, so that you may discern what is the good, pleasing, and perfect will of God." Rom. 12:2. "Sanctify them by the truth; Your word is truth." John 17:17. To proactively renew my

mind and proactively choose God's truth are key for me to have the mind of Christ and be sanctified of misconceptions.

7. "in the hope of eternal life that God, who cannot lie, promised before time began." Titus 1:2.

8. "Every generous act and every perfect gift is from above, coming down from the Father of lights; with Him there is no variation or shadow cast by turning." James 1:17.

9. "Give thanks to the Lord, for He is good. His love is eternal." Ps. 136:1.

10. "For as heaven is higher than earth, so My ways are higher than your ways, and My thoughts than your thoughts." Is. 55:9.

11 Anthony Brown and Pat Barrett, of the band Housefires. "Good Good Father," *Housefires II*. Atlanta: 2014.

12. *Sizing* is the correct technical term. Sizing is applied to the canvas prior to the paint to protect the canvas and avoid the loss of color intensity. Since artists, let alone the general public, do not frequently use the term *sizing*, I invoke a more familiar term, *primer*.

13. These are two favorites: "Moses did everything just as the Lord had commanded him." Ex. 40:16. "I have glorified You on the earth by completing the work You gave Me to do." John 17:4.

14. "Indeed, the Lord's hand is not too short to save, and His ear is not too deaf to hear." Is. 59:1.

15. For more questions refer to chapter 13 and appendix C.

16. "I declare the end from the beginning, and from long ago what is not yet done, saying: My plan will take place, and I will do all My will." Is. 46:10.

17. "It is not that we are competent in ourselves to consider anything as coming from ourselves, but our competence is from God." 2 Cor. 3:5.

18. "His divine power has given us everything required for life and godliness through the knowledge of Him who called us by His own glory and goodness." 2 Peter 1:3.

19. "Every branch in Me that does not produce fruit He removes, and He prunes every branch that produces fruit so that it will produce more fruit." John 15:2.

20 John 17:4.

Chapter 15: Opportunity—A Lifestyle Seizing the Dream

1 "For nothing will be impossible with God." Luke 1:37.

2 "All of you, take up My yoke and learn from Me, because I am gentle and humble in heart, and you will find rest for yourselves." Mat. 11:29.

3 "But as it is written: What eye did not see and ear did not hear, and what never entered the human mind—God prepared this for those who love Him." 1 Cor. 2:9.

4 "Every generous act and every perfect gift is from above, coming down from the Father of lights; with Him there is no variation or shadow cast by turning." James 1:17.

5 I coined the term *grace-rewards* to remind myself that everything is by grace. By grace, God works in me to will and do His good will. God produces fruit if I remain in the Vine. So I go for, and receive, rewards that *Christ earns* living His life in and through me.

6 "If you keep silent at this time, liberation and deliverance will come to the Jewish people from another place, but you and your father's house will be destroyed. Who knows, perhaps you have come to your royal position for such a time as this." Esther 4:14.

7. "You, indeed, have made my days short in length, and my life span as nothing in Your sight. Yes, every mortal man is only a vapor. *Selah*" Ps. 39:5.

8. "Teach us to number our days carefully so that we may develop wisdom in our hearts." Ps. 90:12.

9. "So Methuselah's life lasted 969 years; then he died." Gen. 5:27.

10. Theodore Roosevelt, "Citizenship in a Republic" (speech, Sorbonne, Paris, April 23, 1910). *The Works of Theodore Roosevelt*, Vol. XIII (New York City: Charles Scribner's Sons, 1926), pp. 506-529. Bold emphasis added.
11. William Carey, sermon to the Baptist Association (Friar Lane Baptist Chapel, Nottingham, England, May 30, 1792). As a result of this message men later started the English Baptist Missionary Society on October 2, 1792. Carey became known as the father of modern missions.
12. "My aim is to evangelize where Christ has not been named, so that I will not build on someone else's foundation." Rom. 15:20.
13. "circumcised the eighth day; of the nation of Israel, of the tribe of Benjamin, a Hebrew born of Hebrews; regarding the law, a Pharisee;" Phil. 3:5.
14. Otto F. A. Meinardus. "Paul's Missionary Journey to Spain: Tradition and Folklore." *The Biblical Archaeologist*, Vol. 41, No. 2 (June 1978): pp. 61-63.
15. The breadth of this can be seen in the map titled "Paul's Missionary Journeys" in *The Apologetics Study Bible* (Nashville: Holman Publishers 2007).
16. "and I no longer live, but Christ lives in me. The life I now live in the body, I live by faith in the Son of God, who loved me and gave Himself for me." Gal. 2:20.
17. 2 Cor. 1:10.
18. Daniel honorably served the sovereigns of both the gold and silver kingdoms by remaining loyal to his Sovereign, who would set up the kingdom that would destroy all kingdoms and last forever (Daniel chapter 2).
19. Kevin Belmonte, *William Wilberforce, A Hero for Humanity* (Grand Rapids, MI: Zondervan, 2002), page 18.
20. Bob Beltz, *Real Christianity* (Ventura, CA: Regal Books, 2006), page 11. On October 28, 1787, Wilberforce wrote in his diary, "God Almighty has set before me two great objects: the suppression of the slave trade, and reformation of manners." By *manners* Wilberforce meant what we might call *morals* today.
21. Ibid.,13.
22. "Now to Him who is able to do above and beyond all that we ask or think according to the power that works in us..." Eph. 3:20.
23. "I have fought the good fight, I have finished the race, I have kept the faith." 2 Tim. 4:7.
24. "Fight the good fight for the faith; take hold of eternal life that you were called to and have made a good confession about in the presence of many witnesses." 1 Tim. 6:12.
25. Pastor Debbie Santiago founded the Salt and Sea Mission on Coney Island, and ran the mission for 30 years.
26 "They asked only that we would remember the poor, which I made every effort to do." Gal. 2:10.
27. TBL stands for Triple Bottom Line. The mission of TBL Leadership Partners LLC is to educate and empower people to achieve triple bottom line success: people success, business success, and community success.
28. "For we walk by faith, not sight," 2 Cor. 5:7.
29. For all Daniel knew, he could have been executed in Daniel chapter 1. Within days of conversion, the Jews plotted to kill Paul. Wilberforce realized his dream only three days before his death.

Chapter 16: Compelling Imperative—A Lifestyle Tethered to the Mind of Christ

1. Jim Elliot, entry for 28 October, 1949, in *The Journals of Jim Elliot*, ed. Elisabeth Elliot (Grand Rapids, MI: Fleming H. Revell, 2002) page 174.

2. Allan Harman, *Matthew Henry: His Life and Influence* (Ross-shire, Scotland: Christian Focus Publications, 2012). Kindle edition. Matthew Henry recalled his father's acts of kindness and charity and how he used to say, "He is no fool who parts with that which he cannot keep, when he is sure to be recompensed with that which he cannot lose," a statement very close to Jim Elliot's, made nearly three centuries earlier than Elliot's journal entry.

3. At the time of publication a reproduction of Jim Elliot's original journal entry could be found at http://www2.wheaton.edu/bgc/archives/faq/20.htm. According to the website the underlining, the bracket, and the asterisk were probably added after Elliot's death.

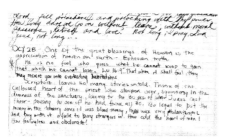

4. "I die every day!" 1 Cor. 15:31b.

5. "Then He said to them all, 'If anyone wants to come with Me, he must deny himself, take up his cross daily, and follow Me. For whoever wants to save his life will lose it, but whoever loses his life because of Me will save it.'" Luke 9:23-24.

6. God's very nature demands an appropriate response. For further expansion on this line of thought, see *How Should We Then Live?* by Francis A. Schaeffer (Wheaton, IL: Crossway Books of Good News Publishers, 2005).

7. "Where can I go to escape Your Spirit? Where can I flee from Your presence?" Ps. 139:7.

8. "'For I know the plans I have for you'—this is the Lord's declaration—'plans for your welfare, not for disaster, to give you a future and a hope.'" Jer. 29:11.

9. "I have told you these things, so that in me you may have peace. You will have suffering in this world. Be courageous! I have conquered the world." John 16:33.

10. "If you do nothing in a difficult time, your strength is limited." Prov. 24:10.

11. 1 Cor. 3:13.

12. "In this, love is perfected with us so that we may have confidence in the day of judgment, for we are as He is in this world." 1 John 4:17.

13. "Set your minds on what is above, not on what is on the earth." Col. 3:2. In life as in sports, head position and focal point greatly influence outcome.

14. Susan Wise Bauer. *The Story of Science: From the Writings of Aristotle to the Big Bang Theory* (New York: W.W. Norton & Company, 2015), page 98. For young learners and rocket scientists who like comic books, try *A Crash Course in Forces and Motion with Max Axiom, Super Scientist (Graphic Science)* by Emily Sohn and Charles Barnett III, illustrated by Steve Erwin (North Mankato, MN: Capstone Press, revised edition 2016), page 7.

Chapter 17: Strategic Compass—A Lifestyle Knowing the Right Direction

1. The highest return comes from investing in an approved *Truventure* strategic summit.

2. For the purposes of this chapter I use the trio of strategic direction, but the astute foresee playing the same game with every block of one's entire *Strategic Pyramid*.

Chapter 18: Strategic Map—A Lifestyle Landing the Vision

1 Jon Kolko. *Well Designed: how to use empathy to create products people love* (Brighton, MA: Harvard Business review, 2014) page 173. Oliver Wendell Holmes is credited to have said, "I would not give a fig for the simplicity this side of complexity, but I would give my life for the simplicity on the other side of complexity."

2 "Now may the God of peace, who brought up from the dead our Lord Jesus—the great Shepherd of the sheep—with the blood of the everlasting covenant, equip you with all that is good to do His will, working in us what is pleasing in His sight, through Jesus Christ. Glory belongs to Him forever and ever. Amen." Heb. 13:20-21.

3 I engage my mind with the mind of Christ and my spirit with the Holy Spirit and claim promises such as, "Send Your light and Your truth; let them lead me" (Ps. 43:3a); "Who is the man who fears the Lord? He will show him the way he should choose" (Ps. 25:12); "You reveal the path of life to me; in Your presence is abundant joy; in Your right hand are eternal pleasures" (Ps. 16:11).

4 See Appendix E for the *Truventure* Preferred Path.

5 If I have spent sufficient quality time with my Creator to answer questions and identify essentials (chapter 13), then much of my *Strategic Pyramid* will come from my gleaned list, but this is a helpful resource not a limitation. New insights are always welcome.

6 *Truventure* is applied strategy. Traction is primary. Categorizing whether something is a strategy or tactic or whatever does not add value at this juncture.

7 Nonessential blocks are placed on a list for later evaluation; it may be essential later in the process. For example, *iron sharpens iron* is not an essential strategy to land my vision, but God made it clear it's an essential supporting block to land my investment strategy.

8 Consider Occam's Razor, the Law of Unintended Consequences, Murphy's Law, and the Principle of Parsimony.

9 *Grant no quarter* means not to allow someone any mercy or indulgence. Originally it meant to refuse to imprison and simply kill one's prisoner. Personally, I love application of this by my Commander to self.

10 "For the flesh desires what is against the Spirit, and the Spirit desires what is against the flesh; these are opposed to each other, so that you don't do what you want." Gal. 5:17.

11 Richard L. Lynch and Kelvin F. Cross, *Measure Up!* (Malden, MA: Blackwell Publishers, 1991), page 65.

12 Insight and rigor are the odd couple of the *Strategic Pyramid* process.

13 Global Media Outreach shares Christ with billions of people at their point of need as they search the internet.

14 Reasons to Believe spreads the Christian Gospel by demonstrating that sound reason and scientific research—including the very latest discoveries—consistently support, rather than erode, confidence in the truth of the Bible and faith in the personal, transcendent God revealed in both Scripture and nature.

Chapter 19: Smart Pyramid—An Examined Lifestyle

1 Douglas Groothuis. *Philosophy in Seven Sentences: A Small Introduction to a Vast Topic* (Downers Grove, IL: InterVarsity Press, 2016), pages 15-16.

2. I underline or bold metrics for several reasons. First, I use many different styles and want to identify every metric. Second, in addition to identification, underlining provides emphasis and focus. Third, it is easier and cleaner to compare actual and target metrics if

they are both underlined. Finally, underlining is an effective way to hold myself accountable to the metric my Lord and I agreed upon.

3. Often strategy is developed within resource constraints, but not in the *Strategic Pyramid* process. The *Strategic Pyramid* lets the vision statement define scope, not resource constraints, and it engages the Almighty, not our own limitations.

4. During strategy development, color coding is useful to identify related blocks with a similar color. But when I get to strategy implementation, I prefer an evaluative color pallet.

5. If asked how I was doing at landing my vision, I could think, *I'm not doing that great, well not failing, but I have a long way to go, hmm?* I might be left wondering. Rather then being left wondering, I would like a quantitative estimate, hence the composite metric.

6. A singular composite metric that accurately assesses the performance of a business, a manufacturing process, or an engineering phenomenon is widely considered the holy grail. In this case it has the added benefit of helping us get everything essential for strategy implementation and an examined life on one page.

7. Example of a "Smart Pyramid" is provided in Appendix D.4.

8. "The Word became flesh and took up residence among us. We observed His glory, the glory as the One and Only Son from the Father, full of grace and truth." John 1:14.

9. "Therefore, no condemnation now exists for those in Christ Jesus," Rom. 8:1.

10. "There is no fear in love; instead, perfect love drives out fear, because fear involves punishment. So the one who fears has not reached perfection in love." 1 John 4:18.

11. "For it is God who is working in you, enabling you both to desire and to work out His good purpose." Phil. 2:13.

12. Henry and Richard Blackaby and Claude King. *Experiencing God: Knowing and Doing the Will of God* (Nashville, TN: B&H Publishing Group, 2008), pages 69, 77, 124, 316. Blackaby popularized the concept of look where God is working and joining Him there.

13. Most of us have been trained in Bethel Sozo. *Sozo* is Greek for the word *salvation,* used a variety of ways: *saved* (Romans 10:9), *healed* (Matthew 9:22), and *delivered* (Luke 8:36). Bethel Sozo takes everything to the Godhead, which coincidently is the essence of my *Truventure.* For an introduction to Bethel Sozo, consider the following resource: Teresa Liebscher, Dawna DeSilva. *SOZO Saved Healed Delivered: A Journey into Freedom with the Father, Son, and Holy Spirit* (Shippensburg, PA: Destiny Image Publishers, 2016).

14. The goal of Truventure Journeying Councils is to quickly go deep and help each other hear God's voice, think strategically, and maximize his or her life, business, and/or ministry. Contact Truventure.com for more information.

Epilogue

1. James Strong, LL.D., S.T.D., *The New Strong's Exhaustive Concordance of the Bible* (Nashville, TN: Thomas Nelson Publishers, 1990), page 87.

2. James Strong, LL.D., S.T.D., *The New Strong's Exhaustive Concordance of the Bible* (Nashville, TN: Thomas Nelson Publishers, 1990), page 76.

Appendix A.1

1. Labor, Influence, Finances and Expertise (Dave Hannah).

2. Hannah Whitehall Smith, *The Christian's Secret to a Happy Life,* (Peabody, MA: Hendrickson Publishers, 2004).

3. Jerry Bridges. *Trusting God* (Colorado Springs, CO: NavPress, 1988) page 18.

4. To each distressed lady who brought a problem to her, the late Bible teacher extraordinaire, Mrs. Ruby Thompson would empathetically respond, *for this we have Jesus.*
5. Jerry Bridges. *Transforming Grace* (Colorado Springs, CO: NavPress, 1994) page 226.
6. "When all has been heard, the conclusion of the matter is: fear God and keep His commands, because this is for all humanity." Eccl. 12:13.
7. "And now, Israel, what does the Lord your God ask of you except to fear the Lord your God by walking in all His ways, to love Him, and to worship the Lord your God with all your heart and all your soul?" Deut. 10:12.
8. "He has shown you, O mortal, what is good. And what does the Lord require of you? To act justly and to love mercy and to walk humbly with your God." Micah 6:8.

Appendix E

1. *Short cuts make long delays*, J.R.R. Tolkien. *The Fellowship of the Ring* (London, George Allen & Unwin, 1954) chapter 4.

Made in the USA
San Bernardino, CA
22 February 2019